W/D

The Shadow of Eternity

Belief and Structure in
HERBERT, VAUGHAN
AND TRAHERNE

Sharon Cadman Seelig

THE UNIVERSITY PRESS OF KENTUCKY

Library of Congress Cataloging in Publication Data

Seelig, Sharon Cadman.
    The shadow of eternity.

    Includes index.
    1. English poetry—Early modern, 1500–1700—
History and criticism. 2. Herbert, George, 1593–
1633—Criticism and interpretation. 3. Vaughan,
Henry, 1622–1695—Criticism and interpretation.
4. Traherne, Thomas, d. 1674—Criticism and inter-
pretation. I. Title.
PR545.M4S4   821'.3'09   80-51018
ISBN 0-8131-1444-6   AACR2

Scholarly publisher for the Commonwealth,
serving Berea College, Centre College of Kentucky,
Eastern Kentucky University, The Filson Club,
Georgetown College, Kentucky Historical Society,
Kentucky State University, Morehead State University,
Murray State University, Northern Kentucky University,
Transylvania University, University of Kentucky,
University of Louisville, and Western Kentucky University.

Editorial and Sales Offices: Lexington, Kentucky 40506

Contents

Acknowledgments

MY THANKS to Mount Holyoke College for a leave of absence and grants-in-aid that first allowed me to undertake this study and that later assisted in its publication; to Richard Johnson, Philip Sheridan, and Sheldon Zitner who read and offered criticism of parts of the manuscript in several stages; to the late James M. Osborn for permission to read the manuscript of Traherne's "Select Meditations" in his collection; to J. A. Mazzeo and Edward Tayler, who guided and encouraged my earliest studies of Vaughan; to the Newberry Library, which provided both financial and scholarly support for that first study; and most especially to my husband and family, who, all along, have understood. I gratefully acknowledge the permission of Oxford University Press to quote from *The Works of George Herbert*, ed. F. E. Hutchinson (1941); *The Works of Henry Vaughan*, ed. L. C. Martin (2d ed. 1957); and *Thomas Traherne: Centuries, Poems, and Thanksgivings*, ed. H. M. Margoliouth (2 vols. 1958).

It's not a matter of peeling away the surface and finding the truth underneath. The truth is on the surface; it's just a matter of finding it there.

Gabriel Josipovici

Time is a sacred thing: it flowes from Heaven, it is a thred spun from thence by the motion and circumvolution of the spheres. It is an emanation from that place, where eternity springs. The right use of it, is to reduce it to its Original: If we follow time close, it will bring us to its Fountain. It is a *clue* cast down from Heaven to guide us thither. It is the younger brother of eternity, the one must be sought in the other. It hath some assimilation to Divinity: it is partly knowable, and partly not: Wee move in it, and wee see it not: It is then most invisible; when most present.

Henry Vaughan's translation of
Nieremberg, *Of Temperance and Patience*

Introduction

IN the years following the rediscovery of metaphysical poetry in the twentieth century, it has become clear that the abundance of definitions and descriptions produced by that initial enthusiasm reflect at least as much the preoccupations of our own time as of that of John Donne. As Frank Kermode has argued, readers who earnestly seek an undissociated sensibility to satisfy their own needs and theories will surely find one, whether in the works of Donne or Milton or Dante.[1] But in our modern preference for wit and cynicism, we have often not fully understood how deeply serious and functional the wit of metaphysical poetry is.[2] Even though we are perhaps more aware than some of our forebears that a jest may be serious, we are less easily convinced, despite the example of Beckett, that such wit may represent a world view as well. Of all that we have been told about metaphysical poetry I find Joan Bennett's words among the most useful: "It would not be wide of the mark to describe metaphysical poetry as poetry written by men for whom the light of day is God's shadow."[3] This modest statement has at least two advantages: it is not a definition and therefore does not propose to tell us what metaphysical poetry is not; and it echoes the words of a writer of great metaphysical prose, Sir Thomas Browne, who also believed that "*lux est umbra dei.*"[4]

The metaphysical cast of mind, even the metaphysical conceit, is not found only among metaphysical poets. It is rather an attitude that is the product of centuries of biblical scholarship and religious meditation, originating in the method of exegesis that related the Old Testament to the New by types and antitypes, that saw in a single passage or event several kinds or levels of meaning, that saw in nature traces of the eternal, that found in the Book of Creatures a reflection of that other Book of God, the Bible. The germ of this philosophical attitude may be traced back to Plato, the methods of exegesis, to the second-century Alexandrian school of Platonism of which Philo Judaeus is the most notable member.[5] The expressions of this point of view are legion, but one might begin with Saint Bonaventure:

All creatures of this sensible world lead the mind of the one contemplating and attaining wisdom to the eternal God: for they are shadows, echoes, and pictures, the traces, simulacra, and reflections of that First Principle most powerful, wisest, and best. . . . They are signs divinely bestowed, which, I say, are exemplars or rather exemplifications set before our yet untrained minds, limited to sensible things, so that through the sensibles which they see they may be carried forward to the intelligibles which they do not see, as if by signs to the signified.

The orderly method of the twelfth-century monk contrasts with the intuitive flashes of the seventeenth-century mystic Jacob Böhme, but their perceptions have a common basis—the belief in a complex but essentially unified reality: "When I take up a stone or clod of earth and look upon it; then I see that which is above, and that which is below, yea the whole world therein." The seventeenth-century Spanish Jesuit Juan Eusebius Nieremberg recalled the origins of the tradition and stated its principle when he wrote: "Plotinus called the world the poetry of God. I add, that this poem is like a labyrinth, which is read in every direction, and gives intimation of, and points to, its author."[6]

This view of the world is not only the basis of medieval mysticism; it is the belief that informs metaphysical poetry. The contrast between the mystical, aesthetic image of Plotinus and the labyrinth full of detailed information of Nieremberg suggests the differences between those two thinkers, yet the elaboration of the meaning of the labyrinth undertaken in the Middle Ages and the Renaissance provides the network of associations to be freely drawn on by the poets of the seventeenth century.[7] The metaphysical poets were not perverse and egotistical exhibitionists who twisted reality to suit their own poetic whims. What appeared to Dr. Johnson "the most heterogeneous ideas . . . yoked by violence together" was for the previous century a form that allowed the discovery of the true nature of reality, a discovery accomplished through the witty insight of the poet. Perhaps the best statement of this notion is found in *Conceit and the Art of Wit*, a treatise by the Jesuit Balthasar Gracián, published in 1642, which defines wit as "an act of the intellect which expresses the correspondence that exists between objects. . . . The conceit consists in a dexterous concord, a harmonious correlation between two or three extreme knowables, expressed by an act of the intellect."[8] It is because such correspondences exist in nature that the poet can express them in his art. "As God created a 'metaphysical' world, so the poet creates 'metaphysical' poems."⁹ The poet creates in the image of God, without whose primary creation his secondary creation could never be; yet the poet's creative act also illuminates the divine creation.

When Donne in "Goodfriday, 1613. Riding Westward" lays out the proposition on which the poem is based—"Let mans Soule be a Spheare, and then, in this, / The intelligence that moves, devotion is"—he appears to be stating only a tentative hypothesis, good for the duration of the poem. But the poem at last forces the reader to acknowledge the hypothesis as truth, by playing on the variety of relationships that exists between the physical and spiritual worlds. On the one hand there seems a contrast or conflict between them: "I am carryed towards the West / This day, when my Soules forme bends toward the East"; yet we see that the same rules apply to souls as to "other Spheares": both are subject to "forraigne motions." Indeed one of the thrusts of the poem is to make us aware how completely such "forraigne motions" dominate—so much so that it is hardly true that the poet's "Soules forme bends toward the East," for he says: "Yet dare I'almost be glad, I do not see / That spectacle of too much weight for mee." Yet Donne's memory, if not his eyes, turns toward the scene, and even the body's apparently negative motion is seen to have positive meaning:

O Saviour, as thou hang'st upon the tree;
I turne my backe to thee, but to receive
Corrections, till thy mercies bid thee leave.

At the heart of this poem that ponders the relative postures of body and spirit, finding them now in harmony, now in opposition, there is a stunning expression of the link between them, and of the link between the worlds of nature and of grace: "Could I behold those hands which span the Poles, / And tune all spheares at once, peirc'd with those holes?" The reader's response involves both protest and recognition: he objects that the two—the divine creator and the suffering Jesus—are very different; but he is forced to recognize, by the form of Donne's statement, which unites the two within a sentence and a couplet, that in the mysteries of the Trinity and the Incarnation they are one. The split between physical and spiritual experienced by the poet, as by all men, is reconciled in Christ. This recognition underlies the further turnings and questionings of the poem, throughout which the tension persists, but also the will to unity. It is the two taken together that mark metaphysical poetry.

The poetry of Donne, Herbert, Vaughan, and Traherne grows out of a sense of reality given brilliant expression by their contemporary, Sir Thomas Browne: "thus is man that great and true *Amphibium*, whose nature is disposed to live not onely like other creatures in divers elements, but in divided and distinguished worlds; for though there bee but one [world] to sense, there are two to reason; the one visible, the other invisible" (*RM* 1:45). Metaphysical poetry, which proceeds by analogy and leads us to discover correspondences, is the truest expression of this amphibious state. But if the theory of correspondences on which metaphysical poetry depended was the product of a long tradition, it was a tradition increasingly threatened in a century that was beginning to favor observation and induction over meditation and analogy.[10] The poets we have nicknamed metaphysicals are not the only ones who thought in such terms, but rather those who were self-conscious in their expression of a world view slipping away forever. This distinction is made by Herbert Read, who, in describing Dante, in contrast to Donne, as one who writes metaphysics in poetry but is not a "metaphysical poet," said, "The world was not a problem to him."[11]

The world was a problem for the English metaphysical poets of the seventeenth century. Their poetry turns on the precarious balance between the divided and distinguished worlds in which they lived, a balance that became ever more difficult to maintain as the century wore on. The metaphysical conceit is not only a discovery about reality; it is a claim about the nature of reality. Such claims were made boldly by Donne, confidently by Herbert, as a last hope by Vaughan, and, in a shift that marks the end of the line, without any sense of difficulty by Traherne.

J.A. Mazzeo and S.L. Bethell have stated admirably the case for the theory of correspondences as the basis of metaphysical poetry, but less attention has been given to the extent to which this belief in analogy shapes individual poems and bodies of poetry. In exploring this question I have chosen to consider not John Donne, whose poems have been the basis for most modern definitions of metaphysical poetry, but rather three poets who, though usually called metaphysicals, have often proved an embarrassment to those who so named them, lacking, as they seem, the audacious wit, the extravagant conceits, the nimble logic, the harsh and sinewy verse of the master. But all of them—Donne, Herbert, Vaughan, and Traherne—share a sense of dual reality without which in a metaphysical poet one might say, in the words of Sir Thomas Browne, "(though I feele his pulse) I dare not say he lives" (RM 1:42). The poetry of each of them represents an exercise, not necessarily in the sense of a formal meditation so usefully outlined by Louis Martz,[12] but more generally, an attempt to shape their lives and verse around the fact of divine presence and influence as they understood it. The varying success they achieved reflects, of course, their individual poetic powers, but also the quality of their religious experience.

I do not mean to suggest that saints inevitably write good poems and sinners bad ones, and I take note of Helen White's warning that mysticism and poetry are in an important sense antithetical, the one a matter of ineffable experience, the other, of expression.[13] But the principle of universal analogy, as distinct from the practice of mysticism, the belief that "though there bee but one [world] to sense, there are two to reason," provides a structure to which both life and verse may conform. The famous tension of metaphysical poetry is not simply a matter of literary expression; it grows out of a paradoxical view of reality. The struggle to attune oneself to that reality is the shaping force in Donne's "Goodfriday," Herbert's "The Collar," Vaughan's "The Search," and Traherne's "Dissatisfaction," even as it appears to have been a dominant force in the lives of the authors.

Yet even as one lists these instances one becomes aware of the striking differences in the poems mentioned, differences that in large part reflect a changing view of the relationship between the two worlds that man inhabits—the realms of body and spirit, nature and grace, darkness and light—and the increasing difficulty in the seventeenth century of making connections between them, of living simultaneously in both. George Herbert, writing of man's amphibious state, described himself as "A wonder tortur'd in the space / Betwixt this world and that of grace,"[14] and his poems convey the full sense of that tension. Traherne, forty years later, is in large measure released from Herbert's dilemma, but also deprived of the richness of his solution. His vision, though splendid, is more nearly single; he finds only joy in discovering "My Soul a Spirit infinit!"[15] The seventeenth century was an age in which many became wits or visionaries but in which few—the metaphysical poets among them—united the two tendencies within themselves. It yielded to an age in which Pope, without pain or passion, could move from the first to the second person and declare man "The glory, jest, and riddle of the world!" But it is the metaphysical poets who make us feel what it is like to be such a creature and it is to the relationship between belief and expression in their work that we now turn.

Basic to this inquiry is the hypothesis that each of the poets considered is a maker of shapes and forms to be seen not only in individual poems, but in his work as a whole, and that the distinctive characteristics of those forms are related to the quality and nature of the poet's religious and cosmological experiences, taken in their broadest senses. My aim is not to deduce biography from poetry but to examine the way in which the poetry itself creates a universe of assent with its own particular laws and limits.

Though the hypothesis of form may seem almost inevitable, the question of the shape of *The Temple, Silex Scintillans,* and Traherne's poems has been long and vigorously debated; various patterns have been asserted and denied, and each work has in its turn been called shapeless or chaotic. While I am convinced that such is not the case, this critical context should serve as a caveat against too hasty or easy discoveries of system. In approaching the text cautiously, as readers attempting to grasp the shape of the poet's work, we are engaged in an undertaking in some ways analogous to the poet's own attempt to perceive his world truly.

I

Between Two Worlds
HERBERT

SINCE the publication of *The Temple* in 1633, many readers have tried to see some pattern in this complex and mystifying body of poems, or if not, to impose one on it. One of the boldest and probably the most vulnerable of these, George Herbert Palmer, arranging the poems by subject matter into twelve groups, wrote: "I believe that such a classification according to the subject matter of the poems, a classification which is also largely chronological, will be found more generally convenient than the ancient arbitrary order; and I even hope that it may render the consecutive reading of Herbert instinctively evolutionary and agreeable."[1] Palmer has located the problem exactly. To read *The Temple* without knowing its pattern, its direction, or its outcome is troublesome. The "ancient arbitrary order," we find, goes against our instincts for clarity and form; it bewilders and perplexes us. But it does not follow that we may by rearrangement solve the problem, for all available evidence indicates that the ancient order is Herbert's own, and that, far from arbitrary, it is the intentional product of his own modification of the first version as found in the Williams Manuscript.[2] Palmer assumes, and modern scholars would agree, that the poems of the Williams Manuscript are earlier than those of the Bodleian Manuscript or the first edition of 1633,[3] but in making his "chronological sequence," he also assumes that Herbert was concerned with certain themes or questions only at certain periods of his life; hence Palmer offers such groups as "Cambridge Years," "Meditations on Abstract Themes," "Doubts about Bemerton," "Suffering," "Death." But while such a pattern may simplify matters, it violates the essential structure of *The Temple*, which is anything but "instinctively evolutionary and agreeable." Herbert, so far as we know, never went beyond his description of the little book as "a picture of the many spiritual Conflicts that have past betwixt God and my Soul, before I could subject mine to the will of Jesus my Master."[4] The very essence of this conflict was frustration; perhaps the most astonishing aspect of *The Temple* is its lack of progress, its absence of order, its chaotic indirection. This is not to deny that there are traces of form or strong indications of movement, nor that Herbert finally submits to his Master. The problem is rather that there are so many apparent patterns, so many diverse movements, so many submissions of the will that finally, *The Temple* may seem to have as many heads as Hydra. It recreates a struggle in which the poet himself often could not discern a pattern, and the fruitful uncertainty these poems produce in their readers is, I suspect, precisely what Herbert would have wished, for it is a reflection of his own.

The Temple as a whole and in individual poems uses to the full the reader's normal desire to comprehend what he is reading, to see its shape and its patterns. Such an impulse is perhaps particularly marked in twentieth-century readers with a fondness for intellectualizing, but it must also have existed for seventeenth-century readers attuned to wit and strong lines. To all such eager readers *The Temple* offers many tantalizing clues, clues that often lead to puzzlement and surprise.

It has frequently been suggested that the seasons of the church year form the basis for the topics and moods of Herbert's work.[5] Yet although this pattern is strongly marked in the first poems on the passion and resurrection of Christ, and although poems for other feasts of the church follow in their proper order ("Whitsunday," p. 59; "Trinitie Sunday," p. 68; "To all Angels and Saints," p. 77; "Christmas," p. 80; "Lent," p. 85), these poems are too few and their relation to surrounding poems too slight to constitute the shaping pattern of *The Temple*.[6] In this as in other instances, the vestiges of a design seem almost to raise expectations precisely in order that they may be frustrated. In the case of the notion that *The Temple* imitates the church year, such frustration is purposeful, for Herbert's year begins not, as we might expect, with Advent, the season of preparation and hope, but with the passion and death of Christ, the essential act of sacrifice on which *The Temple* focuses our attention.[7]

Another intriguing possibility is the suggestion in Herbert's titles of a tripartite structure—"The Church Porch," "The Church," "The Church Militant." These have prompted some critics to see in *The Temple* a hierarchical progression, a representation of the movement of God's church through time to eternity.[8] But to do so is to claim, in flat contradiction to the meaning of the words, that "The Church Militant" stands for the Church Triumphant. It is also to take as the climax of his efforts a poem that is very far from Herbert's best, a portrayal of struggle rather than of triumph or rest.

The physical structure of a church or of a Hebrew temple has also been suggested as an analogue to the form of *The Temple*,[9] yet the order of Herbert's poems seems to contradict what we know about these places of worship. "The Church Porch," full of worldly and prudential morality, may instruct us in the decencies prerequisite to entering the sanctuary, but there the orderly progression ceases, for Herbert does not lead us past the baptismal font and up the aisle but rather directly to the holiest place of all, the altar.[10] Not until later do we see the monuments, windows, floor, lock, and key, and then we are made to see them as metaphors for man's experience.

Other critics have sought the pattern of these poems not in temples made with hands but in the poet's own soul. Joseph Summers and, more recently, Stanley Fish, have stressed the central importance of sacrifice for Herbert.[11] Fish argues that Herbert seeks finally to do away with his sense of self, as distinguished from God, to give up even the experience of giving up. It is a testimony not only to the subtlety of Herbert's poems but to the difficulty of finding words to do them justice that several other modern critics find almost the opposite to be true. Coburn Freer asserts that, contrary to much modern criticism of Herbert, the poet does not lose but rather finds himself in a humble way; Arnold Stein considers Herbert's best poems those in which "the poet confronts and attempts to master his own life or death"; Helen Vendler finds that self-abasement is not Herbert's true note, that it in fact characterizes many of his false starts.[12] Even Fish himself, after pages of almost excessively brilliant analysis, concludes that "letting go is finally not what Herbert's poems do (except for an occasional and therefore suspect success) but what they try to do."[13] And whereas Fish finds the poet bending his whole effort toward renouncing and surrendering the claims of his own ego, Vendler describes him as a humanist who at last comes to understand God by making Him in his own image.[14]

With several of these critics I share substantial areas of agreement, but their sophisticated analyses also suggest how partial a view results when we remake *The Temple* in our own image, taking an aspect of it most congenial to us for the whole. And yet it may be almost impossible not to, for no statement of pattern, of theme, of method does it justice, certainly no summary except perhaps Herbert's own when he called it a picture of his many spiritual conflicts. Moreover, there is something in the very nature of *The Temple* itself that tempts us to make such judgments and descriptions.

I have mentioned the variety of themes and patterns that suggest themselves only to dissolve in complexity, but there is also the apparent simplicity of the text, the plain style and homely terms,[15] the sentiments, above all the titles. Though we have been amply warned by recent scholarship how subtle Herbert is, poems with such titles as "Life," "Death," "Man," "Peace," "Sinne," and "Affliction" constitute a direct and probably irresistible provocation to the reader to guess at the subject or the content of a poem.[16] Such titles suggest large subjects grandly treated; they introduce particular lyrics and parables written in homely language. One is tempted to think that these brief poems must simplify or trivialize, but if Herbert's poems seem to ask easy questions, we should not mistake for the poet's own the quick and obvious answers to which we may be prompted. To induce such responses may be part of Herbert's plan, for when "Life" turns out to be about death, and "Mortification" shows us life in death, we find that we have been outwitted by simple little poems that begin in man's world and lead to God's.

The Temple also presents us with a bewildering variety of voices, by no means all of them to be identified with Herbert's own. Of course there are such obvious uses of persona as "The Sacrifice," in which Christ speaks from the cross, or "Love Unknown" or "Dialogue," in which, respectively, soul and friend or soul and savior discourse. But even in these instances there are surprises: "The Sacrifice" follows "The Altar," which in the very severity of its form focuses attention on the poet himself, on the building of the altar in his heart, on the artistic and spiritual discipline required of him, on the sacrifice he makes to serve God and to write poetry in his praise.[17] It comes as something of a shock, then, to realize that "The Sacrifice" deals not with the poet's renunciation but with Christ's; that the noun of the title is not abstract but specific and proper. Unlike the poet who gives something of his own, Christ gives himself.

This unexpected shift in persona and perspective paves the way for further revelations. The "Deare Friend" of "Love Unknown" appears to be the unknown lover, i.e., Christ, in disguise. The apparently yielding soul who addresses his "sweetest Saviour" in "Dialogue" proves to be subtle, saccharine, and false. The dissertation on the follies of man in "Miserie" (originally titled "The Publican") ends with the confession

"My God, I mean my self." The raging, rebellious voice of "The Collar" responds to the appellation "Child" with a submissive "My Lord." Our reading of these poems is made easier by the shift of mood or attitude with which they conclude, allowing us to take the final position as our point of orientation. But often the mood shifts from one poem to another as well as within a single lyric, so that the expressed attitude of each poem is at least potentially challenged by its context. Moreover, no matter how wise we may be in retrospect, each of us has had initially to encounter each poem alone, without knowing to what criticism its ending may subject its beginning. Nor have all readers passed Herbert's tests with flying colors. A.B. Grosart was unimpressed by "the tinkling pieties of *The Temple*"; D.J. Enright complains of Herbert's flat and unconvincing verse; Bernard Knieger marvels at "the seemingly rather odd phenomenon of an otherworldly Christian using much worldly imagery in a non-pejorative sense."[18] Each of these readers, I would argue, has failed one of Herbert's tests, has misread the voice of one of Herbert's personae as the poet's own. But to say this is not so much to criticize them as readers as to acknowledge the success of Herbert's design, in which each poem is one of a long series of challenges we must meet before we can attempt the next. *The Temple* is not only a picture of the poet's many spiritual conflicts; it is a reenactment of those conflicts within the soul of the reader.

It has been customary to emphasize the tendency of Herbert's poems to return to a stable religious and artistic base, but that is to overlook the very vigorous, indeed violent, athletic experience of reading *The Temple*. Looking from without, one may say that Herbert always comes home to his Master, but reading through *The Temple* one is struck instead by how often the poet comes home only to be discontented there, to find it less secure, less blissful than expected, to find the emotions that gave meaning to his confident declarations suddenly altered. The reader who traces Herbert's course from pride to despair to presumption and from despair to hope again reads feelingly such lines as: "O rack me not to such a vast extent; / Those distances belong to thee" ("The Temper I," lines 9–10).

It may be said that Herbert leads us into temptation that we may be delivered from evil. In doing so he uses the voice of simple piety, too good to be true, too simple to be convincing; he represents formal adherence to patterns in which the heart does not participate; he depicts naïveté of the spirit, sometimes manifested as arrogance, or expressed in the belief that God's gifts can be matched by man's endeavors.

> Surely I will revenge me on thy love,
>   And trie who shall victorious prove.
> If thou dost give me wealth, I will restore
>   All back unto thee by the poore.
>
> ("The Thanksgiving," lines 17–20)

Sometimes, by contrast, such spiritual naïveté is seen in the discovery by an intelligent and worldly speaker of an amazingly simple yet essential truth: "Perhaps great places and thy praise / Do not so well agree" ("Submission," lines 15–16). Such discoveries may make us smile at as well as judge the persona. Among the most amusing of Herbert's voices is that of the literal-minded, rational man, competent in the affairs of this life but at a loss in the things of the spirit:

> As I one ev'ning sat before my cell,
> Me thoughts a starre did shoot into my lap.
> I rose, and shook my clothes, as knowing well,
> That from small fires comes oft no small mishap.
>   When suddenly I heard one say,
>   *Do as thou usest, disobey,*
>   *Expell good motions from thy breast,*
> *Which have the face of fire, but end in rest.*
>
> I, who had heard of musick in the spheres,
> But not of speech in starres, began to muse.
>
> ("Artillerie," lines 1–10)

The speaker, fortified by proverbs and experience of the world, is only temporarily daunted by the speaking star; he tries for twenty more lines to work out a contract agreeable to both parties, divine and human, before he finally resigns, acknowledging the defeat that brings redemption: "There is no articling with thee: / I am but finite, yet thine infinitely." More sophisticated, but finally no less misguided, is the querulous voice of "The Crosse," unable to believe that God will not finally see the wisdom of the speaker's own "designe":

> What is this strange and uncouth thing?
> To make me sigh, and seek, and faint, and die,
> Untill I had some place, where I might sing,
>   And serve thee; and not onely I,

But all my wealth and familie might combine
To set thy honour up, as our designe.
  .   .   .   .
Besides, things sort not to my will,
Ev'n when my will doth studie thy renown:
Thou turnest th' edge of all things on me still,
Taking me up to throw me down.

             ("The Crosse," lines 1–6; 19–22)

In all of these flawed voices there is of course something of the poet.
Herbert had a genuine if not unambiguous desire to submit his will to
God; he was aware of the role of forms of ritual in doing so. He frequently
expressed a desire for useful activity ("Employment," "Businesse"), and
the temptation to believe that he could somehow repay God's mercies to
him is especially apparent in the early poems on the passion. It must often
have been a disappointment to this splendidly educated young man, who
cared rather too much about his dress, who rose to be Orator at Cam-
bridge and had high hopes of a court appointment, who shared the
choleric tendencies of his family, that the power and dignity of the
Herberts might not, through him, be put to the more obvious sorts of uses
in God's service.

    Yet it would be a mistake simply and uncritically to take these voices as
Herbert's own, for they dramatize the spiritual conflicts of which *The
Temple* is the record. If they correspond to aspects of Herbert's character,
they also speak to something within the reader: hence their attractiveness
and their danger. We can never assume we know the identity of the
speaker, whether saint or sinner, penitent or man of worldly wisdom.
Whether we side with him or draw back in disapproval, our spiritual
stature is being measured. Herbert offers us clues—in the structure of a
poem, in the exaggeration of an attitude, in the evenness of meter or the
raggedness of a rhythm, in the balancing of one poem against another—
by which we may read and judge whether "the soul unto the lines ac-
cords" ("A true Hymne," line 20). But we should never underestimate
the difficulty of this task, for the temptations in Herbert are as real as the
solutions; indeed it is doubtful that one who has not experienced both has
truly read *The Temple.*

    Herbert's subtle strategy of temptation and deception, of manipula-
tion of persona, language, and meter, may be detected as early as "The
Church Porch," with which *The Temple* begins. At first this purely

didactic poem seems straightforward enough. It opens with a formula common in the Renaissance, assuring the courtly reader that he may expect profit and delight from *The Temple,* and goes on to preach prudence, virtue, and self-control from a sometimes astonishingly pragmatic and worldly perspective. Even advice on explicitly religious matters is tinged with a worldly standard of measurement and punningly presented in the colloquial language of fashion:

> Resort to sermons, but to prayers most:
> Praying's the end of preaching. O be drest;
> Stay not for th' other pin: why, thou hast lost
> A joy for it worth worlds. Thus hell doth jest
>   Away thy blessings, and extreamly flout thee,
>   Thy clothes being fast, but thy soul loose about thee.
>
> (stanza 69)

Yet another strain, muffled, even disguised, runs through these verses. Herbert begins the poem with an invitation:

> Thou, whose sweet youth and early hopes inhance
> Thy rate and price, and mark thee for a treasure;
> Hearken unto a Verser, who may chance
> Ryme thee to good, and make a bait of pleasure.
>   A verse may finde him, who a sermon flies,
>   And turn delight into a sacrifice.
>
> (stanza 1)

The first four lines might have been addressed to such a promising youth as Herbert was himself. The terms of the discourse—"rate," "price," "treasure"—are unabashedly secular, but they may be turned to another purpose, and indeed, inside "The Church," they will be. It is in fact the method of *The Temple* to begin with such terms as its readers will readily comprehend and, by using them in new ways, to shift their meaning to reveal another kind of truth.

The word "sacrifice" in the seventeenth century had strong literal as well as metaphorical senses. It denoted the slaughter of animals and even of humans as an offering to the Judaeo-Christian God or to pagan deities; it marked the continuity between the Judaic sacrifice of animals to Yahweh and the sacrifice of Christ himself in atonement for man's sin; and it applied to the offering of prayers, thanksgiving, penitence, or devotion to God. Thus Herbert's words immediately suggest that the reading of poetry—in itself a pleasure—may also be an act of devotion and of spiritual edification, and these words allow us to ignore, for the moment, their darker meanings. But the sacrifice understood metaphorically becomes in the course of *The Temple* increasingly literal, for very soon we find that sacrifice is not delightful, but that delight itself is sacrificed, as the persona complains that he has been caught with God's bait of pleasure, enticed, entangled, and betrayed.

"The Church Porch" is ethical rather than sacramental and as poetry unremarkable. Yet its opening lines contain the language—"sweet," "treasure," "pleasure," "bait," "sacrifice"—that will dominate the rest of *The Temple* and be redefined by it. "Sweet," with its biblical echoes of the "sweet savor of sacrifice," as applied to the crucifixion of Christ must have a very different meaning from "sweet" as applied to the sweet youth of "The Church Porch." The bitter irony of such a contrast is the means by which Herbert directs us to new apprehensions of truth, to a vision of a paradoxical and yet redemptive reality, to a world in which "Love is that liquour sweet and most divine, / Which my God feels as bloud; but I, as wine" ("The Agonie," lines 17–18) or, as in "The Sacrifice," in which "Your safetie in my sicknesse doth subsist" (line 227).

Such shifting use of language is sometimes unobtrusive, but pervasive, in *The Temple*. Because Herbert the poet provides us with words that prove more meaningful than the persona has yet suspected, the possibility of judgment and instruction is always ours. Yet there is a very real possibility that we as readers may be no more perceptive than the persona, that we may fall into his errors, that we may take his views, which are no doubt often a reflection of Herbert's state of conflict, for the poet's final vision. The eleven poems on the passion with which *The Temple* begins allow us to see in miniature the instruction of the persona and the illumination of the reader that go on throughout *The Temple* as a whole.[19] They also reflect the two didactic and poetic techniques central to our discussion of Herbert—the transformation of the meaning of words and the establishment of a significant relation between poetic form and statement, between patterns of verse and patterns of life.

"The Altar" marks the opening of "The Church," the heart of *The Temple*;[20] it also strikes a key note, dramatically representing the tension between will and performance, between pattern and participation, basic to the whole work. "The Altar," like "Paradise," and like that other shaped poem "Easter-wings," is a clear example of poetic discipline, of the subjection of line and meter to the rigid requirements of the shape of an altar. As the poet disciplines his verse, so he hopes also to discipline his heart. Not only do his words speak of such control: we feel the difficulty of the task in the hard, monosyllabic rhymes, the constricted dimeter lines that form the upright of the altar. Herbert alludes to the biblical injunction against cutting altar stones with human tools (Ex. 20:25); but he also makes us feel the power of God in the discipline of the verse, cutting across his lines and sentences:

> A HEART alone
> Is such a stone,
> As nothing but
> Thy pow'r doth cut.
> Wherefore each part
> Of my hard heart
> Meets in this frame,
> To praise thy Name.
>
> (lines 5–12)

The first four lines of this passage, though choppy and awkward, are metrically absolutely regular, as Herbert describes God's power to cut the stone that is his heart. Even more difficult, as the irregularity of the next lines suggests, is the shaping of the altar, making "eách párt / Őf mý hárd héart" meet in this frame.

Clearly, the form of Herbert's verse embodies its meaning, but Herbert's comment on what he achieves in writing such a poem is perhaps even more illuminating: "That, if I chance to hold my peace, / These stones to praise thee may not cease" (lines 13–14). In one sense, of course, this is simply a variation on the theme of *ars longa, vita brevis*, reminiscent of Shakespeare's own version: "So long as men can breathe or eyes can see, / So long lives this, and this gives life to thee." But in a more particular sense Herbert has achieved something of significance for himself as a living poet and practicing Christian: he has assumed the posture of praise in a way that will outlast his own abilities, even his own inclinations.

That all who kneel do not effectively pray no one knew better than George Herbert. He need have thought no further than his own parishioners crouched "in hudling, or slubbering fashion, gaping, or scratching the head";[21] moreover his definition of "A true Hymne"—"when the soul unto the lines accords"—suggests by implication the many instances of discord between the two. But despite hypocrisy and discrepancy, Herbert also realized the efficacy both for himself and for those who might be influenced by his example of assuming such a posture.

The Countrey Parson, when he is to read divine services, composeth himselfe to all possible reverence; lifting up his heart and hands, and eyes, and using all other gestures which may expresse a hearty, and unfeyned devotion. This he doth, first, as being truly touched and amazed with the Majesty of God, before whom he then presents himself; yet not as himself alone, but as presenting with himself the whole Congregation, whose sins he then beares, and brings with his own to the heavenly altar to be bathed, and washed in the sacred Laver of Christs blood. Secondly, as this is the true reason of his inward feare, so he is content to expresse this outwardly to the utmost of his power; that being first affected himself, hee may affect also his people, knowing that no Sermon moves them so much to a reverence, which they forget againe, when they come to pray, as a devout behaviour in the very act of praying. (*Works*, p. 231)

In this passage from *The Country Parson* Herbert stresses the parson's physical posture as a reflection of his spiritual state and as an inducement to the same spiritual state in others. But he also sees the posture of prayer with its physical submission as a preparation for and means to his own spiritual activity. If this is true of Herbert's understanding of bodily posture, it is also true of the structure of his verse, which functions both as a model for and an indication of his spiritual life.

Joseph Summers has noted the almost unparalleled variety of verse forms in *The Temple*, [22] but the picture is even further complicated by the poet's shifting relationships with these patterns of life and verse. He is by turns willing, reluctant, aggressively involved, passively withdrawn, dubious, and at last accepting and participating in a pattern essentially divine. There are patterns which he tries to assume but cannot, others which he assumes outwardly but not inwardly, some which he rebels violently against. When in "Easter" his soul celebrates the resurrection of Christ, the lines, though haltingly, effectively imitate that great pattern:

> Rise heart; thy Lord is risen. Sing his praise
> Without delayes,
> Who takes thee by the hand, that thou likewise
> With him mayst rise:
> That, as his death calcined thee to dust,
> His life may make thee gold, and much more, just.

(lines 1–6)

But a few pages later, in "The Temper I," the lines perform what the heart can, all too obviously, no longer participate in:

> How should I praise thee, Lord! how should my rymes
>   Gladly engrave thy love in steel,
>   If what my soul doth feel sometimes,
>   My soul might ever feel!

(lines 1–4)

In this instance even the persona's image of the ideal is shockingly rigid—love engraved in steel. Such an image reinforces the explicit statement: these are the words of a would-be devotee who no longer feels what he professes. Yet the persona also sees the movements in which he is made to participate, movements as yet too great for him, as potentially fruitful:

> Yet take thy way; for sure thy way is best:
>   Stretch or contract me, thy poore debter:
>   This is but tuning of my breast,
>   To make the musick better.

(lines 21–24)

In the light of the poet's struggles in the poems on the passion, it is appropriate that the movements of "Easter" are not aggressive or confident, for they are the first steps of a fledgling soul moving to the rhythm of music he is only beginning to hear. Herbert balances dimeter lines against pentameter ones; the close rhymes, the matching of the action ("likewise," line 3; the as . . . so construction of lines 5–6; the rise . . . risen pattern of line 1) all imply the imitation of an action, the Christian and poet following the steps of his Master. In the first stanza of the poem, the speaker in childlike fashion is taken by the hand. In stanza 2 the lines already move somewhat more confidently as he addresses his lute. Just as the heart moves in imitation of Christ, so the inanimate object of wood and strings moves in sympathy with his rising. Herbert does not stress here, as Vaughan was to do later, the contrast between the elements of nature, which are instinctively right in their responses to the divine tempo, and man, who is willfully mistaken in his choice. Instead inanimate nature supports man in his efforts; the instrument has been taught its art by the divine creator. Even so, man and his instrument are not solely responsible for music, as the prayer with which the song ends indicates: "O let thy blessed Spirit bear a part, / And make up our defects with his sweet art" (lines 17–18).

The second shaped poem of the passion sequence, "Easter-wings," although moving like "The Altar" from long to short to long lines, moves much more freely and easily. It tells the story not of deliberate and conspicuous sacrifice but of man's fall, which paradoxically shall "further the flight in me." The decline is here natural, resulting from the fault of man; the arising is accomplished through the grace of God:

> With thee
> Let me combine
> And feel this day thy victorie:
> For, if I imp my wing on thine,
> Affliction shall advance the flight in me.

> (lines 16–20)

The lines move literally from the abundance of ten syllables ("Lord, who createdst man in wealth and store"), reflecting God's providence, to six syllables ("That I became / Most thinne"), imitating the paltry means of man alone. The lines build syllable by syllable as the soul's force is supplemented by God's. Significantly, the persona no longer cries "Victorie" for himself as in "The Thanksgiving" but feels and sings "thy victorie."

As these early poems indicate, the form of Herbert's verse—its stanza structure, its metrics, its sounds—are vital elements of his dramatic didacticism. They are the means by which Herbert enables us to judge the voices of his personae and the means by which he forces us to perceptions that are unfamiliar, often unwelcome or uncomfortable, in short, the means by which he brings us to his view of divine truth. A case in point is "Praise I," whose limping iambic verse and rigid structure belie its title but point up Herbert's meaning. As the persona goes through the motions of faith and praise, the lines make us feel the lack of fervor and conviction:

> To write a verse or two is all the praise,
> That I can raise:
> Mend my estate in any wayes,
> Thou shalt have more.

> I go to Church; help me to wings, and I
> Will thither flie;

Or, if I mount unto the skie,
I will do more.

(lines 1–8)

Herbert allows us to feel in the dogtrot rhythm and short lines of the first stanza of "Praise I" precisely how true the speaker's words are: "a verse or two is all the praise, / That I can raise." Whether the more optimistic lines that follow may be true, such rhythms also lead us to doubt. The persona describes simple and barren activities in declarative clauses that remain unsubordinated to and unconnected with other clauses ("I go to Church"); he attempts to force connections by juxtapositions, as in lines 5–6 or in the subordinating conditional clause of lines 7–8, but the futility of these gestures is apparent. The "more" with which each stanza ends remains vague, and becomes increasingly hollow with each repetition. To see these with nineteenth-century critics as representative of a seventeenth-century poet's simple piety is surely mistaken. They are the speech of a persona who, though bruised and humbled, is unbroken, who has not ceased to cling to his own conceptions.

Often, in such poems as "Praise I," restriction of line and meter signals sterility and limitation. But Herbert also uses such limited means to show the possibility of yielding to and learning from such restriction. As "The Altar" suggests, a posture at first unnatural and uncomfortable may finally prove true to the inner man. Another instance is "Content," not one of Herbert's best poems but one in which strikingly varied metrics reflect the variation of mood. The speaker of "Content" preaches to his own soul a stoic message rather like that in Vaughan's "The Seed growing secretly." At first the pattern appears rigid, and the soul's movements, as imitated by the lines, are accordingly stilted and awkward. Later the pattern is looser, more flexible; at the same time it is apparent that "the soul unto the lines accords": it moves in perfect harmony with the divinely willed pattern and the verse flows freely and easily. It would perhaps be too simple to say that flexible verse in Herbert is a sign of spiritual health and rigidity a sign of stagnation; or at least one must distinguish flexibility from the chaos of rebellion found in "The Collar," and patient imitation from stubbornness. But Herbert consistently uses the tension inherent in his verse patterns to suggest the state of the persona's soul.

An instance of the persona's willfulness, in which a rigidity of verse testifies to a rigidity of spirit, is "Businesse," in which the "foolish soul who sinn'd today" is briskly catechized in iambic tetrameter couplets and triplets. The poem serves obtensibly to declare the truth about the sinfulness of the soul and the beneficence of God, but its form militates against the emotional experience of the truths it appears to convey. All experience, as the brusque speaker presents it, is divided into questions and answers. This method allows but two possibilities in any given case, and the bold rhetorical format seems to make the answers obvious enough. Yet the soul subjected to this barrage of questions, though we never hear him speak, seems always to have chosen the wrong alternative, and so his condition goes from bad to worse.

> If, poore soul, thou hast no tears,
> Would thou hadst no faults or fears!
> Who hath these, those ill forbears.
>
> Windes still work: it is their plot,
> Be the season cold, or hot:
> Hast thou sighs, or hast thou not?
>
> If thou hast no sighs or grones,
> Would thou hadst no flesh and bones!
> Lesser pains scape greater ones.
>
> But if yet thou idle be,
> Foolish soul, Who di'd for thee?
>
> (lines 6–16)

If the poem's aim is to instill doctrine, it must count as a failure, for one is tempted to sympathize with the silent soul rather than with the busy questioner. But if it reflects intellectual comprehension without emotional participation, it is a brilliant success, a perfect reproduction of the state described in its own final lines: "Who in heart not ever kneels, / Neither sinne nor Saviour feels."

The poem that follows, entitled "Dialogue," presents at first glance a great contrast to "Businesse." Full of the language of emotion, of apparent yielding expressed in feminine rhymes, it seems to embody the emotional response lacking in "Businesse." But in fact its compliance is sham; it represents pride, willfulness, and resistance to the divine will in the guise of penitence and humility. The dramatic and rhythmic structure of the poem provides both a snare for the reader and an illumination:

> Sweetest Saviour, if my soul
>   Were but worth the having,
> Quickly should I then controll
>   Any thought of waving.

(lines 1–4)

So begins the human speaker in "Dialogue," in rhythm deceptively simple and regular, as if his were the voice of purest innocence. But the grammatical superlative—"Sweetest Saviour"—is not matched by the ultimate response, for while affirming his love for his Savior, the speaker hides behind claims of his own unworthiness and steadfastly refuses to yield his soul. The alternation between masculine and feminine endings suggests determined stubbornness under apparent yielding, as does the paradox of lines 3–4: the speaker would *control* "any thought of *waving*," that is, wavering. The point is further reinforced and complicated by the confusion of wave, waive, and waver which creates a paradox of action and inaction: "waving" may indicate a state of instability or a generous insistence on an inferior position; an avoidance of duty or a rejection of an offer.[23] These multiple meanings serve to indict the speaker who, in pretending modesty, refuses Christ's offer, evades his duty, and wanders from the true path.

The persona continues to put his version of reality before us in language and meter that allow us to see what he hopes to ignore:

> But as I can see no merit,
>   Leading to this favour:
> So the way to fit me for it
>   Is beyond my savour.
> As the reason then is thine;
>   So the way is none of mine:
> I disclaim the whole designe:
>   Sinne disclaims and I resigne.

(lines 17–24)

"Savour" denotes understanding,[24] but punningly recalls sense rather than reason. The persona's narrow statement of the case, which ignores his "Sweetest Saviour," also calls our attention to his blindness: in relying on his own "savour" he is but one letter from the redeeming truth. Throughout the poem, claims of nonparticipation and inaction have a stubbornly active quality: to "disclaim the whole designe" (line 23) is to refuse God's redemption. But the parallel form of line 24 ("Sinne disclaims and I resigne") raises another question. If both sin and the persona have given up trying to control his fate, he then "waves," that is, strays and wanders without direction. But how can the persona speak for sin without suggesting (a notion the parallelism and rhymes reinforce) that in this disclaimer the speaker's sinful self yet dominates? Whatever the persona's intention, the divine voice takes him at his word and teaches him to spell it in a new way. True resigning is seen, not in the hard masculine rhymes of stanza 3 but in the feminine ones of stanza 4 that describe the action of Christ:

> That is all, if that I could
> Get without repining;
> And my clay, my creature, would
> Follow my resigning.

(lines 25–28)

The balance so carefully maintained throughout the poem is tipped by one who has parted, not only with his "glorie" but perhaps more important, given the values of this poem, with his "desert"; the voice of tenderness breaks through the language of commerce, at last moving the stubborn and hypocritical speaker and upsetting the neat division of stanzas: "Ah! no more: thou break'st my heart" (line 32). It is not the beginning but the end of "Dialogue" that supplies what was missing in "Businesse," as it teaches what it truly means to kneel.

Such poems as "Dialogue" and "Businesse" use language and meter to undermine the position of the persona and to force a recognition, in him and in the reader, of a new view of reality. In the early poems on the passion, as has frequently been noted,[25] the persona must be detached from his attempts to match or measure the sacrifice of Christ. He gradually comes to state this impulse in other terms and finally, as in "Dialogue," to relinquish it.[26] But the progress of these poems is unsteady and irregular, for the persona's moments of yielding, though frequent, are impermanent and the means of instruction almost always unexpected. Nevertheless there is throughout The Temple a movement from a rigid or fruitless adherence to patterns, to a violation and questioning of them, to a final yielding to and embracing of the divine form. Such a yielding, which depends not only on meter and persona, but on a radical transformation of language and a skillful use of poetic structure, may be seen in embryo in "The Agonie," perhaps the most complex and interesting poem of the passion sequence.

As is true of many another of Herbert's poems, "The Agonie" at first seems inappropriately named. The title leads us to expect a definition or perhaps a picture of agony, whereas the first lines offer nothing of the sort. They begin calmly enough in the world of reason, philosophers, and objective inquiry. Here are no mysteries, nothing resists measurement; man can even, as the aggressive persona of the previous poems would rejoice to hear, walk "with a staffe to heav'n." Only in the slower pace of line 4 and in the language of line 6 is there a hint that the swinging, balanced meter does not mark the straight and narrow way that leads to life but rather the broad and easy way to destruction.

> Philosophers have measur'd mountains,
> Fathom'd the depths of seas, of states, and kings,
> Walk'd with a staffe to heav'n, and traced fountains:
> But there are two vast, spacious things,
> The which to measure it doth more behove:
> Yet few there are that sound them; Sinne and Love.
>
> (lines 1–6)

We have not found the subject nor the tone we expected, but the air of assurance and level of generality of this poem may well lull us into a sense of security. "Agonie" is forgotten; this poem can hardly touch us, but we will listen with mild interest to the definition of "Sinne and Love."

> Who would know Sinne, let him repair
> Unto Mount Olivet; there shall he see
> A man so wrung with pains, that all his hair,
> His skinne, his garments bloudie be.
>
> (lines 7–10)

But Herbert has prepared a rude surprise for us. Before we reach the anticipated definition—"Sinne is that presse and vice, which forceth pain / To hunt his cruell food through ev'ry vein" (lines 11–12)—Herbert forces us to see, not sin, but Christ; and only as we protest that we have been deceived do we realize that we have indeed seen sin—seen it through its effects. The definition of sin, when it finally comes, does not contradict the experience of the first four lines of stanza 2, but it reverses our expectations of passive and active. The structure of Herbert's stanza makes us understand sin, not as a theological concept, but by its fruits, as the source of human and divine suffering.

Herbert similarly subverts our expectations in stanza 3: after the first two stanzas, the reader might reasonably expect love, unlike sin, to be a positive quality; but before we can recognize love as "that liquour sweet and most divine" (line 17) we must realize that it is "that juice, which on the crosse a pike / Did set again abroach" (lines 14–15). The structure we have been trying to grasp is now clear: stanza 1 states the subject; stanza 2 defines sin; stanza 3 defines love. But the apparent rationality of this scheme, as deceptive as the tone of the opening, is destroyed by the experience of the poem. The reader is not allowed to draw circles around the abstract concepts of sin and love but is forced to sound them, to know them, to taste them. The title is after all accurate, for we are drawn deeply into the *agon* of the poem; its symmetry allows no returning to the objective stance of the opening, no easy way out; one must go through its process, one must experience forcefully, though vicariously, Christ's agony in order to read the poem. The neat parallel structure works like a metaphysical conceit, a yoking of opposites, as it demonstrates the inevitable relationship between sin and love, between joy in God's grace and a sense of Christ's suffering. Man characteristically seeks to forget the one aspect and remember the other, but the poem has shifted our perspective from human arrogance to divine suffering, and its conclusion enforces a dual awareness: "Love is that liquour sweet and most divine, / Which my God feels as bloud; but I, as wine" (lines 17–18).

Yet even within this parallel structure Herbert's language is discriminatingly accurate. "Who would know Sinne" contrasts with "Who knows not Love," the conditional with the declarative. We all in fact know sin in that we are all sinners, but we also choose to know it. In the spirit of philosophical inquiry suggested by stanza 1, we may in this particular case choose to know sin without understanding its consequences. And just as we are all sinners, we are all beneficiaries of God's love, though we may not feel or acknowledge it. This deeper knowledge is what Herbert seeks to instill, as he echoes the words of the psalmist, "O taste and see that the Lord is good" (Ps. 34:8). He would make us feel along our pulses the paradoxes of theology, the dual reality at the heart of the universe.

Like "The Agonie," a good many of the poems of complaint of *The Temple* move from a focus on man's activities to a sense of divine passion and compassion; in so doing they recreate the very language in which they are written and the universe in which they exist. An early example is the brief sequence "Deniall" and "Christmas," which opens with a statement of human misery that judges God by man's short yardstick.

> When my devotions could not pierce
> Thy silent eares;
> Then was my heart broken, as was my verse:
> My breast was full of fears
> And disorder.
>
> (lines 1–5)

Because the persona hears with his own ears no response to his prayers, he assumes that God is deaf to his appeals. But the synecdoche—"silent eares"—indicates his own misperception, for he expects speech from the organ of hearing, action from the instrument of compassion.[27] The sheer number of metaphors in "Deniall" and the frequency of images of displacement convey chaos and misdirection. "My bent thoughts, like a brittle bow, / Did flie asunder" (lines 6–7). Herbert's images create cumulatively the picture of a man with soul and body literally distracted and dissolved:

> My heart was in my knee,
> But no hearing.
>
> Therefore my soul lay out of sight,
> Untun'd, unstrung.
>
> (lines 19–22)

It has often been noted that Herbert's prayer for harmony between God and his soul ("O cheer and tune my heartlesse breast," "Deniall," line 26) is met in the mending of the rhyme in the last line of that poem. But it is answered even more fully when the soul that lay "Untun'd, unstrung" sings to his Lord in "Christmas." If *The Temple* were really organized around the calendar of the church year, one would expect such a poem to be preceded by Advent meditations, by preparation for the Redeemer's coming. But clearly nothing could be further from the persona's mind at the beginning of "Christmas."

> All after pleasures as I rid one day,
> My horse and I, both tir'd, bodie and minde,
> With full crie of affections, quite astray,
> I took up in the next inne I could finde.
>
> (lines 1–4)

The context is thoroughly secular. Herbert uses the language of the hunt in riding "after pleasures," "with full crie of affections." There is also more than a hint of kinship between man and beast, who are "both tir'd, bodie and minde." This notion is reinforced in lines 11–12, in which Herbert speaks of "my dark soul and brutish" and begs, "To Man of all beasts be not thou a stranger."[28] Here the "full crie of affections" conveys the unruliness of those passions that are not subject to reason, and "quite astray," which appears first to refer to "my horse and I," is finally seen to modify the "I" of line 4: in other words, the persona does not merely make a mistake, his horse does not simply take the wrong fork; rather the bestial element within him leads him astray.

But as often in *The Temple*, losing one's way is the necessary prelude to finding it:

> There when I came, whom found I but my deare,
> My dearest Lord, expecting till the grief
> Of pleasures brought me to him, readie there
> To be all passengers most sweet relief?
>
> (lines 5–8)

The need for oxymoron—"the grief / Of pleasures"—suggests that there is something wrong with our perception of reality and our use of language, that our pleasures are griefs, our griefs pleasures. This moment of discovery brings another reversal: contrary to what one might have gathered from the longing and pleading of the preceding poems, it is not man who waits for God, but God who waits for man. "My dearest Lord" has been there, "expecting," all along. Although the energies of both persona and reader have been fully invested before this, the action of "Christmas" comes as a surprise to both, for it shifts the center of attention from man's activity to God's, widening our scope of vision to let in something of the divine, by which light we are seen to be not earnest seekers but wanderers.

An even richer instance of the use by a persona of language that is limited and ambiguous and that yet implies for the reader a broader context and fuller meaning is the sonnet "Sinne I."

> Lord, with what care hast thou begirt us round!
> Parents first season us: then schoolmasters
> Deliver us to laws; they send us bound
> To rules of reason, holy messengers,
> Pulpits and Sundayes, sorrow dogging sinne,

Afflictions sorted, anguish of all sizes,
Fine nets and stratagems to catch us in,
Bibles laid open, millions of surprises,
Blessings beforehand, tyes of gratefulnesse,
The sound of glorie ringing in our eares:
Without, our shame; within, our consciences;
Angels and grace, eternall hopes and fears.
Yet all these fences and their whole aray
One cunning bosome-sinne blows quite away.

Ostensibly the poem says: we are cared for by a loving and provident God who, through parents, schoolmasters, churches, and all the experiences of our lives, provides for our spiritual welfare; but all this strategy is undermined by sin. The ending of this poem contrasts with the generally positive orientation (i. e., towards the divine) which is characteristic of the majority of Herbert's poems; here sin has the last word and holds great power. But if we look carefully at the language of the poem, we may be even more puzzled, for many of the words Herbert uses are deeply ambiguous, depending for meaning on their context and our perspective. The "care" of line 1 seems to refer to God's providence, his carefulness for our welfare; but as we read further we may wonder if, from the persona's perspective, he is not girt about with care in the sense of trouble and worry. The primary meaning for fence in the seventeenth century is a protective pale, or defense,[29] but such a structure is positive only if one feels oneself to be on the right side of it, and the reader may well be uncertain whether the deliverance of line 3 points toward greater freedom or toward bondage. Life as this sonnet describes it is either a long series of blessings or a perpetual captivity. Those things to which the speaker is bound are positive: "laws," "rules of reason," "holy messengers"; yet bondage itself is full of negative implications. Moreover, these positive qualities are interspersed with disturbingly negative ones: "sorrow dogging sinne," "Afflictions sorted, anguish of all sizes." In fact this sonnet, which Coleridge admired for "the purity of the language and the fullness of the sense,"[30] is a complicated link in an immensely complicated process, one that uses words to suggest the very opposite of what they may originally signify to us.

To understand the poem at all we must recall the relationship between law and grace articulated by Paul in Romans.[31] Paul emphasizes our bondage to the law and our freedom through the grace of God; nevertheless the law was for the Hebrews a guard against sin and self-destruction.

The rules of reason, though perhaps unloved by schoolboys, are the means by which they learn to use their humanity to the full, by which they learn to judge between right and wrong. And in fact the poem outlines the process of maturing in which the child moves from externally imposed restrictions (by parents, schoolmasters, rules of reason, lines 1–4) to a state of maturity in which internalized principles govern response: "tyes of gratefulnesse, ... / Without, our shame; within, our consciences." The universe as a whole is governed by Providence, and as the poem progresses, representing the gradually expanding horizon of maturity, and perhaps the path to the freedom of grace and of obedience, the picture is increasingly positive. But in the last couplet the safeguards that made such freedom possible are shattered; closer to man even than the defenses of Providence is his "cunning bosome-sinne."

Paul's own discussion of the nature of the law, positive or negative, in the first eight chapters of Romans resembles in detail the language and attitude of "Sinne" and may in fact be the basis of it. Paul stresses that we are necessarily servants, whether of sin or of righteousness, of grace or of the law: "But God be thanked, that ye were the servants of sin, but ye have obeyed from the heart that form of doctrine which was delivered you. Being then made free from sin, ye became the servants of righteousness" (Rom. 6:17–18). Paul acknowledges also the difficulty of finding language appropriate to the subject: "I speak after the manner of men because of the infirmity of your flesh" (Rom. 6:19). He considers explicitly the problem suggested by Herbert's use of language, namely how that which is good—the law—can have negative consequences:

What shall we say then? Is the law sin? God forbid. Nay, I had not known lust, except the law had said, Thou shalt not covet. But sin, taking occasion by the commandment, wrought in me all manner of concupiscence. For without the law sin was dead. For I was alive without the law once: but when the commandment came, sin revived, and I died. And the commandment, which was ordained to life, I found to be unto death. For sin, taking occasion by the commandment, deceived me, and by it slew me. (Rom. 7:7–11)

Paul's explanation of the goodness of the death-dealing law will hardly arouse much enthusiasm in the breast of natural man, who may well find his use of language tortured and confused, if not contradictory. Indeed Paul's position is dictated more by the need to reconcile Christian and Jewish doctrine than by the strict rules of logic. The reader may have similar problems with the voice of Herbert's sonnet which, though apparently that of the grateful believer, is nevertheless tainted by the sin of which it speaks. It sees God's grace through the perspective of this world, in which divine providence appears as a snare, a net, a tie, in which the functions of protection and imprisonment are confused. This is not to say that the speaker intends a negative statement—quite the contrary—but that the fallen language he must use—"catch," "shame," "fears"—makes a purely positive statement impossible, either for him or for us as hearers.[32]

Our difficulties with the language of this sonnet point to the complexity of a method by which words are used in ever richer senses and by which their contexts become clearer to both persona and reader. If we recall lines 1–6 of "The Church Porch," in which the verser promised to "Ryme thee to good, and make a bait of pleasure," we will note an unobtrusive anticipation of "Fine nets and stratagems to catch us in." The first statements of these paradoxes—like Donne's "silken snares and silver hooks" in "The Bait"—emphasize the positive, allowing reader and persona to dwell on the adjective or adjectival phrase, but later poems force a recognition of the negative meanings of the central nouns—bait, nets, stratagems.

Yet Herbert's language is potentially redemptive as well as judgmental, for although his sonnet concludes with the temporary victory of sin, it implies by contrast the spiritual development outlined by Paul, one in which the word "deliver" clearly denotes freedom: "But now we are delivered from the law, that being dead wherein we were held; that we should serve in newness of spirit, and not in the oldness of the letter" (Rom. 7:6); "For ye have not received the spirit of bondage again to fear; but ye have received the spirit of adoption whereby we cry, Abba, Father" (Rom. 8:15).

The suspicion that I may be forcing the meaning of "Sinne I," finding it negative where it is positive, or positive where it is negative, or complex where it is simple, will, I think, be alleviated by noting that it directly precedes "Affliction I," which expands and makes explicit many of the ambiguities of "Sinne I." The "afflictions sorted, anguish of all sizes" which may puzzle the reader in an apparently positive context make sense in the light of the series of five poems which constitute a spiritual autobiography in miniature and redefine the meaning of affliction.[33] As John Donne declared, "affliction is a treasure, and scarce any Man hath enough of it."[34] The persona of these poems at last comes to see his own afflictions in a positive light, but the process by which he does so is neither easy nor natural. In the first poem the persona recounts how he has been deceived (as he now thinks) by the apparent pleasure of serving God:

> When first thou didst entice to thee my heart,
>   I thought the service brave:
> So many joyes I writ down for my part,
>   Besides what I might have
> Out of my stock of naturall delights,
> Augmented with thy gracious benefits.
> . . . .
> Thus argu'd into hopes, my thoughts reserved
>   No place for grief or fear.
>
> (lines 1–5, 15–16)

But after the initial experience of bliss, the persona finds himself at cross-purposes with God: "Thus doth thy power cross-bias me, not making / Thine own gift good, yet me from my wayes taking" (lines 53–54). Yet even in the conclusion to this poem, the persona makes a statement that allows us to see that this is a world, not in which the punishment is made to fit the crime, but in which sin and punishment are one: "Ah my deare God! though I am clean forgot, / Let me not love thee, if I love thee not" (lines 65–66). Similarly, in "Sinne I," Herbert's phrase, "sorrow dogging sinne," implies that the one necessarily follows upon the other.

The sequence of "Affliction" poems concerns not so much self-knowledge as an understanding of the nature of reality, of the paradoxes upon which the persona's life depends. "Affliction II" opens with a prayer: "Kill me not ev'ry day, / Thou Lord of life" (lines 1–2); which leads to an explicit statement: "as thou art / All my delight, so all my smart" (lines 12–13). "Affliction III" goes further, not only to see God as the source of pain and delight, but to see that each is involved in the other in a purposeful way:

> My heart did heave, and there came forth, O God!
> By that I knew that thou wast in the grief,
>   To guide and govern it to my relief,
>   Making a scepter of the rod.
>
> (lines 1–4)

In the fourth poem sorrows continue, battering the soul until even this sense of direction is lost: the persona's abject state may be compared to the dark night of the soul of Saint John of the Cross.

> Nothing performs the task of life:
> The elements are let loose to fight,
> And while I live, trie out their right.

(lines 16–18)

Yet by the end of the poem, the persona envisions his regeneration.

Positive endings to expressions of despair are common in Herbert, but it is even more significant that the final poem in the sequence begins positively because the persona has redefined security as a state that arises out of affliction rather than one that is distinguished from it. The beautiful opening lines combine images of containment and safety (the ark) with those of flexibility. The persona survives by yielding to a situation in which he is sheltered from, though not spared, floods and tempests. He inhabits a universe governed by laws different from those he had previously understood.

> My God, I read this day,
> That planted Paradise was not so firm,
> As was and is thy floting Ark; whose stay
> And anchor thou art onely, to confirm
> And strengthen it in ev'ry age,
> When waves do rise, and tempests rage.

("Affliction V," lines 1–6)

The ark is not only the image of God's protection of Noah and of the ark of his covenant with the people of Israel, but also of the church of Christ. Part of the liberation achieved in "Affliction V" seems to result from the persona's realization that his experience is not unique: he is relieved by something he reads; he is part of a community and a tradition. He no longer uses the desperate first person singular pronoun: "I" occurs only once, in line 1, where it connects the persona to this community, and is thereafter replaced by the first person plural. It is out of this sense of belonging to Christ's church on earth that the last confident lines emerge:

> Affliction then is ours;
> We are the trees, whom shaking fastens more,
> While blustring windes destroy the wanton bowres,
> And ruffle all their curious knots and store.
> My God, so temper joy and wo,
> That thy bright beams may tame thy bow.

(lines 19–24)

The sequence of "Affliction" poems has accomplished a reversal of attitudes and of language; it ends with an explicit paradox (line 20), and also with a paradoxical image. The words "bow" and "bright beams" of line 24 both suggest a rainbow, but the context suggests a conflict between the two. The rainbow above Mount Ararat was the sign of God's covenant with the sons of Noah; the bow is also the archer's weapon of destruction. Herbert's words "tame thy bow" suggest the bow's destructive qualities, but after the flood the colors of the bow of the covenant will tame the destructive force of the rain, the expression of God's wrath. The point is that finally the two, positive and negative, are one.

The Temple as a whole accomplishes just such a reversal as these examples suggest—a reversal of preceptions on the part of the persona and the reader. Because the reality that Herbert places before us is in a sense constant, it may be said that the outcome of his verse is certain. But one could with equal accuracy say that the outcome of Rorschach test is certain—since all elements in the test itself are constant—or that a photographic negative is equivalent to a positive print—the values of light and dark are simply reversed. The early poems of The Temple tend to reveal only light or only dark, to represent only blessings or only despair: the persona, failing to grasp the relationship beteen the two, sees reality either as simple or as double and divided, until at last he comes to understand that reality is a thoroughly paradoxical whole, but one that is ultimately redemptive.

As Herbert redefines the meaning of affliction in the series of poems by that name, so he also transforms the meaning of mortification—or rather of life itself—for these two are finally seen to be one. The six stanzas of "Mortification" represent the stages of man's life—birth, childhood, youth, maturity, age, and death—but the poem is an even more striking image of the perpetual movement of death within that which we call life. In fact death is the secret pattern, the hidden reality of life. It operates as a kind of undertow through Herbert's stanzas: the first part of each stanza announces a phase of man's life; the second counters with an image of death. "Death," which ends the seventh line of every stanza, rhymes with "breath," which ends the third line of every stanza, thus suggesting the inseparability of the two and the movement of one towards the other. Nor is movement in this case merely figurative: the latter half of almost every stanza contains an image of physical motion or an imperative to it and an image of man passively subject to that motion: "Which do consigne and send them unto death" (line 6); "Successive nights, like rolling waves, /

Convey them quickly, who are bound for death" (lines 11–12); "A chair or litter shows the biere, / Which shall convey him to the house of death" (lines 29–30). Such movement toward mortality is sometimes barely perceptible, but inevitable; it is not man's choice but his destiny. It affects even those infants "whose young breath / Scarce knows the way." Man, even though unwittingly, can perform no action that does not lead to his final end: "When boys go first to bed, / They step into their voluntarie graves" (lines 7–8). Man is part, though unconsciously, of a grand ceremonial procession. It is Herbert's intention to make us aware of our place in that process so that we may no longer be passive but active, so that life will not be an unconscious process of dying, but rather that dying will be the conscious choosing of life.[35]

> Man, ere he is aware,
> Hath put together a solemnitie,
> And drest his herse, while he has breath
> As yet to spare:
> Yet Lord, instruct us so to die,
> That all these dyings may be life in death.
>
> (lines 31–36)

Herbert creates awareness of mortality with the explicit statement of lines 31–36; his poem is, for the reader, part of the divine means of instruction. But even more persuasive than such declarations is the structure of the poem itself—the balance between the forces of life and of death, the shocking way in which each stanza, apparently about life, is really about death, the swift movement of the latter half of each stanza, accelerated by an abundance of liquids and open vowels, in contrast to the slower movement, closed syllables, and irregular meter of the first half. The fourth line of each stanza ends with a colon or semicolon and in three of six stanzas is metrically irregular: "Scárce knóws thĕ wáy" (line 4); "Mákes thĕm nòt deád" (line 10); "Schóolĭng hĭs eýes" (line 22). Both meter and punctuation suggest the pause and the disorder of this life before the strong tide of death dominates the latter part of each stanza:

> When boyes go first to bed,
> They step into their voluntarie graves,
> Sleep bindes them fast; onely their breath
> Makes them not dead:

> Successive nights, like rolling waves,
> Convey them quickly, who are bound for death.
>
> (lines 7–12)

In the poems I have been considering, Herbert teaches us to use language in a new way, placing his words in divine contexts that radically alter their meaning, and, as is particularly evident in such poems as "The Agonie" and "Mortification," skillfully employing the formal elements of his verse—its sound, metrics, structure, and juxtapositions—in these didactic reversals. The truth in Herbert is always twofold; it spans heaven and earth; it condemns and heals. What we from our limited perspective have taken to be opposites, separated as earth from heaven, are in Herbert's poems bound together by line and syntax, which parallel the binding force of God's grace, and by paradox and oxymoron, which reveal unity beneath our narrow view of antithesis.

Take, for example, the little poem "Bitter-sweet":

> Ah my deare angrie Lord,
> Since thou dost love, yet strike;
> Cast down, yet help afford;
> Sure I will do the like.
>
> I will complain, yet praise;
> I will bewail, approve:
> And all my sowre-sweet dayes
> I will lament, and love.
>
> (lines 1–8)

The title states a clear opposition that seems to be reinforced by the structure of the lines, divided by the medial caesura and by "yet." But curiously, the words and phrases so juxtaposed are not opposites. The Lord loves, yet strikes; but he does not hate. While casting down, he does not raise up, but he does "help afford." The poet, while bewailing, may not be able to rejoice, but he can approve. He can even, in the final line, advance from the opposition of "yet" to the tension of "and" joining "lament" and "love." In other words, the poet lives, not in the midst of a contradiction that would destroy him, but within a paradox that chastens and gives life.

The poet's ability to survive what at first seems a hostile reality, in which he is struck and cast down, is the direct result of the divine action that he imitates, just as the pattern of the second stanza repeats the first. In stanza 1 he articulates a cause-effect relationship between God's actions and his own: "Since thou . . . Sure I"; therefore what sounds in stanza 2 like independent action stated in independent clauses is but a reflection of the divine action of the first stanza. But the juxtapositions within stanza 2 ("complain yet praise"; "bewail, approve")—if the poems we have been reading are any guide to the meaning of this one—seem to represent not a coexistence within the persona of two different responses to his situation but rather the transformation of one into the other (as in the "Affliction" poems affliction is transformed to delight, as in "The Agonie" love is felt by God as blood, by man as wine). The oxymora of "Bitter-sweet" offer a specific instance of how divine grace transforms man's action from complaint to praise, from wailing to acceptance, just as *The Temple* as a whole works to reveal to poet and reader the reality beneath appearances, the life-giving view from eternity.

In the passion poems the persona labors to act, to match God's sacrifice with his own, but the healing vision that he finally achieves in the last poems is often the result of his defeat, never of his own efforts; it is always the gift of God's grace.[36] Such a vision is embodied in "Prayer," which spans heaven and earth with an ease entirely appropriate to its subject but which expresses that vastness within the narrow room of a sonnet. Not only does the whole poem arch the span, but individual lines juxtapose heaven and earth, suggesting a movement or common ground between them. Herbert balances phrase against phrase, using alliteration and assonance for emphasis; he sets lines broken by caesura against unbroken lines, as in the first quatrain:

> Prayer the Churches banquet, Angels age,
>   Gods breath in man returning to his birth,
>   The soul in paraphrase, heart in pilgrimage,
>   The Christian plummet sounding heav'n and earth.

The effect is a dynamic balance of slow and rapid movement, a sense of vastness contained, of ponderousness offset by speed. These oppositions derive from and reflect God, who created "the six-daies world" which, by his grace, can be transposed "in an houre"; who having breathed his breath into man now receives it back again; who sends manna down that it might be exalted.

In this description I do not wish to underestimate the contrasts and violence of the poem,[37] nor to imply that "Prayer" suggests a kind of passivity. On the contrary, the poem covers great distances in space and time; it may even be said to begin in eternity and to conclude there, to move from the peace of paradise to man's challenge against it, and on to a reassertion of order that takes into account the preceding disorder. It describes a universe that includes war as well as love, discord as well as concord. The poem is itself an oxymoron, written in one of the tightest, most restrictive of poetic forms, but syntactically and rhetorically a series of riddling epithets, neither connected by conjunctions nor bound together in clauses.[38] Such an unusual union suggests the nature of prayer itself: it is something in which man participates but of which he understands very little, in which God understands and receives all. It suggests the sort of accommodation to man—without loss of divine majesty—that Herbert defines in the poem immediately following "Prayer":

> But by way of nourishment and strength
> Thou creep'st into my breast;
> Making thy way my rest,
> And thy small quantities my length;
> Which spread their forces into every part,
> Meeting sinnes force and art.
>
> ("The H. Communion," lines 7–12)

"The Churches banquet, Angels age," "Heaven in ordinarie, man well drest," prayer is an activity in which men and angels unite; it is the continuous activity of heaven and the best activity of man, the intersection of two orbits. Like "the fruit of this, the next worlds bud" in "Sunday," such images create mystery without vagueness because they give us a firm basis for understanding in this world while clearly pointing to what is beyond our understanding in the next. As the sonnet's lack of completed statement and its riddling epithets imply, prayer cannot be defined. But when this riddling poem is understood—or rather when the mystery of prayer is understood—it is not by the poet who no longer needs metaphor,[39] but by God himself who hears and understands prayer, who has conceived the whole riddle and who comprehends the great swinging movements from earth to heaven. If man understands at all, it is only insofar as he, like the poet at the end of *The Temple*, also enters into the kingdom of heaven. "O could I love!" cries Herbert in "A true Hymne." The answer reverses the direction of the action as it points to the Prime Mover: "God writeth, *Loved.*"

"Prayer" and "Bitter-sweet" incorporate high and low, love and anger, joy and sorrow to find a unity in heaven and earth. They also represent Herbert's use of forms of verse to create meaning, in particular to show man's actions as a reflection—as opposed to an imitation—of divine actions. This is not to suggest, in the manner of the persona of the passion poems, that man can act as Christ does, but that through divine grace he is *seen* to do so. The power of such a vision is suggested in "Faith," where it is represented rather crudely, from a human perspective.

> I owed thousands and much more;
> I did beleeve that I did nothing owe,
> And liv'd accordingly: my creditor
> Beleeves so too, and lets me go.
>
> (lines 13–16)

In this early poem Herbert separates somewhat more clearly than in later lyrics the steps of the process by which man is credited with a righteousness that he does not merit.

> When creatures had no reall light
> Inherent in them, thou didst make the sunne
> Impute a lustre, and allow them bright;
> And in this shew, what Christ hath done.
>
> (lines 33–36)

The notion of reflected merit is dominant both as a theological and as a poetic principle in the poems that conclude *The Temple*, and a good many of them reveal divine truth through curiously shifting perspectives and reflections. One of the most intriguing and complete in its embodiment of the new perception toward which *The Temple* moves the reader is "The Odour." Here Herbert carefully distinguishes man's powers from God's, yet links the two inseparably. In contrast to his position in the passion poems, the speaker no longer hopes for a significant change in his own accomplishments and merits, but rather for a change in the way God regards him:

> My *Master,* shall I speak? O that to thee
> My *servant* were a little so,
> As flesh may be;
> That these two words might creep & grow
> To some degree of spicinesse to thee!
>
> (lines 11–15)

Herbert's expression of his desire, though heartfelt, is extremely cautious and modest: flesh cannot be what it is not; it can at best be in "some degree" pleasing to God. But the poem goes on to remind us that it is "*My Master*, which alone is sweet" (line 21) and that any sweetness in the poet is but reflected. The structure of the poem reinforces this truth by making the reader move in circles. The rhyme words of the first and last lines are identical; lines 1 and 5 rhyme also with line 3; lines 2 and 4 in each stanza rhyme exactly, sometimes polysyllabically ("reflection" / "imperfection"), sometimes contrastingly ("pleasing" / "displeasing"). The sense as well as the syntax moves from the subject through the object to the subject again, emphasizing that one—"*My Master*"—is the source and object of all.

> With these all day I do perfume my minde,
> My minde ev'n thrust into them both:
> That I might finde
> What cordials make this curious broth,
> This broth of smells, that feeds and fats my minde.
>
> (lines 6–10)

As prayer is "Gods breath in man returning to his birth," so all sweetness and devotion proceed from Christ:

> For when *My Master*, which alone is sweet,
> And ev'n in my unworthinesse pleasing,
> Shall call and meet,
> *My servant*, as thee not displeasing,
> That call is but the breathing of the sweet.
>
> (lines 21–25)

The words and the rhymes reenact the scene: "sweet" of line 21 meets "sweet" of line 25 in "meet" of line 23; quite literally, "That call is but the breathing of the sweet," since the one is an echo of the other. Only in this reflected sweetness, through Christ's atonement, can man meet God, "As sweet things traffick when they meet" (line 27).

This is a remarkable poem, not only in the degree to which its verbal structure creates its meaning, but in its expression of a new lack of struggle and activity on the part of the poet. He has learned what John Donne meant when he said: "Every thing is immediatly done, which is done when thou wouldst have it done. Thy purpose terminates every action."[40] Despite his earnestness he now rests wholly within the context of

God's law, which like the laws of optics acts with or without our permis-sion. But the changing of perspective in Herbert's poem is no optical illusion; it is the true vision of heaven created by God's mercy. In "The Odour" man does not see through a glass darkly but rather finds true identity only insofar as he is a reflection of Christ.

A similar discovery of identity by means of a different technique is made in "Jesu." Quite literally a spelling poem, it teaches how truly "Thy word is all, if we could spell" ("The Flower," line 21). The simple process of putting four letters together may, with apparent incongruity, recall kindergarten; but precisely this primitive and therefore elemental and necessary experience is what the poem seeks to convey, for in the spelling of "Jesu," as in the spelling of sacrifice, we are all, persona and readers, the merest beginners. As with the other words *The Temple* has taught the reader to spell, "Jesu" can be learned only through the heart, not the mind. Its meaning is found not in a definition but in an action, in God's loving deed: "I ease you." Unless one is the object of the transitive verb of the clause, he will not understand the word; but in the very receiving of the action he is changed and healed, as the poem moves from the past tense of brokenness to the present of grace.

> When I had got these parcels, instantly
> I sat me down to spell them, and perceived
> That to my broken heart he was *I ease you*,
> And to my whole is JESU.
>
> (lines 7–10)

What we are, says Herbert, determines the way we see him, but the very act of seeing, here of spelling, is enough to make us whole.

Whereas earlier poems have shown us duality, the relationship be-tween earth and heaven, the last poems of *The Temple* emphasize the reversal of our vision—the saving transformation that occurs when our life is viewed from eternity. In "Aaron" the sinful man, through Christ ("who is not dead, / But lives in me while I do rest") becomes the true priest. Death, which was "once an uncouth hideous thing" because "We lookt on this side of [it], shooting short," is now "grown fair and full of grace." The poet, who was once caught in "Sinnes Round" without hope of escape, now weaves "A wreathed garland of deserved praise." Although in "A Wreath" the poet still speaks of his "crooked winding wayes," he now finds in them the straight line of life leading to God. The poem itself, with the second half of each line repeated in the line following, moves in a linked circle, an emblem found in many of these last poems, working as they do by repetition and reflection. Herbert had early called the Bible "the thankfull glasse, / That mends the lookers eyes" ("The H. Scriptures I," lines 8–9); now all reality is subsumed by such a healing vision. Man has not succeeded in moving upwards; rather he has seen that he already exists within the redeeming circle of God's providence.

Perhaps the most succinct example of this new vision is found in the odd little echo poem "Heaven," wherein the misleading shell falls away from words to reveal their truth, as "wholly" becomes "holy," and "delight," "light." The echo speaks of heaven, but the words in which it speaks are those of earth, transformed to point to God's truth. The echo, repeating but part of a word in rhyme, is both a representation of the imperfection of our knowledge and an image of the perfect circle of God's eternity.

> Are holy leaves the Echo then of blisse?
>   *Echo.* Yes.
> Then tell me, what is that supreme delight?
>   *Echo.* Light.
> Light to the minde: what shall the will enjoy?
>   *Echo.* Joy.
> But are there cares and businesse with the pleasure?
>   *Echo.* Leisure.
> Light, joy, and leisure; but shall they persever?
>   *Echo.* Ever.
>
>   (lines 11–20)

The Temple, I have been suggesting, is not only a book made up of poems; it is in some sense a single poem. One of its chief subjects is words, the meaning of words, the true apprehension of meaning. Its purpose is not only self-expressive but didactic. But as one might gather from the lines of "The Church Porch" examined earlier, Herbert's chief didactic means is not the declarative sentence but the pleasant snare. In his use of imagery, meter, and structure, in his creation of a persona with whom we may sympathize or whom we may judge, Herbert appeals not merely to our intellects but to our emotions and our senses, teaching us not through what we know and think, but through what we feel. Like his kinsman Sidney, Herbert wrote for fallen man; he knew that poetry is especially useful "since our erected wit maketh us know what perfection is, and yet our infected will keepeth us from reaching unto it."[41]

The Temple is not a work whose pattern can be grasped from without, though it offers many tantalizing clues that tempt us to try and thus to become involved with it. Nor is it merely random and arbitrary in its arrangement, subject to clarification and rationalization by some such rearrangement as that of George Herbert Palmer. *The Temple* is not a chaos but a maze; it is in Donne's phrase "a little world made cunningly," an array of perspectives, values, and attitudes within which the truth is to be discerned.

Critics often write as if these truths always were discerned, as if Herbert wrote no poem that does not represent a solution rather than, or as well as, a problem. But the solutions are often those of the persona rather than of the poet and hence often fallible and suspect. Even when truth is grasped or acknowledged, that vision is often temporary, to be lost again at the beginning of the next poem. The unity and the complexity of *The Temple* consists precisely in its presentation of a world in which the truth is perceivable but not always perceived, in which battles won in the first poem must be fought again even in the last, in which themes are constant but comprehension and treatment of them are not.

The Temple, as it records the struggle of will between Herbert and his Master, always presents us with two views of reality—the heavenly and the mundane, that of Christ and that of the sinner. Sometimes one is dominant, sometimes the other; sometimes they are set in deliberate contrast; sometimes the opposing view is present only by implication, to be inferred by the reader. But the important point is that both are always present, even as *The Temple* as a whole moves from one to the other. Hence even in the last poem, which represents Herbert's final submission, his entry into the joys of the heavenly kingdom, the battle is hard fought; the soul is still reluctant, "guiltie of dust and sinne." And hence, in the last poems, the truth that we perceive is the truth that the persona and reader have been surrounded by throughout. *The Temple* as a whole moves the reader out of the wilderness into the heavenly city. It does so with the central image of the Eucharist, present throughout, first in "The Altar," the place of sacrifice and suffering; then in "The H. Communion," "Love-joy," "The Bunch of Grapes," "The Invitation," "The Banquet," and at last in "Love III," in the heavenly communion. As the language of the Anglican liturgy recalls ("Christ our Passover is sacrificed for us: therefore let us keep the feast"),[42] the symbols of the sacrifice and the banquet are typologically united; but whereas the altar emphasizes the earthly aspect of suffering, the banquet reflects the eternal triumph.

Heaven and earth, joy and sorrow, linked forcibly and with difficulty in such poems as "The Agonie," are at last joined easily in "Love III" as the poet, who has so often and so long resisted, yields to God's grace. The focus has shifted from man to God, from the altar built by God's servant to Christ as the servant of man. The fences, the bondage of "Sinne" so ambiguously presented are now seen for what they are:

> What open force, or hidden CHARM
> Can blast my fruit, or bring me HARM,
> While the inclosure is thine ARM?
>
> ("Paradise," lines 4–6)

The contrast between the first and last poems, however much "such beginnings touch their end," marks the shift from earthly to heavenly perspective toward which *The Temple* has been moving and toward which it moves the reader.

In his final submission of the will—"So I did sit and eat"—the poet acknowledges his dependence on God's mercy and grace. Judging and being judged, we as readers are similarly at the mercy of these poems, subjected to an experience not of verbal meanings only, but of structure, image, rhyme, and rhythm as well. The record of the poet's entanglement by God also becomes a means to lure and instruct the reader. Herbert's "fine nets and stratagems," his "millions of surprises" work to convict of sin and misapprehension, to show the inadequacy of human actions and conceptions, and at last, through a remarkably rich experience of language and structure, to reveal the truth in whose presence we have lived blindly all along:

> Such sharpnes shows the sweetest FREND:
> Such cuttings rather heal then REND:
> And such beginnings touch their END.
>
> ("Paradise," lines 13–15)

II
The Shadow of Time
VAUGHAN

IF THE poems of *The Temple* tease and entice the reader, first allowing false perceptions of order and later leading him to see the truth that shapes not only Herbert's poems but his life, Vaughan's *Silex Scintillans* may well seem without any coherent plan at all. Whereas Herbert interpolated later poems with those of the Williams Manuscript to form *The Temple* as we know it, Vaughan simply added his more recent poems to the unsold sheets of the first edition, which with a new title page and preface became the second edition of 1655.[1] One can detect in Herbert at least traces of, if not complete adherence to, a liturgical calendar, but Vaughan's poems—despite such titles as "The Morning-watch," "The Evening-watch," "The Passion," "Christs Nativity," "Easter-day," "Ascension-day," "White Sunday," "Trinity-Sunday," and "Palm-Sunday" —reveal no such overall scheme. Moreover, whereas Herbert's liturgical poems conform to the ecclesiastical order, beginning with the passion and moving through the church year to All Saints' Day, Vaughan's do not.

In trying to grapple with Vaughan, the reader may at first be struck most forcefully by his acknowledged and deeply felt debt to Herbert himself, "whose holy *life* and *verse*," says Vaughan, "gained many pious *Converts*, (of whom I am the least)" (*Works*, p. 391). Vaughan like Herbert sees his verses as a sacrificial offering to God, and although his stridently righteous tone contrasts unpleasantly with Walton's account of Herbert's last days, he too is concerned about the benefits to his readers of the record of his own spiritual struggles.[2] In "The Match," Vaughan explicitly answers Herbert's hope, expressed in "Obedience," that "some kind man would thrust his heart / Into these lines" and join him in resigning all to God. Indeed, *Silex Scintillans* as a whole is a response to *The Temple*; even the subtitle, "Sacred Poems and Private Ejaculations," is borrowed from that work. But this is only the beginning. Of the 134 titles in *Silex Scintillans*, 26 are taken verbatim from Herbert and another 9 appropriated with only slight variations. A number of Vaughan's poems are written on subjects or biblical texts treated by Herbert; others borrow lines, phrases, techniques; some (like "Idle Verse") seem a mere tissue of several of Herbert's poems.

But to concentrate on such indebtedness to Herbert is not to discover the best in Vaughan. "How fresh, O Lord, how sweet and clean / Are thy returns," writes Herbert in one of his most beautiful poems, "The Flower." "How rich, O Lord! how fresh thy visits are!" echoes Vaughan in "Unprofitablenes," and then, as the reader's heart sinks, continues, "'Twas but Just now my bleak leaves hopeles hung / Sullyed with dust and mud." Other more positive and more inspired lines follow, but regardless of its merits, the poem is doomed by its echoes of one so very different in mood and intention; how can a lament over man's unprofitableness match a celebration of God's mercy? However sincere Vaughan's gratitude to Herbert, the poems in which he borrows most heavily are often weak and unsatisfactory, for the best qualities of Vaughan are very different from the best qualities of Herbert.

The openings of *The Temple* and *Silex Scintillans* provide a striking and instructive contrast. Herbert begins with "The Altar," an image of sacrifice and obedience, expressed in stark, simplified, disciplined poetic form. Vaughan begins with "Regeneration," a vision of the Christian's progress from darkness through judgment to rebirth, complicated in its language and syntax, in its shifting levels of reality, in its use of a persona who teaches the reader and is taught by the experience he describes. Herbert's chief aim, pursued first in "The Altar" and throughout *The Temple*, is the bending of his will to God's, whereas Vaughan desires more ardently to see God than to obey him. "Remove me hence unto that hill, / Where I shall need no glass," Vaughan prays; he wishes, "O that I were all soul."[3] For Herbert the problem is precisely in his soul, which he knows to be stubborn and rebellious; for Vaughan, attracted by Hermetic philosophy and Neoplatonism, man's frailty, his mortality, his fleshly nature is the most serious concern.[4] This is not to say that Vaughan does not believe in sin, but that man's disobedience does not stimulate either his imagination or his intellect as it does Herbert's or Donne's.[5] In moving from Donne, for whom sin was a fearsome obsession, and Herbert, who struggled to rid himself of the claims of his own ego, to Vaughan and Traherne, we move from poetry of will and obedience to poetry of vision, to poetry written by men who, in sharp contrast to their predecessors, no longer felt keenly the dilemma of Paul: "The good that I would I do not, but the evil which I would not, that I do" (Rom. 7:19). The early poems of *The Temple* focus on Christ's passion, showing the divine sacrifice as central and man as unwilling to bow to it. Vaughan's early poems, like his later ones, focus on death, judgment, and immortality.[6] But whereas Herbert's eucharistic images unite the end and the beginning of *The Temple*, Vaughan's final poems are far more disparate than Herbert's, dependent on a variety of natural, traditional, and personal motifs. Herbert's poems frequently grow out of a liturgical context; Vaughan, though a layman most loyal to the Church of England and deeply distressed by what it suffered in the Civil War, seems to feel the link with God's people throughout history even more strongly than his fellowship in the contemporary church. Just as "Regeneration" deals less with the traditional motif of pilgrimage and more with visions of election and a longing for the vision of God himself, so most of Vaughan's poems tell us relatively little about the struggles of the individual Christian in this world, except that his life is not as it was "in those early days," for now we "see not all clear." He regrets keenly, in poems like "Corruption," the loss of that easy access to God recorded in the Old Testament, when "Angels lay *Leiger* here: Each Bush, and Cel, / Each Oke, and high-way knew them."

Vaughan's poems record again and again his search for a focus, a point of orientation for his life, his soul, his understanding. In "Distraction" he cries, "O knit me, that am crumbled dust! the heape / Is all dispers'd, and cheape"; and in "The Seed growing secretly" he laments, "Life without thee is loose and spills." This emphasis on vision and illumination, typified by the conclusion of "Regeneration" ("Lord, then said I, *On me one breath, / And let me dye before my death!*") has led a number of critics to call Vaughan a mystical poet, but the use of this term has also provoked vigorous dissent.[7]

Whether or not Vaughan had mystical experiences is at this point impossible to prove. Discussion of the question is further obscured by the extreme vagueness of the term mystical, which is sometimes (and I think properly) used to refer to a quite exceptional ecstatic experience, such as that celebrated by Teresa of Avila, or to the cultivation of such experience through prescribed patterns of meditation; and at other times is used so loosely as to mean only generally religious, having a sense of the divine. By the evidence of his poems, Vaughan, more than Donne or Herbert, earnestly sought the transcendent experience of the divine in this life, but the evidence of the poems is equally strong that he seldom, if ever, achieved it. His works reveal more of the longings than the experiences of the mystic, but for our purposes the point is that such longings or visions, whether actually granted or merely sought, influence the structure of his poems, for it is toward such a transcendent conclusion that they characteristically move. This basic pattern takes a variety of forms— the progression from emblematic visions to the hope of a final revelation in "Regeneration," the contrast between the "great ring of pure and endless light" of eternity and the "vast shadow" of time in "The World," the failure to glimpse the light, to find a unifying principle, that mars so many of his poems.

For Vaughan as for Browne and for Herbert, the material world is a reflection of the immaterial; the Book of Creatures teaches the lessons of that other book, the Bible; light is the shadow of God. But Vaughan differs from Herbert in that he not only accepts the principle that the material world reflects the immaterial, but also takes light as his chief metaphor for divinity.

> Since in these veyls my Ecclips'd Eye
> May not approach thee, (for at night
> Who can have commerce with the Light?)
> I'le disapparell, and to buy
> But one half glaunce, most gladly dye.
>
> ("Vanity of Spirit," lines 30–34)

> When on some *gilded Cloud*, or *flowre*
> My gazing soul would dwell an houre,
> And in those weaker glories spy
> Some shadows of eternity.
>
> ("The Retreate," lines 11–14)

> To put on Clouds instead of light,
> And cloath the morning-starre with dust,
> Was a translation of such height
> As, but in thee, was ne'r exprest.
>
> ("The Incarnation, and Passion," lines 5–8)

One might multiply these examples many times, for Vaughan's poetry is filled with images of light—radiant, flashing, glimmering, fading. But significantly, as these examples also indicate, Vaughan is as conscious of the loss of light as he is of its presence; light is for him but the *shadow* of God and it is in the land of shadow, of "weaker glories," that he resides:

> Farewell you Everlasting hills! I'm Cast
> Here under Clouds, where stormes, and tempests blast
>   This sully'd flowre
> Rob'd of your Calme, nor can I ever make
> Transplanted thus, one leafe of this t'awake,
>   But ev'ry houre
> He sleepes, and droops, and in this drowsie state
> Leaves me a slave to passions, and my fate;
>   Besides I've lost
> A traine of lights, which in those Sun-shine dayes
> Were my sure guides, and only with me stayes
>   (Unto my cost,)
> One sullen beame, whose charge is to dispense
> More punishment, than knowledge to my sense.
>
> ("Mans fall, and Recovery," lines 1–14)

That "sullen beame" that Vaughan so resents would appear to be his conscience.[8] His description of it as more a source of "punishment, than knowledge" testifies to the gulf between him and Herbert, for it is illumination rather than obedience that Vaughan seeks.

While Herbert's poems subject the reader to a succession of changing moods and experiences, Vaughan's characteristically contrast a former positive state—either in his own personal experience or in that of mankind as a whole—with his present unhappy one, often without giving the reader the full measure of that happier state. Herbert's poems tend to move from negative to positive, from disobedience to submission, from misperception to understanding; Vaughan's, from a positive past to a negative present, or from a negative present to a hoped for but unachieved future; and if, in the manner of Herbert, Vaughan ends on a positive note, such an ending is more frequently achieved through prayer or hope or rhetorical polish, and that often forced, than through experience.

Although Herbert's poems are anything but simple, the complexities they gradually reveal are nevertheless firmly controlled by the poet, as they unfold within a clear and purposeful structure. Though often mystifying, Herbert's poems are never merely confusing; their meanings are neither random nor infinite—only extremely rich and full. Whereas one often takes a poem by Herbert to be simpler than it is and only later discovers its fuller meaning, one's initial reaction to many of Vaughan's poems may well be puzzlement and confusion: the point, the principle of organization, the syntax—all may be unclear. And on better acquaintance these do not resolve themselves into simplicity, or even into systematic intricacy, but into a multiplicity of meanings and possibilities that may seem almost infinite, suggested by but not limited by the poet. Vaughan uses words capable of a variety of senses depending upon the context, so that the words remain, like the title of his poems, *Silex Scintillans*, "sparkling flint," gems set in foil, magnificent, but often excessively bright or allusive. Some of Vaughan's poems remain diffuse, never finding the focus they need, but the best of them are rich, subtle, and suggestive, governed by a very different sort of economy from George Herbert's. For Vaughan, as for Herbert, the true light is behind the shadow if only man can perceive it, but Vaughan is so caught up in the search for that light that his poems reflect chiefly the darkness and frustration of his experience. Moreover, whereas Herbert frequently provides a persona with whom the reader may stumble and fall while the poet maintains ultimate control, Vaughan writes almost exclusively in his own voice, so that whatever safety and clarity might be derived from distance is lost.

An example of how Vaughan's own particular spiritual experience shapes a poem is "Disorder and frailty." The poem, whose rising-falling-rising pattern never allows the reader to feel himself at rest, vividly and persuasively conveys the uncertainty and instability of the poet's position. The first four lines of each stanza show man's progress, real or imagined, the result of his own inclination or of divine prompting; the next nine lines at first show hesitation, which then accelerates into decline, in a movement reinforced by short, rhyming, run-on lines. The fourteenth line of each stanza reasserts the positive, and the fifteenth, unrhymed, line laments the poet's state. The second stanza is typical of the whole:

> I threaten heaven, and from my Cell
> Of Clay, and frailty break, and bud
> Touch'd by thy fire, and breath; Thy bloud
> Too, is my Dew, and springing wel.
>   But while I grow
> And stretch to thee, ayming at all
>   Thy stars, and spangled hall,
>   Each fly doth tast,
>   Poyson, and blast

My yielding leaves; sometimes a showr
Beats them quite off, and in an hour
      Not one poor shoot
      But the bare root
Hid under ground survives the fall.
      Alas, frail weed!

(lines 16–30)

The nervous, rapid motion between positive and negative that shapes the poem is reinforced by images of the contrasts to which the plant is exposed: "winds" (line 7), "thy . . . breath" (line 18); "bit with frost" (line 7), "touch'd by thy fire" (line 18); "Dew" (line 19), "showr" (line 25); "springing wel" (line 19); "the fall" (line 29). These are among Vaughan's favorite images; he uses them here in pairs, the elements of which are united by a common principle (e.g., winds / breath) but which differ widely in their effect, to stress the poet's vulnerability and God's redemptive power. Man is fostered by God's breath, touched by his fire, destroyed by winds and frost. But whereas God has power to create or destroy, the poet's power is strictly limited. Even his ostensibly positive activity, his upward motion, is negative: "I threaten heaven"; his "sleeping Exhalation" (line 31) soon becomes "sickly Expirations" (line 42); and only under divine influence does the ambiguous "and from my Cell / Of Clay, and frailty break" (in which "break" may indicate either daybreak or rebellion, a denial of his nature or a release of new energy) become clearly positive: "and bud / Touch'd by thy fire and breath."

The power of this poem is increased by the richness and resonance of its images—the basic metaphor of man as a plant (itself a biblical notion; see, for example, Ps. 103:15) is reinforced by other more obviously biblical images of God's spirit and man's frailty to provide an underlying theme for the poem: "Thy bloud / Too, is my Dew, and springing wel"; "the bare root / Hid under ground survives the fall." The "springing wel" suggests the living water of John 4:10–14; "the fall" is not merely the shower of rain, but man's own decline into sin; and the seasons of spring and fall, also suggested here, are not natural phenomena but the gifts of God's mercy: "Thy bloud / Too, is my Dew."

The image of intense but ongoing cycles of life that characterize plants may appear hyperbolic and rashly optimistic when applied to man, who knows but one death. Vaughan's images resemble and may have been inspired by George Herbert's in "The Flower": "And now in age I bud again, / After so many deaths I live and write." But Vaughan's lines also identify the poet with a life larger than his individual experience. His own story, referred to in the first lines of stanza 1 and the last lines of stanza 3, suggests the history of the human race:

> When first thou didst even from the grave
> And womb of darknes becken out
> My brutish soul, . . .
> . . . . .
> Leaving me dead
> On my first bed
> Untill thy Sun again ascends.
>
> ("Disorder and frailty," lines 1–3, 42–44)

Man arose from primeval darkness and it is to this darkness that he is in danger of returning if, as in "The Constellation," he breaks the slender link " 'Twixt thee, and me; And oftimes creep / Into th' old silence, and dead sleep" ("Disorder and frailty," lines 10–11).

The cycle of life and death, of rising and falling, established in "Disorder and frailty" is not broken but rather redeemed in the last stanza, in which the ordinarily negative middle lines become a prayer that God will prevent the pattern we have observed from recurring.

> Let not perverse,
> And foolish thoughts adde to my Bil
> Of forward sins, and Kil
> That seed, which thou
> In me didst sow,
> But dresse, and water with thy grace
> Together with the seed, the place.
>
> (lines 50–56)

And in place of the final unrhymed lament for man that has concluded each previous stanza we find words both healing and rhymed: "tune to thy will / My heart, my verse" (lines 59–60).

Vaughan at his best, as well as Vaughan at his worst, is a poet in search of a clearer vision, a means of orientation. He repeatedly and often brilliantly conveys the notion of man disordered, chaotic, needing to be bound together by some outside power—in his case by God. An epitome of this tendency is "Distraction," which turns on the Latin as well as the English sense of its title. It portrays the poet quite literally disintegrating into fragments, lacking the magnetic center by which he can assert his own unity and integrity. The poem begins "O knit me, that am crumbled dust! the heape / Is all dispers'd, and cheape" and goes on to assign the cause:

> The world
> Is full of voices; Man is call'd, and hurl'd
> By each, he answers all,
> Knows ev'ry note, and call.
>
> (lines 11–14)

"Distraction" deals with man's refusal to obey God in prosperity, but these lines might also be taken as a description of Vaughan's own difficulties in finding a center for his belief and his poetry. Some of his poems so answer "ev'ry note" that they fail to find their own dominant key. Endlessly allusive, richly suggestive, they sometimes appear to mean so much that their meaning is blurred and diffuse.

An instance of Vaughan's excessive and diffuse allusiveness is his sonnet "H. Scriptures," which very likely owes its title to Herbert's two sonnets on the same subject and its method to Herbert's "Prayer I." Vaughan does not, like Herbert, abandon sentences altogether, but he does bestow upon his subject a good many mysterious phrases.

> Welcome dear book, souls Joy, and food! The feast
> Of Spirits, Heav'n extracted lyes in thee;
> Thou art lifes Charter, The Doves spotless neast
> Where souls are hatch'd unto Eternitie.
>
> In thee the hidden stone, the *Manna* lies,
> Thou art the great *Elixir*, rare, and Choice;
> The Key that opens to all Mysteries,
> The *Word* in Characters, God in the *Voice*.
>
> O that I had deep Cut in my hard heart
> Each line in thee! Then would I plead in groans
> Of my Lords penning, and by sweetest Art
> Return upon himself the *Law*, and *Stones*.
> Read here, my faults are thine. This Book, and I
> Will tell thee so; *Sweet Saviour thou didst dye!*

The richness of the poem's allusions makes it a fascinating example of the scope of Vaughan's interests. Lines 1–2, "The feast / Of Spirits, Heav'n extracted lyes," echo the epitomizing images of Herbert's "Sunday."[9]

"The Doves spotless neast" recalls the traditional image of the Holy Spirit as a dove, but the concluding phrase, "where Souls are hatch'd unto Eternitie" is an extension of Hermetic as well as biblical accounts of the creation of the world.[10] A like synthesis of sources is apparent in the second quatrain: the hidden stone suggests the secret of the philosopher's stone, as does "the great *Elixir*," but it may also derive from the stone that the builders rejected (Mark 12:10), which signifies Christ. Manna is explicitly biblical, the food by which God fed the Israelites in the wilderness (Ex. 16), as the Bible is the soul's food in the wilderness of this life. Vaughan's nice pun on Logos, "The *Word* in Characters," with its witty notion that in the Bible the Word, i.e., Christ, is spelled out so that man may understand him, extends the notion of lines 1–4 that this book is a bridge between the physical and the spiritual, the mundane and the transcendent.

But though Vaughan's language is richly allusive and his formulations intriguing, the contrast with Herbert is illuminating. Whereas Herbert's sonnet "Prayer I," despite its riddles, has a clear inner dynamic, an unmistakable unity, Vaughan's "H. Scriptures" is loosely organized, and its movement from the opening welcome to the final almost defiant declaration of salvation (again including a phrase taken from Herbert) is rather forced and artificial. The words have perhaps too many meanings: the stones of line 12 (the tablets of the Law) rather confusingly recall the stone of line 5 without creating a useful contrast; "God in the *Voice*" of line 8, which is parallel to "The *Word* in Characters," may refer to the message of John the Baptist, who described himself as "the voice of one crying in the wilderness" (Matt. 3:3), but the parallel does not enrich the meaning of either phrase. The notion that man has a surprise for God (lines 13–14) may work within Herbert's well-established framework of personae, but in the octave of Vaughan's "H. Scriptures," the result is simply a rather awkward confusion as to who is being addressed—the Bible (as in lines 9–12) or Christ himself (as in lines 13–14). Moreover, the joy expressed at the Savior's death lacks the necessary motivation because it is not set in the context of judgment for sin. In short, Vaughan's language is especially interesting to a reader of his other poems, to a seeker of his biblical, Hermetic, and poetic sources, but it does not result in a poem that is in and of itself very effective.

Yet it is also the response within Vaughan's poetry to so many notes, its rich and shifting levels of reference, that fascinate the reader and constitute Vaughan's peculiar attraction. He is a poet of minor keys, of imperfectly executed virtuoso passages, of disappointments, but also of surprises. In "Buriall," for example, Vaughan does not descend to the bone scraping so often found in seventeenth-century meditations on mortality, but he nevertheless provides a startling image of his fate after death, as he prays:

> Watch o're that loose
> And empty house,
> Which I sometimes liv'd in.

(lines 8–10)

The poem shifts disconcertingly from the familiar, even the clichéd, to the bizarre, as it moves from "the first fruits of the dead," "the wages of my sinne," to "that loose / And empty house." Words that have lost their force suddenly come vividly alive, as the "ruin'd peece" acquires physical reality:

> a ruin'd peece
> Not worth thy Eyes
> And scarce a room but wind, and rain
> Beat through, . . .

(lines 11–14)

A series of comforting, soporific abstractions abruptly becomes an account of man's physical disintegration:

> Thou art the same, faithfull, and just
> In life, or Dust;
> Though then (thus crumm'd) I stray
> In blasts,
> Or Exhalations, and wasts
> Beyond all Eyes . . .

(lines 23–28)

For a moment Vaughan appears to align himself with Herbert, to reveal, despite his sense of his own dissolution, a certainty of the divinely ordered context within which that dissolution occurs. "The world's thy boxe: how then (there tost,) / Can I be lost?" (lines 31–32). But the box Vaughan imagines the world to be is much larger than its Herbertian counterpart, and the divine control less clearly evident, just as the structure of Vaughan's poems is looser than Herbert's. Even when they represent the struggles of a blind and willful persona, Herbert's poems imply a divine standard; but however much Vaughan believes in God's providence, the perspective as well as the voice of "Buriall" is that of struggling mortality:

> But the delay is all; Tyme now
> Is old, and slow,
> His wings are dull, and sickly.

(lines 33–35)

In Vaughan's own words, "the delay is all." The poem, despite its theoretical sense of order and its longing for the final event that would make this order a personal reality, conveys a sense of confusion and disorientation characteristic of "that deep / And senseless sleep / The wages of my sinne" (lines 3–5) in which the poet finds himself. The poem finds an ending only by looking to a heaven that it never reaches:

> Yet he
> Thy servant is, and waits on thee,
> Cutt then the summe,
> Lord haste, Lord come,
> O come Lord *Jesus* quickly!

(lines 36–40)

Vaughan's verse frequently represents a failure of order and coherence—not because he lacked craft or rhetorical ability, but because the failures of his spiritual experience are faithfully set down in his poems. But Vaughan's search for meaning, for vision, with all its disappointments, is no less ardent than Herbert's, though differing in emphasis. It is even more difficult to find a consistent movement or development in *Silex Scintillans* than in *The Temple*, but easier to see Vaughan's concentration on three main themes or topics. The first of these is the Book of Creatures, in particular the idea of creaturely obedience contrasted to human willfulness, as seen in "Man" and "The Constellation"; this grouping includes also meditations on natural emblems, as in "The Bird," "The Tempest," "The Waterfall," "The Showre." Second, there are meditations on biblical passages or incidents, such as "Mans fall, and Recovery," "The dwelling-place," "The Night," "Jacobs Pillow, and Pillar." Finally there are poems about divine revelation and the poet's relationship to God, such as "The Retreate," "Peace," "The Pilgrimage," "The Seed growing secretly," and "Childe-hood."[11] These three designations are of course emphases, not hard-and-fast categories;

indeed, Vaughan's finest and most mature poetry is precisely a fusion of them all, achieved in poems in which the complexity of his thought is matched by the richness of his verse.

A great many of Vaughan's poems, as those critics who saw in him a precursor of the Romantic movement were quick to point out, deal with nature, although as the same critics sometimes neglected to say, with nature as man's teacher in a quite un-Wordsworthian way.[12] The early enthusiasm for Vaughan as a precursor of Wordsworth ignored the essential difference between the seventeenth-century poet's emblematic view of nature and the nineteenth-century poet's pantheistic vision, between a notion of creation as a hieroglyph and a "sense of something far more deeply interfused." Yet while easy assumptions of a direct influence or even a basic likeness have properly been discredited, the connection with Wordsworth nevertheless contains a grain of truth. That Vaughan rather than Herbert was seen as a forerunner of Wordsworth is the result not simply of Vaughan's use of certain motifs—for example, childhood and nature—but of his treatment of those motifs. Vaughan's images are predominantly conventional, as is the meaning he derives from them, but the process by which that meaning is derived suggests a personal encounter, even a unique individual discovery.[13] Sometimes, as in Vaughan's poem "The Storme," which begins "I see the use" (i.e., the moral or application), a natural event or object is only a point of departure for the preaching of morality; at other times the poet's meditations on nature play a part in his discovery of a spiritual truth—or so it seems from the way the natural image functions in the poem. For example, in "Rules and Lessons," which may be Vaughan's answer to Herbert's didactic poem "The Church Porch," the poet firmly prescribes behavior ("never sleep the Sun up; Prayer shou'd / Dawn with the Day," lines 7–9), but also clearly expects the reader to be moved and inspired by God's traces in creation.

> Walk with thy fellow-creatures: note the *hush*
> And *whispers* amongst them. There's not a *Spring*,
> Or *Leafe* but hath his *Morning-hymn*; Each *Bush*
> And *Oak* doth know *I AM*; canst thou not sing?
>
> (lines 13–16)

As in the works of Vaughan's medieval predecessor Bonaventure and of his contemporary Browne, there is a two-way relationship between God's two books, an instructive link between the worlds of nature and grace. That Christ is called the morning star leads us from the known to the unknown, from the physical to the spiritual, but while it tells us something about Christ, it also alters our view of this world, making us see in it the world of which it is only a shadow, and thus the earth which points to heaven is not to be merely despised in favor of that heaven but studied and perhaps, in later manifestations of the Book of Creatures motif, delighted in.

The notion of the Book of Creatures was originally and primarily theological and devotional: our understanding of the nature of God and the principles of doctrine may be reinforced by study of the creation. We see the world not for its own sake, but as a testimony of the divine. But potentially this notion may lead in exactly the opposite direction—toward an appreciation of this world at the expense of the next. Vaughan of course does not go so far, and his methods and his conclusions are orthodox; but in attempting to catch the divine meaning of creation, he attends more closely to it than do earlier metaphysical poets. The result is not a clearer view of nature, certainly not a Baconian sense of its reality, but a more clouded, more problematic view of the divine-human relationship.

"Man" is perhaps Vaughan's clearest and most concise statement of his reading of the Book of Creatures: nature provides a divine lesson, a pattern for man's activities which he, the only irregular being in creation, persistently ignores. Four brief stanzas with almost metronomic rhythm and alternating rhyme forcefully convey

> . . . the stedfastness and state
> Of some mean things which here below reside,
> Where birds like watchful Clocks the noiseless date
> ′ And Intercourse of times divide,
> Where Bees at night get home and hive, and flowrs
> Early, aswel as late,
> Rise with the Sun, and set in the same bowrs.
>
> (lines 1–7)

The poem contrasts such regularity with the meaningless and lamentable motion of man who "knocks at all doors, strays and roams" (line 22). Vaughan prays that "God would give / The staidness of these things to man" (lines 8–9), but so fully does the meter project the orderliness of nature that the reader can scarcely feel man's plight at all, however much the poet laments it until, perhaps on reflection, he finds that the monotonous metrical regularity projects also the pointless existence of man who "ever restless and Irregular / About this earth doth run and ride" (lines 17–18). The mechanical quality of the poem, which may make the ideal of creaturely obedience less appealing than Vaughan intended, also underscores the ineptitude of man, who, far from surpassing such primitive patterns, is not even able to match them:

> He knocks at all doors, strays and roams,
> Nay hath not so much wit as some stones have
> Which in the darkest nights point to their homes.
>
> (lines 22–24)

Though "mean things," the creatures are not simply automatic in their motions; Vaughan's description of them as steadfast, watchful, and staid implies the power of choice, but unlike man, these lower beings "To his divine appointments ever cleave" (line 10).

Yet in this image of the creatures' faithfulness it is characteristically their peace rather than their obedience that attracts Vaughan.

> I would (said I) my God would give
> The staidness of these things to man! for these
> To his divine appointments ever cleave,
> And no new business breaks their peace;
> The birds nor sow, nor reap, yet sup and dine,
> The flowres without clothes live,
> Yet *Solomon* was never drest so fine.
>
> (lines 8–14)

The division between peace and obedience is precisely what distinguishes Vaughan's poem from other treatments of this subject. The passage from the Sermon on the Mount to which Vaughan's language refers (Matt. 6:26–29), in urging a reliance on divine Providence, establishes the essential connection between the two: "Wherefore, if God so clothe the grass of the field, which to day is, and tomorrow is cast into the oven, shall he not much more clothe you, O ye of little faith? . . . But seek ye first the kingdom of God and his righteousness; and all these things shall be added unto you" (Matt. 6:30, 33). In the poems of Herbert also the connection between peace and obedience is always clear; the poet in his disobedience finds no peace; he struggles, as in "The Collar" or "The Thanksgiving," either to free himself from the confines of God's will and his conscience or, more frequently, to submit to the divine pattern. But in the poems of Vaughan, who was either unable or unwilling to follow his sources on this point, the link between theology and emotion is weaker; "Man" stresses not sin but disorder, disorientation, and discomfort. Moreover, in Vaughan's lament, man scarcely seems to have the option of the obedience that brings peace:

> Man is the shuttle, to whose winding quest
> And passage through these looms
> God order'd motion, but ordain'd no rest.
>
> (lines 26–28)

"Man" seems to have in abundance the quality I earlier found lacking in Vaughan: orderly in the extreme, it is focused around a clear conception of the difference between man and the other creatures. It is both stanzaically and metrically regular, and its language, often wittily anthropomorphic, seems perfectly disciplined. Yet all this is just the trouble, for the conception that Vaughan expresses, though conventional, is too simple to do justice to his own distressing situation. At best the poem provides a negative analysis of man's situation: the minor note on which it ends offers no solution, nor does the poem as a whole give much sense that the poet has been touched by the plight he describes.

If "Man" is too easy a statement of human difficulties, "The Constellation," though written on the same theme, betrays no such signs of excessive regimentation; it reveals if anything too complicated a perception of the subject and too great an involvement in it. As before, nature is an image of the divine order that man refuses to obey, and Vaughan's first smoothly flowing lines do justice to the beautiful image of the constellation they describe: "Fair, order'd lights (whose motion without noise / Resembles those true Joys . . ." (lines 1–2). But the first signs of difficulty in sense and in meter occur as the poet tries to articulate the precise relationship between the heavenly body and its earthly observers: "Whose spring is on that hil where you do grow / And we here tast sometimes below" (lines 3–4). The metaphor expressed in these four lines, if not mixed, is at least very muddled, and it points to a rather tenuous sense of the relationship between heaven and earth. Though Vaughan's original intention would seem clear, the result is not. The lights of the constellation resemble the joys of heaven; yet it is difficult to see one simply as a representation of the other, for both come from the same hill. To complicate the image further, one springs, establishing the notion of a fountain of joys (this idea begins as a dead metaphor in line 3 and comes to life somewhat suddenly and awkwardly in line 4 with "tast"), while the other grows, a notion expressed with an organic verb not particularly appropriate to the "fair, order'd lights" which in line 1 move noiselessly and almost mechanically.

One such stanza as this might be taken as the result of a momentary failure of attention, but throughout the poem man's inability—or unwillingness—to receive the divine revelation, to perceive the ideal, in fact undermines the description of the ideal itself: "And we here tast sometimes below." Vaughan is concerned in this poem both with what is and with what is perceived. He expresses this concern deliberately in the choice of his image—the constellation is there whether man chooses to see it or not—yet Vaughan emphasizes not the reliability of the transcendent ideal but the fragmentary, flickering quality of man's perception:

> He grops beneath here, and with restless Care
> 　First makes, then hugs a snare,
> Adores dead dust, sets heart on Corne and grass
> 　But seldom doth make heav'n his glass.

(lines 17–20)

The relation between man and God is already indirect, channeled through such visible images as the constellation, but now man turns from that glass, or reflection of the truth, to "dead dust," "Corne and grass," to a false idol that he "first makes, then hugs." In contrast to the "Fair, order'd lights" of heaven created by God, Vaughan describes an order devised by man to entrap himself. As God's creature, man is kin to both high and low in the scale of being, but rather than looking heavenward, man attunes himself to the lower end of the scale—to "Musick and mirth." "Musick"—as in the music of the spheres and the Ptolemaic notions of harmony—is of course originally also an image of heavenly order, but it is here distorted and perverted, just as mirth is a perversion of "those true Joys."[14]

Much of the poignancy of this poem arises from its use of such slightly skewed images as these, for the images that function other than we would have expected and the analogies gone awry are in fact a vivid reflection of the human misperceptions that Vaughan laments and that make poetic articulation of the problem so difficult. Even when man attempts to learn from the constellation, Vaughan finds that, perverted "by a black self-wil" (line 37), he cannot:

> Perhaps some nights hee'l watch with you, and peep
> When it were best to sleep,
> Dares know Effects, and Judge them long before,
> When th'herb he treads knows much, much more.
>
> (lines 25–28)

Man ought to observe the constellation, but as these lines suggest, there is even a wrong way of doing that; a scientific, as opposed to a meditative, approach only suggests how inferior man's arrogant rationality is to the instinct of lower creatures. Although the constellation, the image of heavenly order, is intended as a fixed point of reference, its actual function in the poem is somewhat different. Not only does it move physically from east to west, sometimes seen, sometimes not (lines 9–12), but its significance is not entirely constant or predictable. Man's inability to focus on the heavens is parallel to Vaughan's own attempt to find a satisfactory metaphor to express his plight.

The poem's apparently loose organization seems to follow the poet's changing perception of these "Fair, order'd lights." The first eight stanzas maintain a kind of balance between heaven and earth; each of them glances now at one and now at the other, maintaining a sense of relationship even as it articulates man's misuse of that relationship. But in stanzas 10–12 Vaughan moves to an agonized and bitter description of the current disorder of church and state in England which not only upsets the balance established in stanzas 1–8 toward the earthly sphere but also moves the focus of the poem from mankind to Englishmen. One cannot doubt Vaughan's acute concern for his country, but the particularity of that concern undermines his ability to write a poem about the plight of mankind; indeed it almost destroys his ability to write a poem at all, for stanzas 10–12 violate the pattern of the poem quite as much as the human waywardness Vaughan describes: "Thus by our lusts disorder'd into wars / Our guides prove wandring stars" (lines 45–46).

The final stanzas return to an image of order and to the pattern of balance between earth and heaven. Vaughan concludes with a prayer that the one may imitate the other, that England may resemble the fixed stars of the constellation.

Yet O for his sake who sits now by thee
　　All crown'd with victory,
So guide us through this Darknes, that we may
　　Be more and more in love with day;

Settle, and fix our hearts, that we may move
　　In order, peace, and love,
And taught obedience by thy whole Creation,
　　Become an humble, holy nation.

　　　　　　　　　　　　　　　　　(lines 49–56)

Although these stanzas reassert the balance of the poem in favor of light, the poem and poet never fully recover from the experience of darkness, largely because the darkness remains real and present, and the light, ethereal and unachieved. "The Constellation," though not one of Vaughan's very best poems, is altogether characteristic of his dilemma: he is the poet of light surrounded by darkness, a man caught in complexities that the artist could not always shape and control.

Sometimes, as in "Man," Vaughan uses natural emblems in traditional ways; sometimes, as in "The Constellation," he loses his way in the processes of individual discovery; but his best poems avoid both these extremes to forge a unique synthesis from the poet's own experience. Among the most interesting of Vaughan's nature meditations, and a poem that shows his divergence from Herbert, is "I walkt the other day." This is one of the group of nine untitled poems in *Silex Scintillans* that very likely lament the death of Vaughan's brother and perhaps later of his wife.[15] These poems progress from an almost metronomic rigidity reflecting the poet's blankness and grief ("Come, come, what doe I here?") to an increasing ability to find images of the resurrection in his own experience. In "Come, come" the poet struggles to overcome his negative thoughts, denying the images of death and sterility that occur to him:

　　　　Perhaps some think a tombe
　　　　　　No house of store,
　　　　But a dark, and seal'd up wombe,
　　　　　　Which ne'r breeds more.
　　　　　　Come, come!
　　　　Such thoughts benum;
　　　　But I would be
　　　　With him I weep

A bed, and sleep
To wake in thee.

(lines 21-30)

In "I walkt the other day," the tomb, the bed, and sleep have been transformed to a "gallant flowre," an image of incubating life awaiting the resurrection.

"I walkt the other day," as one would expect from its seventeenth-century origin, uses nature, here specifically a flower in winter, in a thoroughly tendentious way. Yet despite one's educated tendency to believe that the flower grew out of the moral, rather than the moral out of the flower, the structure of the poem tempts us to believe otherwise, as it reenacts the process of the poet's discovery to create a surprise for the reader. In this respect Vaughan's poem differs markedly from Herbert's "Peace," which in some ways it resembles. In Herbert's poem the speaker sets out expressly to search for "Sweet Peace," and in his search moves through a number of ostensibly natural settings, all of which clearly imply a human or moral counterpart: "I sought thee in a secret cave" (perhaps suggesting the life of a hermit); "I . . . going did a rainbow note" (pointing to nature itself?); "Then went I to a garden, and did spy / A gallant flower" ("The Crown Imperiall" or court?). At last the persona learns that the "repose / And peace which ev'rywhere / With so much earnestness you do pursue" is to be found only within the garden of the Prince of Salem, within God's Church and through his Holy Communion.

In Herbert's poem the narrative is obviously only a framework within which various life choices are presented and rejected as a prelude to the true choice that concludes the poem. "Peace" is skillfully constructed; the images of fading and death of the first three stanzas are redeemed by the images of life, the "twelve stalks of wheat" that spring from the Prince's grave in stanza 5; and the peace sought for is not found in any simple conceptual formula such as I have given above, but in the taking of grain, the making and eating of bread—in other words, in an experience of Christ. Yet despite the validity and intensity of Herbert's poem, it emerges as a kind of parable of his experience rather than as a representation of it; one believes not in its literal truth but in its significance. In Vaughan there is no divorce between the two: his poem does not simply present a goal accomplished but recreates the experience of discovery.

The opening of "I walkt the other day" suggests that Vaughan did in fact spend a period in daily meditation on nature. In doing so he would have conformed to the suggestion of his brother Thomas, clergyman and alchemist, who urged: "In the summer, translate thyself to the fields, where all are green with the breath of God, and fresh with the powers of heaven. Learn to refer all naturals to their spirituals by the way of secret analogy."[16] Under the apparently simple guise of a walk in the fields, Vaughan creates a constantly changing frame of reference within which the flower is transformed from an inanimate object to an image of man, first generally and then, with frightening particularity, to an image of the poet's loved ones and himself.

> I walkt the other day (to spend my hour)
> Into a field
> Where I sometimes had seen the soil to yield
> A gallant flowre,
> But Winter now had ruffled all the bowre
> And curious store
> I knew there heretofore.
>
> Yet I whose search lov'd not to peep and peer
> I'th' face of things
> Thought with my self, there might be other springs
> Besides this here
> Which, like cold friends, sees us but once a year,
> And so the flowre
> Might have some other bowre.
>
> Then taking up what I could neerest spie
> I digg'd about
> That place where I had seen him to grow out,
> And by and by
> I saw the warm Recluse alone to lie
> Where fresh and green
> He lived of us unseen.
>
> Many a question Intricate and rare
> Did I there strow,
> But all I could extort was, that he now
> Did there repair
> Such losses as befel him in this air
> And would e'r long
> Come forth most fair and young.

This past, I threw the Clothes quite o'r his head,
    And stung with fear
Of my own frailty dropt down many a tear
    Upon his bed,
Then sighing whisper'd, *Happy are the dead!*
    What peace doth now
    Rock him asleep below?

                                              (lines 1–35)

From the very beginning of the poem certain points are left unre-
solved, certain words undefined, and it is precisely around these points
and words that meaning gathers. Vaughan's opening places us on a rather
casual, intimate footing with him, but it does not tell us what sort of hour
he usually spends, whether in pursuit of nature, exercise, or God; indeed
Vaughan proceeds as if we ought to know the answer and so forces us to
consider the question. We know from "The Constellation" how impor-
tant the difference between these alternatives is, but here Vaughan's
answer is that the pursuits of nature and of God, when truly followed, are
one: "And yet how few believe such doctrine springs / From a poor
root."[17]

There are other questions as well: is "gallant flowre" simply a name or
also a description? Does the poet "whose search lov'd not to peep and
peer / I'th' face of things" find such peering rude and indecent or does he
prefer to go deeper, beneath "the face of things"? Does he walk in a field
or, as such words as "bowre" and "curious store" suggest, in a garden
created for his delectation? Does the phrase "cold friends" (line 12),
amidst images of winter and death, refer to the world of men or of plants?
In most of these cases, the answer is both: Vaughan's images work to bring
together the physical reality and the meaning within it; the suggestion
that "there might be other springs / Besides this here" implies not only
other seasons but other sources and levels of life.

Yet the process of creating meaning in this poem is an especially subtle
one. The poem's involvement in physical detail may owe something to
the new science, but that alone is insufficient to answer the questions it
raises. Nor will our familiarity with emblems and poetic techniques
enable us to read "I walkt the other day" without a trace of wonder. The
"gallant flowre" emerges as both the clearly functioning central image of
the poem and a source of mystery, but it is a source of mystery not only for
the persona but also for the poet and the reader, because the poet's image
is not of his own making. In taking the flower as an image of the resurrec-

tion Vaughan uses a conceit framed by the witty creator; its sense is perfectly clear, but its depths of meaning are ultimately unfathomable. Even after the poet has uncovered the flower physically, he has not uncovered its secret—for the mystery of nature is parallel to the miracle of resurrection. Unlike some of the poems considered earlier, "I walkt the other day" conveys awe without confusion; the whole is unified by the connections between light and shadow, God and creation. Vaughan does not dwell on these connections, play with them, or hyperbolize them as Donne might have; they simply shape his poem so that the reader is less aware of the poet's cleverness than of the unity of God's world.

In the last three stanzas, whose run-on lines comprise a single sentence, the reader is drawn inexorably upward by an art that reflects divine providence:

> O thou! whose spirit did at first inflame
>   And warm the dead,
> And by a sacred Incubation fed
>   With life this frame
> Which once had neither being, forme, nor name,
>   Grant I may so
>   Thy steps track here below,
>
> That in these Masques and shadows I may see
>   Thy sacred way,
> And by those hid ascents climb to that day
>   Which breaks from thee
> Who art in all things, though invisibly;
>   Shew me thy peace,
>   Thy mercy, love, and ease,
>
> And from this Care, where dreams and sorrows raign
>   Lead me above
> Where Light, Joy, Leisure, and true Comforts move
>   Without all pain,
> There, hid in thee, shew me his life again
>   At whose dumbe urn
>   Thus all the year I mourn.

(lines 43–63)

Without seeming to do so, certainly without insisting on the point, Vaughan here rings the changes on light and shadow, visible and invisible, as he shows how, in creation, man sees what is invisible, the divine light "Which breaks from thee." Nothing is here yoked by violence together: rather the poem grows out of a calm acceptance of paradox by which life in this world is made bearable. God's spirit not only warms but incubates the dead; the ascents are hidden but can be followed; the day that can be seen breaks from one that is invisible, yet is in all visible things. In "I walkt the other day," Vaughan manifests the kind of insight described by such theorists as Gracián and Tesauro, the discovery by the poet of what God himself has implanted in creation. For Gracián the conceit "is an act of the understanding that expresses the correspondence which subsists among the objects."[18] In this poem indeed Vaughan presents himself not as maker but as discoverer. He makes use of correspondences that he did not invent and that he does not fully fathom; yet that lack of understanding does not mar the poem. Though the poem fully acknowledges the limits of the poet's understanding, these limits are marked not by bafflement and frustration but by trust "That in these Masques and shadows I may see / Thy sacred way." Like the poet's faith, the poem is organized around the relationship between what is seen and what is not seen, and in it, to the reader's satisfaction and the poet's, light is the shadow of God. That shadow is seen and the true light believed in without the disturbing eclipses of "The Constellation."

Despite Vaughan's reputation in the nineteenth century as a poet of ✳ nature, at least as many of his poems are primarily biblical as are natural in subject and orientation.[19] Besides his metrical Psalms (Ps. 121, 104, and 65), there are numerous meditations on a specific scene or passage (such as "Isaacs Marriage," "Jesus weeping," "The hidden Treasure") and several poems (such as "Corruption" and "The dwelling-place") in which Vaughan sees himself and mankind within a broad biblical context. But despite their number, these poems do not necessarily represent Vaughan at his best. The metrical Psalms are unremarkable and the meditations on individual passages are often simply exclamatory and moralistic without being persuasive; frequently the lesson has little relation to the incident on which it is based and little felt connection with the persona of the poem. A case in point, "Isaacs Marriage," is far better when it expatiates on the patriarch's virtues ("Religion was / Ray'd into thee, like beams into a glasse") than when it denounces the divergence between the age of Isaac and our own: "Praying! and to be married? It was rare, / But now 'tis monstrous."

Although Vaughan's satirical poems have been praised by one of his ablest critics, in fact his genius lies not in satire, in pointing up discrepancies,[20] but in his imaginative grasp of unity, conveyed through images that, by functioning in more than one context, establish connections not previously known to exist. In "Isaacs Marriage" Vaughan happily soon digresses from the scene itself, which prompts such negative comparisons with his own time, to the surrounding celebration of heaven and earth (itself a metaphor for the ascent of Isaac's soul) in which

> The thankful Earth unlocks her self, and blends,
> A thousand odours, which (all mixt,) she sends
> Up in one cloud, and so returns the skies
> That dew they lent, a breathing sacrifice.
>
> (lines 59–62)

Nature is bound to man, earth to heaven; the whole cycle of creation is a symphony of praise, and the word sacrifice, which Herbert's persona found so hard to learn, becomes in Vaughan's poem as natural as breathing, an almost inevitable expression of a harmonious universe.

But if Vaughan's genius is in making connections, his poems also record the great difficulty he had in doing so. And as he reminds us in the preface to the second edition of *Silex Scintillans*, his poems, like Herbert's, are "hymns"; they proceed not from the desire to write poetry but rather from the attempt to discover and articulate spiritual truth. Perhaps not surprisingly, then, Vaughan's best biblical meditations are those in which he establishes a vital connection between the biblical setting and his own life. Yet his point of contact differs from Herbert's, for unlike his mentor Vaughan is not deeply moved by the Passion; his one poem on the subject is more exclamatory than convincing, forced in rhyme and awkward in meter; but he does want urgently and profoundly, as other poems reveal, to feel some contact with God, in particular with the God of the Old Testament. He returns repeatedly to the days after the Fall when God revealed himself directly and when angels still frequented the earth.

> Sure, It was so. Man in those early days
>   Was not all stone, and Earth,
> He shin'd a little, and by those weak Rays
>   Had some glimpse of his birth.
> He saw Heaven o'r his head, and knew from whence
>   He came (condemned,) hither,

And, as first Love draws strongest, so from hence
His mind sure progress'd thither.

("Corruption," lines 1–8)

These lines, like the whole of "The Retreate," have generally been read as an instance of Vaughan's Platonism or Hermeticism, while his treatment of childhood has suggested to some critics that he believed in man's essential innocence and ultimate perfectibility.[21] But the point of this opening is just the reverse: it seems to respond to a previous speaker, one who apparently is so devastated by the effects of the Fall that he can hardly believe that man was ever otherwise. Vaughan does not dispute the Fall, but rather affirms it, and in so doing affirms the goodness of God's original creation. "The Retreate" does not glorify childhood itself but treats it as a symbol of man's original innocence, just as "Corruption" does not deny the Fall but celebrates the "early days" that immediately followed it.

Vaughan is wholly orthodox in his acceptance of the notion of man's sin, but, as his blurring of the distinction between prelapsarian and postlapsarian experience in "Corruption" shows (until line 9 one is not actually sure that the Fall has occurred), he is less interested in the theology of man's situation than in its emotional and psychological impact. Hence he does not choose for his subject Eden, which is perhaps too far removed from his own experience, but rather a scene graced by vestiges of Paradise.

Nor was Heav'n cold unto him; for each day
The vally, or the Mountain
Afforded visits, and still *Paradise* lay
In some green shade, or fountain.

(lines 21–24)

In the midst of these traces of heavenly bliss, Vaughan dwells on man's alienation, his separation from his surroundings; because he is heaven-born and "shin'd a little," "things here were strange unto him"; on the other hand, Vaughan also underscores the unbreakable connections between fallen man and earthly mortality. Man's best efforts are physical ("Swet, and till") and fruitless; they produce only "a thorn, or weed." But man is himself something of a plant, as the verbs "Seed" and "fel" (meaning felled) suggest. Vaughan applies them in the first instance to man, and only in the second to plants; his language, which fuses the organic and transcendent, conveys his complicated sense of man's state.

> Things here were strange unto him: Swet, and till
>   All was a thorn, or weed,
> Nor did those last, but (like himself,) dyed still
>   As soon as they did *Seed*,
> They seem'd to quarrel with him; for that Act
>   That fel him, foyl'd them all,
> He drew the Curse upon the world, and Crackt
>   The whole frame with his fall.

(lines 9–16)

"Corruption" moves from past to future, from Genesis to the Apocalypse. To do so successfully it must transform and redeem its opening images of natural growth and light. Vaughan makes us aware of this necessity, and lets us know that the moment has come, but the transformation does not occur. "Corruption" is sharply divided into three sections, the first recapturing the early days when man still "shin'd a little" (lines 1–28), the second representing his present desperate state (lines 29–38). The third section, which logically ought to be positive and redemptive, is truncated and unsatisfactory, limited to two lines that express hope rather than reality.

> Almighty Love! where art thou now? mad man
>   Sits down, and freezeth on,
> He raves, and swears to stir nor fire, nor fan,
>   But bids the thread be spun.
> I see, thy Curtains are Close-drawn; Thy bow
>   Looks dim too in the Cloud,
> Sin triumphs still, and man is sunk below
>   The Center, and his shrowd;
> All's in deep sleep, and night; Thick darknes lyes
>   And hatcheth o'r thy people;
> But hark! what trumpets that? what Angel cries
>   *Arise! Thrust in thy sickle.*

(lines 29–40)

The image of the rainbow that once marked God's covenant with man and the image of the hovering dove, the creative spirit of God that in Genesis moved upon the face of the water and in Hermetic texts brooded and hatched the world are here darkened and perverted. Even the final glorious consummation is postponed by a vivid contemplation of man's present hopeless state, so that when it comes or appears to be coming, the moment is dramatic but not ultimately convincing.

Although "Corruption" is much more tightly constructed than "The Constellation," the problem for the poet remains the same. Both poems contrast the darkness and despair of man's earthly existence with the bliss and order of heaven, and in the final lines both expect such beauty and joy to transform the earth. But however orthodox such a conclusion may be, the number of times it may be used successfully is limited, as those sects that have fixed the day of the apocalypse discover to their sorrow. For with the angel's cry, the poem ends, and other poems, concerned with the mundane necessities of continuing life, follow. Whether or not such poems convince the reader, they surely suggest frustration for the poet whose spiritual life is here recorded.

Although *Silex Scintillans* as a whole lacks the superb orchestration of *The Temple*, there is a general movement within it, and a subtle change of attitude on the part of the poet of which "Corruption" (Part I) and "The dwelling-place" (Part II) are partially representative.[22] "Corruption," which takes the Old Testament as its starting point, deals with the human condition generally and looks for redemption in an external divine act. "The dwelling-place," a meditation on the New Testament, dismisses external nature as a means of access to the divine in favor of the individual's inner communion with God.

> My dear, dear God! I do not know
> What lodgd thee then, nor where, nor how;
> But I am sure, thou dost now come
> Oft to a narrow, homely room,
> Where thou too hast but the least part,
> My God, I mean my sinful heart.
>
> (lines 11–16)

In the second part of *Silex Scintillans*, Vaughan increasingly emphasizes ⚡ the inner light of faith rather than a vision or an external event, and although this is a development from the early distinction between visible and invisible, light and shadow, there is in later poems greater stress on the hiddenness of the Christian experience. In "The Ass" Vaughan speaks of the world "where frail visibles rule the minde" and prays that he may "minde those things [he] cannot see." He also stresses the need for meekness and humility, scornfully referring to the Puritans—"Who saint themselves, they are no Saints" ("St. Mary Magdalen")—and contrasting their arrogance with the passivity of Abel, whose death prefigures the healing death of Christ, "Who pray'd for those that did him kill!" ("Abels blood"). Most remarkable, Vaughan so far abandons his early position in "Corruption" as to argue in "Jacobs Pillow, and Pillar" that our present state is better than that of the patriarchs. Using orthodox notions of typology, he writes:

> Thou from the Day-star a long way didst stand
> And all that distance was Law and command.
> But we a healing Sun by day and night,
> Have our sure Guardian, and our leading light;
> What thou didst hope for and believe, we finde
> And feel a friend most ready, sure and kinde.
> Thy pillow was but type and shade at best,
> But we the substance have, and on him rest.
>
> ("Jacobs Pillow, and Pillar," lines 47–54)

Vaughan is perhaps most often thought of as the poet of ecstatic vision, the mystic who "saw Eternity the other night." But a closer look at *Silex Scintillans* reveals far fewer such poems than his reputation would lead us to expect; even these few are of a very particular kind. "The World," for example, despite its brilliant beginning, concerns precisely what its title indicates: not the "great *Ring* of pure and endless light," which is dispatched in the first three lines, but rather "Time [which] in hours, days, years . . . / Like a vast shadow mov'd." "The Pilgrimage" is a prayer for vision rather than a record of it. "The Retreate" does not celebrate a present or even a recent vision but rather looks back to exclaim: "Happy those early dayes! when I / Shin'd in my Angell-infancy." In the untitled lament for loved ones who have died, beginning "They are all gone into the world of light," Vaughan imagines heaven but never claims to see it; the point of the poem is the contrast between what his friends now experience in heaven and what he knows here on earth:

> They are all gone into the world of light!
>   And I alone sit lingring here;
> Their very memory is fair and bright,
>   And my sad thoughts doth clear.
>   .   .   .   .
> I see them walking in an Air of glory,
>   Whose light doth trample on my days:
> My days, which are at best but dull and hoary,
>   Meer glimering and decays.
>
> (lines 1–4; 9–12)

Vaughan continually stresses the limitations of his vision and his knowledge; for nature, though often the means through which man understands something of God, is also the veil that hides God from the poet, whose experience is all too clouded. Throughout *Silex Scintillans*, Vaughan, as at the end of "Corruption," continues to hope for the vision of God, but increasingly his poems show him dealing with that unfulfilled hope in more limited and traditional ways and in particular finding consolation in the written word of God.

Silex Scintillans, as the record of the poet's inward struggles, shows him reaching an accommodation of his visionary desires to the frustration of daily life. The result is not merely resignation, but a redefinition of experience, a firmer belief that God may be seen through the shadow, no matter how deep that shadow at times appears. It is out of this clear sense of correspondences between heaven and earth, and of relationships between spheres of experience that some of Vaughan's finest and most distinctive poems emerge—poems such as "Regeneration," "The Night," "The Seed growing secretly," and "The Agreement." These are poems that cannot easily be classified as natural or biblical, but that represent a mature fusion of the two.

"Regeneration," the poem with which Vaughan chose to begin *Silex Scintillans*, is both rich and imaginatively unified, a brilliant blending of traditional images and individual experience, of the world of nature and the world of the emblem. In reading the poem one is never entirely certain which world one inhabits, for Vaughan's language moves oddly between them, but neither does the poem allow us to doubt that a relationship between the two realms exists. Its landscape is presented in such detail that we might take it for reality, but these very details are so puzzling that we are forced to look for their symbolic meanings; when we do so we find that images apparently natural take us ever deeper into the religious experience of man.

Like some of its artistic and religious prototypes—*The Divine Comedy*, *The Romance of the Rose*, and *The Faerie Queene*—"Regeneration" records a dreamlike vision in which the persona or pilgrim has a dual function—to experience (with wonder) and to guide the reader in understanding something that yet remains mysterious. Vaughan's firm handling of so complex a persona is clear evidence of his control over his material—a control that he always struggled for but by no means always achieved—and evidence of a certain maturity and coherence in the religious experience from which the poem proceeds. I do not wish to confuse poetry with prayer or to pretend that success in the one guarantees it in the other, but to assert that just as in any other sort of writing one is more likely to write clearly if one has a firm notion of one's subject, so in writing devotional poetry, in which the poet attempts, in Herbert's and Vaughan's words, to write "a true hymn," the focus and clarity of the poem are related to the focus and clarity of the experience. Vaughan's beginning to write religious poetry in the late 1640s has been attributed to a religious conversion, an interpretation sharply disputed by Kermode and Marilla. [23] But surely there is evidence in *Silex Scintillans*, when it is compared with Vaughan's earlier *Poems* (1646) and with *Olor Iscanus* (1651), of a quickening of religious interest, call it what one will. Vaughan himself called it a conversion (*Works*, p. 391). Yet more to the point than terminology is the way in which in such poems as "Regeneration" Vaughan begins to make sense of his experiences, experiences not only of vision, but of loss, denial, and frustration.

Even before we reach "Regeneration," Vaughan provides a preliminary treatment of its theme in the emblem on the title page of the edition of 1650: a heart of stone, having been burned by divine fire and struck by a heavenly hand, weeps tears of blood. In accompanying Latin verses, Vaughan explains his emblem and his title as he describes the conversion of his stony heart to flesh. He reiterates the theme in a dedicatory sonnet that shows both the influence of Herbert and Vaughan's transformation of that influence to reflect his own concerns.

> My God! thou that didst dye for me,
> These thy deaths fruits I offer thee;
> Death that to me was life and light,
> But dark and deep pangs to thy sight.
> Some drops of thy all-quickning blood
> Fell on my heart; those made it bud
> And put forth thus, though Lord, before
> The ground was curst, and void of store.
> Indeed I had some here to hire
> Which long resisted thy desire,
> That ston'd thy servants, and did move
> To have the[e] murthred for thy love;
> But Lord, I have expell'd them, and so bent,
> Beg, thou wouldst take thy Tenants Rent.

(p. 394)

The notion of the poems of *Silex Scintillans* as a response to Christ's sacrifice strongly resembles Herbert's view; the image of the tenant with his rent recalls "Redemption" (as well as Christ's parable of the unjust servants and the lord of the vineyard, Matt. 21:33–41); and the mystical reciprocity between life and death in lines 3–4 is of the same kind as that between blood and wine in "The Agonie." Yet the central image of the "all-quickning blood," though it may owe something to Herbertian images of growth and to biblical notions of the redemptive power of Christ's blood (Rev. 7:14), is in its almost alchemical, mystical workings distinctively Vaughan's own.

In "Regeneration" itself Vaughan links these images of rebirth to the traditional metaphor of the Christian pilgrimage by which man moves toward enlightenment and salvation. Like "Mans fall, and Recovery" or "Corruption" or "The Retreate," "Regeneration" is neither simply autobiography nor convention: it is a recapitulation of the history of mankind in the experience of the poet. It shows the persona moving from bondage and darkness to an awakening accomplished through judgment (stanza 3); he is then led and instructed by grace (stanzas 4–9); at last he longs for a heavenly vision not provided in the poem itself.[24]

In the first stanza, indeed in the first line, Vaughan, using the language of law and of nature, clearly indicates that the speaker is still in his spiritual infancy:

> A Ward, and still in bonds, one day
> I stole abroad,
> It was high-spring, and all the way
> *Primros'd*, and hung with shade;
> Yet, was it frost within,
> And surly winds
> Blasted my infant buds, and sinne
> Like Clouds ecclips'd my mind.

At first glance these lines seem to describe the contrast between the poet's negative inner state (frost, bondage) and the burgeoning external world ("high-spring," "*Primros'd*"). But matters are not so simple, for by the second stanza what appeared to be external nature is seen to be an image of the poet's mind—and a deceptive one at that. Moreover, the natural images Vaughan uses are ordered and artificial, and they suggest man's responsibility for his situation.

As man appears to move into the world of nature, that world is described increasingly in human terms. *"Primros'd"* (a noun made into a verb and used as an adjective) and "hung with shade" (a phrase that recalls the stage settings of a theater) suggest a scene designed for a purpose rather than one taken from life. Vaughan speaks of "frost" and "winds"; yet these are not unthinking forces but "surly" adversaries, and the buds they blast are the persona's "infant" buds. The intermingling of object and signification is so complete that the last two lines of the first stanza may be read in two quite different ways: a simile followed by a metaphoric verb, as if the poet's mind were the external sky—"Sinne, like Clouds, ecclips'd my mind"—or a metaphor enclosing a simile, as if the metaphor were literal, internalized truth—"sinne-like Clouds ecclips'd my mind."

The opening of stanza 2—"Storm'd thus"—continues the ambiguity: at first glance the poet seems to be saying: "I was stormed"; but if one remembers Herbert's "The Collar," in which the poet storms before he submits to God, and if one notes that in "Regeneration" the storm is the storm of sin, one may find the meaning "I stormed" implicit here as well. In fact Vaughan storms and is stormed; for in sinning—in being assailed or possessed by sin—he lays himself open to destruction. The ward, the innocent under protection, is not so innocent after all; he is in bondage to sin, and his walk is a "monstrous, mountain'd thing." "Meere stage, and show," continuing the theatrical suggestion of "hung with shade," indicates an outward appearance inconsistent with reality; it also suggests movement, since "stage" may mean a level of development, thus implying completion or perfection in the future. In all this Vaughan is not, I think, being careless or merely confusing. His language and syntax must serve a dual purpose—to do justice to the experience of regeneration, and to communicate that experience to the (perhaps) unregenerate reader. He writes the poem after the experience but he writes from the perspective of the pilgrim on his journey, one who, like the reader, as yet sees only through a glass darkly.

In comparing himself to a pilgrim Vaughan clearly, in this poem where tenor and vehicle are so easily interchanged, places himself in the tradition of Christian pilgrims from Dante to Bunyan. But again, intermingling the literal and the figurative, Vaughan both employs this convention as an important element in the structure of his poem and yet appears to overlook it. He seems to think of an actual pilgrim on an actual path—not the Christian pilgrim of metaphor—and thus what is already a metaphor becomes the vehicle of his simile:

> And as a Pilgrims Eye
> Far from reliefe,
> Measures the melancholy skye
> Then drops, and rains for griefe.

(lines 13–16)

In this spiritual landscape the melancholy sky reflects the pilgrim's feelings; but as his eye measures the horizon, it too becomes part of the weather it surveys. He seems first to lower his eyes; he "drops" them; but as one reads further, this verb, taken with the one following, implies the drops of the rain—"drops, and rains for griefe." These drops, the pilgrim's tears, are the water of regeneration that will bring the new spring, and in stanza 3, where the soul moves upwards by sighing, an expression of penitential emotion becomes a means of propulsion:

> So sigh'd I upwards still, at last
> 'Twixt steps, and falls
> I reach'd the pinacle, where plac'd
> I found a paire of scales,
> I tooke them up and layd
> In th'one late paines,
> The other smoake, and pleasures weigh'd
> But prov'd the heavier graines.

(lines 17–24)[25]

Repentance and struggle bring the pilgrim to the end of the first stage, religion according to the law. According to the Pauline explanation of law and grace, one is in bondage to the law, the instrument by which man realizes his true condition, until he comes of age spiritually.[26] The scales, the standard by which the poet's efforts and actions are weighed, reveal, contrary to our expectations, that "smoake, and pleasures" are on the heavier side of the balance—that is, the poet's "late paines," his efforts to be righteous, are of less weight than these trifles. If we recall that "the wages of sin is death" (Rom. 6:23), it seems that these vanities, part of a sinful life, may have heavy consequences, bearing the soul to damnation in the center of the earth, or, in other terms, to the center mentioned in stanza 8.

Because man, having been judged by the law, must be saved by grace, the speaker is now mysteriously led eastward, in the direction Christians traditionally turn in worship, toward Jerusalem, to the rising place of the "unthrift Sunne." The voice may be that of God's saints or of his angels; the guiding function is that of the Holy Spirit, who appears later in the poem.

> With that, some cryed, *Away*; straight I
> Obey'd, and led
> Full East, a faire, fresh field could spy
> Some call'd it, *Jacobs Bed*;
> A Virgin-soile, which no
> Rude feet ere trod,
> Where (since he stept there,) only go
> Prophets, and friends of God.

(lines 25–32)

The persona, no longer a ward in bonds, moves to a place where he, like Jacob, can encounter God. It is important that he no longer steals abroad, as if in rebellion; he is led and he obeys, as if acknowledging his sonship—his obedient relationship to a loving God, rather than his wardship or bondage to sin. His action expresses the paradox of Christian freedom. The false spring is superseded by a "new spring," the transcendent reality created by God's grace. Following the severe judgment of the scales, it comes to the poet freely, without his effort.

> Here, I repos'd; but scarse well set,
> A grove descryed
> Of stately height, whose branches met
> And mixt on every side;
> I entred, and once in
> (Amaz'd to see't,)
> Found all was chang'd, and a new spring
> Did all my senses greet.

(lines 33–40)

The grove becomes a woodland temple, a place for the kind of divine revelation, under an oak or by a well, so often longed for by Vaughan.[27] Here communion with the divine is represented through images of a garden of spices, a sensuous experience ("Thus fed my Eyes") reminiscent of the Song of Solomon, to which Vaughan refers in the epigraph.

> The unthrift Sunne shot vitall gold
> A thousand peeces,
> And heaven its azure did unfold

Checqur'd with snowie fleeces,
The aire was all in spice
And every bush
A garland wore; Thus fed my Eyes
But all the Eare lay hush.

(lines 41-48)

The "vitall gold," a phrase with roots in alchemy as well as an image of divine grace, is splashed lavishly across the scene. Its "unthrift" reflects the difference between God's gracious prodigality and his severe judgment.

Vaughan has experienced judgment and regeneration—the letter that kills and the spirit that gives life, the winter of his sin and the new spring created by God's grace. The rest of the poem presents images of that grace in the form of visual parables, three mysterious representations of the problematic doctrine of election. If, as the poem has shown, and as Protestant doctrine teaches, grace is freely given, if it is the result of God's mercy rather than of human effort, the question must arise: why are some souls saved and others damned? The traditional answer is that since no one deserves grace, we should rather be grateful for God's mercy than critical of its distribution.[28] Although this is Vaughan's answer also, "Regeneration" does not preach or declare doctrine; it records and reenacts the poet's experience. If we are to come to a better understanding of grace, it must be by puzzling out with the persona what he sees.

Only a little Fountain lent
Some use for Eares,
And on the dumbe shades language spent
The Musick of her teares;
I drew her neere, and found
The Cisterne full
Of divers stones, some bright, and round
Others ill-shap'd, and dull.

(lines 49-56)

The garden as a place of divine-human encounter is a *topos* of long standing: Vaughan would very likely think of the Garden of Eden, in which God walked in the cool of the day, the sensuous gardens of the Song of Solomon, and possibly of the enclosed and fountained gardens in medieval representations of the Annunciation.[29] His fountain recalls the Neoplatonic fountain of souls, the sparks of light that descend from God and return to him, but here the souls are represented by the "divers stones" in the cistern. [30] Vaughan's chief source for the image is probably 1 Peter 2:5: "Ye also, as lively stones, are built up a spiritual house, an holy priesthood"; although Thomas Vaughan, in another instance of the regeneration theme, wrote, "Be ye transmuted . . . from dead stones into living philosophical stones." [31] In the manner of parables, there are two kinds of stones and hence of souls: some have the symbolic virtues of brightness, roundness, and quickness; others are dark, heavy, lifeless, and misshapen—mere stones lacking the breath of God.

> The first (pray marke,) as quick as light
>   Danc'd through the floud,
> But, th'last more heavy then the night
>   Nail'd to the Center stood.

(lines 57–60)

What appears only a simile suggesting rapidity of motion—"as quick as light"—in fact ties life or quickness (as in the phrase "the quick and the dead") to that light that proceeds from the Father who is the source of all life.

As both narrator and actor, Vaughan urges us to "pray marke" the actions of the stones; nonetheless he, or rather the persona of the poem, fails to understand this experience. He is then presented with another vision, "as strange," and of the same meaning as the first:

> It was a banke of flowers, where I descried
>   (Though 'twas mid-day,)
> Some fast asleepe, others broad-eyed
>   And taking in the Ray.

(lines 65–68)

This vision, like that of the stones, reveals varying degrees of responsiveness to the source of grace. The flowers that are awake are those receptive to God's spirit, "the Ray" that is both light and divine influence. The thoroughly emblematic representation of this scene forms a striking contrast to Vaughan's treatment of nature in other poems, where (as in "Man," "Cock-crowing," or "And do they so?") lower creatures respond instinctively to God and to light as his symbol. Vaughan probably thought of the story of the wise and the foolish virgins (Matt. 25:1–13) in which the wise virgins were ready to welcome the bridegroom, a type of Christ, with lighted lamps even in the dead of night. As with this parable, the *schema* in the garden represents absolutes of salvation and damnation. When the persona first entered the grove and found the garden, "All the Eare lay hush"; now, signaling the last stage of the revelation and of the poem, a sound like the rushing wind of Pentecost (Acts 2) is heard. The persona, as always taking for natural what the reader knows to be supernatural, looks around him to see what response there has been to this wind.

> I turn'd me round, and to each shade
> Dispatch'd an Eye,
> To see, if any leafe had made
> Least motion, or Reply.
>
> (lines 73–76)

The persona's attempt to trace the wind is parallel to what must have been his musings and wonderings over the other two visions: Why are some stones "quick" and others "more heavy then the night"? Why are some flowers "fast asleepe" (even at "mid-day") and others "broad-eyed / And taking in the Ray"? Why are some souls saved and others damned? What is the explanation of God's grace? The persona seeks to answer spiritual questions through mundane reality, to see by the light of his reason, but the answer he receives is one of faith: man cannot comprehend God or predict the workings of his grace:

> But while I listning sought
> My mind to ease
> By knowing, where 'twas, or where not,
> It whisper'd; *Where I please.*
>
> (lines 77–80)

This answer clearly echoes the language of John 3:8: "The wind bloweth where it listeth, and thou hearest the sound thereof but canst not tell whence it cometh and whither it goeth: so is every one that is born of the Spirit."

The persona does not pause to ponder this exclusion of rational or "just" explanations. Instead, in the final lines of the poem he takes a leap that is typical of Vaughan's work as a whole and consistent with the previous development of this poem. The persona has progressed from his wardship, the state of being in bonds, through judgment, to abundant grace, to the garden where man meets God. The shadowy and shining symbolic visions of the garden and the voice of the wind, the life-giving breath of God, have brought him close to the truth. Now he asks for the final blessing, the vision of God in this life. The death before death of which he speaks is the ecstasy in which the soul stands outside the body, a state in which one sees not "through a glass darkly" but "face to face" (1 Cor. 13:12). Vaughan concludes: "Lord, then said I, *On me one breath, / And let me dye before my death!*" (lines 81–82).

This paradoxical and complex poem concerns itself with vision: in it the persona acquires a new vision of reality; he sees particular visions— the grove, the garden, the fountain—that reveal as well as conceal; but significantly, and characteristically for Vaughan, "Regeneration" does not end in vision, in complete revelation, but only in the hope of it. Aesthetically complete, the poem nonetheless projects human frustration, even as it uses language in all its complexity to express the inadequacy and ambiguity of language. Although Vaughan uses the central image of the pilgrimage in "Regeneration" and although he shows judgment as the essential prelude to God's mercy, his emphasis is on divine grace and man's vision of God. Donne and Herbert agonize over their own disobedience and struggle to bring their recalcitrant wills into accord with the divine will; Vaughan is far less oppressed by a sense of his own sin. In this respect he owes more to the Neoplatonic and Hermetic search for enlightenment and the mystical hope for union with God than to the Protestant desire for salvation with its stress on sin and judgment; and in this he departs from the pattern of Donne and Herbert and moves toward the ecstatic vision of Traherne, who saw so much of the light of God that he sometimes lost sight of the earthly light that is God's shadow.

But Vaughan, as "Regeneration" brilliantly shows, was in Browne's phrase "that great and true *Amphibium*, whose nature is disposed to live not onely like other creatures in divers elements, but in divided and distinguished worlds." His language and syntax are not fixed in any one realm; his world of "frost within," of "sinne / Like Clouds," of the Old Testament grove that becomes a fountained garden, is bound together by the unifying forces of his imagination and of the tradition of Christian iconography within which he finds himself. Despite a remarkable complexity of concept and technique, "Regeneration" is a coherent and unified expression, a significant achievement in the work of a poet whose persistent problem was focus, orientation, revelation. As he describes a vision that is meaningful, instructive, yet limited, Vaughan is artistically in control, having made sense of what he sees only through a glass darkly.

If "Regeneration" is characteristic of the visionary longings of *Silex Scintillans*, especially of Part I, "The Seed growing secretly" represents the accommodation Vaughan found to the frequent disappointments of mundane existence. In earlier poems Vaughan characteristically seeks the fullness of vision; in his later ones he finds now a satisfying glimpse of what will be—or at least, he claims to be satisfied with that glimpse. Yet "The Seed growing secretly," rather like "The Constellation," shows the considerable difficulty Vaughan had with this personal and poetic stance. The seed of the title is Vaughan's image of the soul disciplined to the Christian life, leading a kind of hidden existence that shows no outward signs of success but is nevertheless under God's protection. The image of the seed suggests entirely new criteria for the religious life, implying that its strength is in inverse proportion to its show:

> Glory, the Crouds cheap tinsel still
> To what most takes them, is a drudge;
> And they too oft take good for ill,
> And thriving vice for vertue judge.

> (lines 37–40)

Such a notion must have appealed to a poet who had all too few explicit signs of divine favor, but it represents a considerable shift from Vaughan's assertion that he would "to buy / But one half glaunce, most gladly dye" ("Vanity of Spirit"), or from his urgent prayer:

> Either disperse these mists, which blot and fill
> My perspective (still) as they pass,
> Or else remove me hence unto that hill,
> Where I shall need no glass.

> ("They are all gone into the world of light," lines 37–40)

Vaughan's image of the seed, the hidden greenness, differs from its biblical counterpart in that the seed of Mark 4:26–27 to which Vaughan refers is not so much hidden as mysterious and unexplained: "So is the kingdom of God, as if a man should cast seed into the ground; And should sleep, and rise night and day, and the seed should spring and grow up, he knoweth not how." Moreover, the parable following this passage is an image of success: it compares the kingdom of heaven to the mustard seed, which, "when it is sown . . . groweth up, and becometh greater than all herbs, and shooteth out great branches, so that the fowls of the air may lodge under the shadow of it" (Mark 4:32). But Vaughan's representation of the ideal Christian life, far from resembling these models of growth, is strangely similar to the root gone underground in "I walkt the other day"—an image of death, of the sleep that precedes the resurrection. Vaughan's attitude has of course many antecedents in Christian tradition and in contemporary practice. If it seems to ignore Christ's command to "let your light so shine before men, that they may see your good works, and glorify your Father which is in heaven" (Matt. 5:16), it finds support and perhaps inspiration in the otherworldliness and self-abnegation of John's gospel: "Except a corn of wheat fall into the ground and die, it abideth alone: but if it die, it bringeth forth much fruit. He that loveth his life shall lose it; and he that hateth his life in this world shall keep it unto life eternal" (John 12:24–25). Even following the dissolution of the monasteries in the sixteenth century, the retired life was held as an ideal on religious and philosophical grounds by many in seventeenth-century England, and for one of Vaughan's Royalist sympathies it may have seemed the only remaining possibility.[32] Although such a view of contemplation and withdrawal suggests making a virtue of necessity and seems to question Vaughan's motives, one cannot overlook the tension in Vaughan's poem between assertions of the sufficiency of God's grace and pleas for more, between praise of the superiority of the life of devotion and envy of the life of the world.

The ambiguity of the poet's situation is reflected in the structure of "The Seed growing secretly" and in its somewhat uncertain use of images. Vaughan claims in stanza 1 to have a precious and enviable gift; yet in the next stanza he complains of the lack of it:

> If this worlds friends might see but once
> What some poor man may often feel,
> Glory, and gold, and Crowns and Thrones
> They would soon quit and learn to kneel.
>
> My dew, my dew! my early love,
> My souls bright food, thy absence kills!
> Hover not long, eternal Dove!
> Life without thee is loose and spills.

(lines 1–8)

A closer look at stanza 1 reveals uncertainty even there: the poet whose theme has so often been the vision of God begins the poem as if to declare that he has been granted such a vision, but significantly alters the verb in line 2 to convey something rather less definite, as he moves from "see" to "feel." This pattern is repeated in the next three stanzas, in which it appears that the gift is only remembered and indefinite, but urgently sought by the speaker.

> Somthing I had, which long ago
> Did learn to suck, and sip, and taste,
> But now grown sickly, sad and slow,
> Doth fret and wrangle, pine and waste.
>
> O spred thy sacred wings and shake
> One living drop! one drop life keeps!
> If pious griefs Heavens joys awake,
> O fill his bottle! thy childe weeps!
>
> Slowly and sadly doth he grow,
> And soon as left, shrinks back to ill.

(lines 9–18)

The brilliant "Life without thee is loose and spills" (line 8) points to God as the vital organizing principle in the poet's life, as in his verse. But the influence is inconstant; the metaphor changes in the next stanza to an indeterminate "Somthing I had" (line 9), which by stanza 4 has become "thy childe" who "weeps" (line 16); in the last two lines of stanza 5 the plant image dominates again: "O feed that life, which makes him blow / And spred and open to thy will!"

Vaughan's two chief images in this poem, the child and the seed or plant, both suggest man's vulnerability. They reinforce each other, indeed shade into each other. Yet Vaughan's use of them also suggests some uncertainty about their ultimate meaning, for the image of the plant conveys neglect quite as much as fostering, and even the representation of the child makes us doubt that man's needs will be met. These images of the seed or plant and the child succored by the dew are intensified and united by an image of heaven at the center of the poem that takes the reader to the source of both:

> For thy eternal, living wells
> None stain'd or wither'd shall come near:
> A fresh, immortal *green* there dwells,
> And spotless *white* is all the wear.

(lines 21–24)

Vaughan's multiple adjectives ("eternal, living"; "fresh, immortal") may seem redundant, but in fact, as they explain eternity in terms of time, they point up the difference between them. Green in this world is a symbol of life and hope, but it is also the color of transitory life, of plants. What is here fresh and green must die, whereas in heaven green is the color of immortality. In this world perhaps only that which is already dead may be said to be eternal; in heaven living and eternal are synonymous. The white and the green, symbols of heavenly purity and immortality brought together in lines 21–24, echo throughout the poem, and the one seems to suggest the other:

> Dear, secret *Greenness!* nurst below
> Tempests and windes, and winter-nights,
> Vex not, that but one sees thee grow,
> That *One* made all these lesser lights.
>
> (lines 25–28)

The italicizing of "*Greenness*" and "*One*" emphasizes the link between the seminal principle in man and its divine source. Yet the blurring of this central image again suggests the poet's doubts over this very point. "Dear, secret *Greenness!*" he exlaims. Dear certainly to the poet, but dear also to God? The seed is "nurst below / Tempests and windes, and winter-nights," but the poet does not say by whom. The one who "sees thee grow" appears rather an observer than a tender nurse. And if he "made all these lesser lights" (the mention of which comes as something of a surprise to one occupied with "Tempests and windes, and winter-nights") where is his power now?

When Vaughan again takes up the theme of light as connecting man to God, more surprises and uncertainties ensue:

> If those bright joys he singly sheds
> On thee, were all met in one Crown,
> Both Sun and Stars would hide their heads;
> And Moons, though full, would get them down.
>
> (lines 29–32)

The logic of this statement may be faultless, but the poem lends it no support, for there has been in fact very little evidence of the "bright joys" of the major premise. Vaughan's vision perhaps owes something to Joseph's dream (Gen. 37) in which the sun, moon, and stars bowed down to him, but in contrast to that prophetic vision, Vaughan's poem is couched in the much weaker subjunctive. Moreover, even if the Christian were to be honored in the fashion of Joseph's dream, he must remain lowly, avoid glory, and even shun light.

In the latter part of the poem Vaughan shifts from the Christian's perception of himself to his appearance before others and in the process creates either a new distinction or a confusion.

> What needs a Conscience calm and bright
> Within it self an outward test?
> Who breaks his glass to take more light,
> Makes way for storms into his rest.

(lines 41–44)

Vaughan here contrasts the calm and bright conscience with external light—the one necessary, the other not. But it is hard to see external light, so lately and so persistently a symbol of divinity, as undesirable. Moreover, Vaughan's rhetorical question, often the sign of a weak position, shifts the grounds of his argument: the question was originally not of "an outward Test" but of bare sufficiency for life: "one drop life keeps!"

My point is not that Vaughan is being logically inconsistent, for the standards for poets are not the same as those for philosophers, but that he is poetically unconvincing because he is emotionally unconvinced. His images, instinctively chosen, convey his felt meaning vividly, but will not bear the construction he tries to put upon them, as they come into conflict with other images or proverbial statements, as for example in stanza 9:

> Let glory be their bait, whose mindes
> Are all too high for a low Cell:
> Though Hawks can prey through storms and winds,
> The poor Bee in her hive must dwel.

(lines 33–36)

The high mind and the hawks stooping at glory arouse no aversion, nor do the "poor Bee" and the "low Cell" emerge as particularly desirable. One can see what meaning the image is intended to convey, but also that it does not do so. Vaughan attempts to resolve the issue by bringing together his own metaphors of secret growth (which have proved somewhat unreliable) and biblical ones of fruitfulness:

> Then bless thy secret growth, nor catch
> At noise, but thrive unseen and dumb;

Keep clean, bear fruit, earn life and watch
Till the white winged Reapers come!

(lines 45–48)

Yet the secret growth, the embryonic seed to which Vaughan clings, is juxtaposed with, but not finally reconciled to, the sense of abundance and fruition in "the fields . . . white already to harvest" (John 4:35) and waiting for the angelic reapers.

The problem of metaphor and connotation here is intimately related to Vaughan's method. If light is the shadow of God, then light may appropriately be used as the poetic image of God—"My souls bright food, thy absence kills!"; but if light is the light of this world, it may be a danger rather than a blessing: "Who breaks his glass to take more light, / Makes way for storms into his rest" (lines 43–44). Such a split is of course not unique to Vaughan; the problem is as old as Platonism. But it may be that Vaughan, writing in a very old tradition, one that would not much longer endure, was in an especially difficult position.[33] The medieval and Renaissance metaphor of the Book of Creatures takes for granted that the lessons found in nature will be those found in Scripture; hence the reading of nature is based far less on individual imagination than on convention. Whereas emblematic writing neatly controls the problem of the suitability of metaphor by its conventionality, by concentration on moral meaning rather than on the details of similitude, Vaughan's tracing of God's steps in "these Masques and shadows" involves him in an examination of the masque and shadow, the appearances that may be ambiguous and unpredictable in their connotations.[34] Making use of a variety of traditions, Vaughan discovers that the vehicle of a single metaphor may have different tenors in different contexts and that the philosophic systems Christianity has assimilated in its movement through history may be in conflict with it.

Vaughan seems on firmer ground spiritually and in firmer control of his metaphors in "The Agreement." Here he no longer seeks the kind of unique individual vision that he begs for in "Regeneration"; he speaks of an experience he has had and continues to have ("And this I hourly finde," line 55), one channeled through that "beamy book," the Bible. Although this context protects Vaughan to some extent from the vagaries of his own emotions, the poem does not celebrate something merely institutionalized: the point of the first two stanzas is that the poet now

comes to terms personally with something that has already been ac-
complished.

> I wrote it down. But one that saw
> And envyed that Record, did since
> Such a mist over my minde draw,
> It quite forgot that purpos'd glimpse.
>   I read it sadly oft, but still
>   Simply believ'd, 'twas not my Quill;
>
> At length, my lifes kinde Angel came,
> And with his bright and busie wing
> Scatt'ring that cloud, shewd me the flame
> Which strait, like Morning-stars did sing,
>   And shine, and point me to a place,
>   Which all the year sees the Suns face.

(lines 1–12)

"The Agreement" balances the Bible against the poet's private cove-
nant with God. At first it appears that the validity of the agreement—or the
relationship between God and man—depends on man's acceptance of
that agreement, his memory of it, his sense of its reality. But we soon see
that even that sense, that acceptance, depends on God, who not only
keeps the record of the promise but enables the poet to see it. Vaughan's
dependency and his reconciliation to it in this poem come closer than
anything we have seen to Herbert's position at the end of *The Temple*. But
in "The Odour" man was reconciled to God through a simple reflection
of the divine goodness, while in "The Agreement" man's vision of God is
curiously indirect though remarkably convincing. The poet's angel
comes—at length—to show him "the flame" which points him "to a
place, / Which . . . sees the Suns face." This sequence might well make
the reader feel as if he were receiving at best a third copy of that original
experience, for the poet does not claim to see God, but only the sun,
which is of course an image of the divine and a pun on son as well, but
nonetheless is a metaphor rather than reality. Yet the images of light,
flame, stars, brightness, the use of parallel construction, and the repeti-
tion of conjunctions (lines 8, 11) convey the sense that the copy is at least
clear and legible, that the poet himself reaches the place to which he is
pointed, that he himself "sees the Suns face." This conviction is some-
how reinforced by a circularity and reciprocity in Vaughan's images that

suggest God both as the initiator of an action and the agent by which it is accomplished in man:

> Thine are the present healing leaves,
> Blown from the tree of life to us
> By his breath whom my dead heart heaves.
>
> (lines 20–22)

> My thoughts, when towards thee they move,
> Glitter and kindle with thy love.
>
> (lines 17–18)

There is a further degree of integration in Vaughan's use of a language rich in biblical allusions to characterize the Bible, emphasizing that the truth he now apprehends is apprehended by the agency of that truth itself. The rather odd behavior of flames and morning stars (lines 9–10) finds its origin in Job 38:7: "When the morning stars sang together, and all the sons of God shouted for joy"; in Revelation 22:16, Jesus himself is "the bright and morning star"; and Psalms 104:1 praises the God "Who maketh his angels spirits; his ministers a flaming fire." The mount with its "white Ascendents" depends on the many biblical references to mountains as holy places set aside for the worship of God, to Mount Zion, the mountain of the Lord, to the picture of the just ascending God's holy mountain, to the mountain from which Christ ascended into heaven.[35] "The Agreement" also abounds in biblical images of fruitfulness and prosperity ("Thou art the oyl and the wine-house," line 19) that recall the staple measures of wealth and the ceremony of anointing in the Old Testament ("Wine that maketh glad the heart of man, and oil to make his face to shine," Ps. 104:15). The Bible is "the faithful, pearly rock," a phrase that suggests the rock from which Moses drew water in the desert (Num. 20:8–11), and the rock upon whom the psalmist depended: "The Lord is my rock, and my fortress, and my deliverer, my God, my strength in whom I will trust" (Ps. 13:2).

Besides the use of concrete biblical images, much of the vividness of Vaughan's poem derives from his treating metaphors as if they were literal fact.

> O beamy book! O my mid-day
> Exterminating fears and night!
> The mount, whose white Ascendents may
> Be in conjunction with true light!
>
> (lines 13–16)

The mount at the center of Vaughan's astrological pun on conjunction and ascendents is the Bible, but the language and the action of climbing also suggest Mount Zion, which, as the Old Testament records, the worshipers of God literally ascended. The use of a biblical metaphor for worship (the ascent of Mount Zion) to characterize the reading of the Bible creates a marvelously circular image, and as one tries to untangle it one is struck by the extent to which metaphor is truth. In Vaughan's terms, only as one reads the "beamy book" does one become a true worshiper, and by joining in an act that links the past and the future, ascend the mount which is the Zion that was and is to come: "But in the last days it shall come to pass, that the mountain of the house of the Lord shall be established in the top of the mountains, and it shall be exalted above the hills; and people shall flow unto it" (Micah 4:1). Vaughan's language emphasizes this continuity in the book that is both in time and beyond it, an incarnation of the infinite in the finite: "Thine are the present healing leaves / Blown from the tree of life to us" (lines 20–21). The tree of life reaches back into the past to Eden, yet it signifies life eternal; such life, though forfeited by our first parents, is present in the healing power of its leaves which, in lines 23–24, are seen to be the leaves of the Bible. And within five lines the word "leaves" has changed meaning in a way that suggests not the poet's cleverness but the persistence of divine truth and fidelity, which expresses its concern for mankind differently in different contexts.

But if Providence involves us in a dynamic cycle of goodness, there is a cycle of evil for which the Bible provides the images as well. Vaughan brilliantly rings the changes on his chosen metaphors of book and breath, Logos and Spirit, contrasting divine light- and life-giving qualities with the deception and self-deception of those powers that oppose them:

> Most modern books are blots on thee,
> Their doctrine chaff and windy fits:
> Darken'd along, as their scribes be,
> With those foul storms, when they were writ.

> (lines 25–28)

"Blots" continues the book metaphor; the images of faulty writing and the darkened page suggest the extent to which modern books and modern scribes are removed from the truth and light. The "chaff" of false doctrine recalls biblical images of the wicked and of their separation from the good: "They are as stubble before the wind, and as chaff that the storm carrieth away" (Job 21:18). The windy fits of false doctrine contrast with the life-giving breath of the Spirit. The curious circularity of these lines implies that false doctrine is its own destruction, that the windy fits will blow away the chaff.[36] The precise origin of darkness is never stated: "when" designates simultaneity rather than cause; but the resulting impression is of darkness encroaching on everything, while darkened man has no thought beyond himself: "While the mans zeal lays out and blends / Onely self-worship and self-ends" (lines 29–30).[37]

Vaughan's insistence on the physical quality of experience, on the book as a material entity, on light as the shadow of God—and thus on the relationship between the physical and the spiritual—makes him go beyond the traditional notion of Christ as the Logos, the Word, to create such a brilliant oxymoron as "Gods bright minde exprest in print" (line 24) or "Thy lines are rays, the true Sun sheds" (line 35). Such an attitude yields also the extraordinary combination of biblical image and physical property in "Thy leaves are healing wings he spreads" (line 36), in which the physical position of the material book becomes emblematic, even as the line recalls "The Sun of righteousness [that] shall arise with healing in his wings" (Mal. 4:2).

Characteristically, evil, or what Donne and Herbert would have called sin, is represented by Vaughan as darkness, obscurity. Vaughan does mention sin rather abstractly in stanza 8:

> O God! I know and do confess
> My sins are great and still prevail,
> Most heynous sins and numberless!

(lines 43–45)

But he quickly finds that "thy Compassions cannot fail" (line 46), and his sin seems less central to his concern than the forgetfulness that afflicts him (lines 1–6) or the false and destructive zeal that possesses others (lines 25–30). In contrast to the patterns of such poems as "The Constellation" or "The Seed growing secretly," the perpetually threatening forces of darkness are here answered throughout by the forces of light. Vaughan "hourly" finds reason for hope, and the divine sufficiency, forever giving but never spent, is the recurring emphasis of this poem. "Ever the same, whose diffus'd stock / Entire still, wears out blackest nights" (lines 33–34). Vaughan's stress on divine power is joined in the conclusion of "The Agreement" with an explicit statement of the reason behind the preceding images of circularity:

So thou, who didst the work begin
(For *I till drawn came not to thee*)
Wilt finish it, and by no sin
Will thy free mercies hindred be.
  For which, O God, I onely can
  Bless thee, and blame unthankful man.

(lines 67–72)

The cheerful resignation Vaughan expresses now may recall George
Herbert's surrender to God in the last poems of *The Temple*; but Vaughan
finds comfort even as he looks forward to the fulfillment of a promise,
whereas Herbert enacts its final dramatic consummation. To the last
Herbert is engaged in a fierce struggle of the will, yielding only in the last
line of the last poem, while Vaughan, more confident and more de-
tached, has already yielded and now rests in his assurance.

Vaughan has not had the great ecstatic experience that he prayed for at
the end of "Regeneration," but he has found a new way of seeing—one
based on correspondences not only between this world and the next but
between the great body of experience that is the Christian tradition and
his own individual experience. Like Herbert he is a "wonder tortur'd in
the space / Betwixt this world and that of grace"; but in such poems as
"The Agreement" he finds rest because he finds a way of understanding
the present in terms of the past and the future—indeed, a way of under-
standing eternity through time. The body of Vaughan's religious poetry
records his search for a way of seeing, even in a time of not seeing. He sees
through the Book of Creatures; he exclaims in "The Waterfall," "What
sublime truths, and wholesome themes, / Lodge in thy mystical deep
streams!"; yet the physical embodiment of truth is only an intermediary,
as the conclusion to that poem emphasizes:

O my invisible estate,
My glorious liberty, still late!
Thou art the Channel my soul seeks,
Not this with Cataracts and Creeks.

(lines 37–40)

Despite his reputation as a poet of nature, Vaughan finds even more
satisfying connections in such traditional and biblically oriented poems
as "The Agreement" and "The Book," poems based on persistent at-
titudes rather than unique individual experiences. And perhaps most
brilliantly, he finds God through the paradoxes of "The Night," in which

the biblical account of Nicodemus coming to Jesus by night becomes the basis for a splendid virtuoso performance on the theme of light and darkness as images of God. "The Night" does not confuse image and meaning in the manner of "The Seed growing secretly," nor does it simply reverse Vaughan's usual values; rather it uses these values to point to the divine mystery. Vaughan employs the shifting connotations of light and dark to write a poem less about the nature of God than about man's perception of him, not like Herbert to show a reversal of vision that enables the poet to see what was always there, but to affirm and rest content even in the midst of darkness. In "The Agreement" Vaughan represents the relationship between divinity and our understanding of it; he makes clear the distinction between inner and outer, between truth and perception, as he speaks of the "beamy book . . . exterminating" both "fears and night," but he also shows how divine power forges a positive link between the two: "My thoughts, when towards thee they move, / Glitter and kindle with thy love" ("The Agreement," lines 17–18). Reading these lines one may recall Herbert's "Jesu," in which God's grace literally enabled man to act, yet one must be struck by the contrast between Vaughan's rather elegant images of scintillating light and Herbert's emphatic picture of elemental experience. In "The Night" Vaughan does not so much articulate divine-human connections in explicit statements as suggest them through his firm control of oxymoron and paradox.

Because light is usually taken as the symbol of goodness in general and of God in particular, scholars have looked for external influence to explain the paradoxical reversal of "The Night," and a number of them have cited the mystical writings of Saint John of the Cross and Pseudo-Dionysius the Areopagite as the most likely sources.[38] In *The Dark Night of the Soul*, John describes God as surrounded by darkness, that is, by man's inability to comprehend him, and sees God as nevertheless communicating to man through this "obscurity." And in the *Ascent of Mount Carmel*, the mystic speaks of "the understanding being blind and in darkness, walking in faith alone; for beneath this darkness the understanding is united with God, and beneath it God is hidden."[39] Vaughan shares with John of the Cross the belief in a God who is beyond human understanding, obscure and incomprehensible; yet Vaughan's persistent hope is to transcend human limits, to see God in this life, whereas John expects complete revelation only when "that which is perfect is come" (1 Cor.

13:10). Both writers emphasize God's communication of himself in darkness, but whereas John speaks of the metaphorical darkness in which man exists, Vaughan goes on to stress the juxtaposition of opposites, the presence of light in darkness as a symbol of the incarnation. There are further similarities in the meditative canticle in which John, like Nicodemus, goes out on a dark night to meet "the Beloved," especially in the latter stanzas of the canticle, richly reminiscent of the Song of Solomon, which describe the kind of peace in darkness that the English poet is seeking. Yet before claiming influence, one should recall that the two poets share a most significant source—the light and dark symbolism of the Bible and the love poetry of the Song of Solomon.

Beyond general resemblances to John of the Cross, there seems widespread scholarly agreement that Vaughan owes his most striking individual phrase—"a deep but dazling darkness"—to the suggestion of Pseudo-Dionysius the Areopagite, who prayed: "Guide us to that topmost height of mystic lore which exceedeth light and more than exceedeth knowledge, where the simple absolute, and unchangeable mysteries of heavenly Truth lie hidden in the dazzling obscurity of the secret Silence, outshining all brilliance with the intensity of their darkness, and surcharging our blinded intellects with the utterly impalpable and invisible fairness of glories which exceed all beauty!"[40] Yet there are also significant differences between Vaughan's views and those of Pseudo-Dionysius, for whom darkness is not a characteristic of God any more than is light, and who employs negation only to stress the inadequacy of all human categories when applied to the infinite deity. Although such a tendency to find all terms for God inadequate and misleading may have prompted Vaughan's use of imagery with shifting connotations, one need hardly seek external explanations for a practice so common in Vaughan.

Indeed, the most striking similarities to "The Night" are found in Vaughan's own prose meditation "At the Setting of the Sun or the Soul's Elevation to the true light" from *The Mount of Olives* (1652):[41]

A heavie night sits in the noone-day upon those souls that have forsaken thee; They look for light, and behold darknesse; for brightnesse, and they walk in obscurity. They grope for the wall like the blind, as if they had no Eyes; They stumble at noone-day as in the night, they are in desolate places as dead men. But on those that walk with thee an everlasting day shines. . . . As long as thou art present with me, I am in the light, but when thou art gone, I am in the shadows of death, and amongst the stones of emptinesse. When thou art present, all is brightnesse. . . . Abide then with me, O thou whom my soul loveth! Thou Sun of righteousnesse with healing under thy wings arise in my heart; . . . make thy light there to shine in darknesse, and a perfect day in the dead of night. (*Works*, p. 151)

The images of physical and spiritual light and darkness in this passage are drawn chiefly from biblical sources;[42] Vaughan's juxtaposing of them in ways that resemble "The Night" but not John of the Cross or Pseudo-Dionysius suggests that his sense of paradox is independent of these sources, that the Bible itself is his chief inspiration, and that the ability to find light in darkness was not simply a momentary poetic achievement but a fact of Vaughan's mature religious experience.

The opening stanzas of "The Night," like Vaughan's prose meditation, treat darkness as an image of willful ignorance and spiritual blindness and light as the image of God; they also raise the possibility that light, in the sense of spiritual enlightenment, may exist in the midst of darkness.

> Through that pure *Virgin-shrine,*
> That sacred vail drawn o'r thy glorious noon
> That men might look and live as Glo-worms shine,
>   And face the Moon:
> Wise *Nicodemus* saw such light
> As made him know his God by night.

(lines 1–6)

"Wise Nicodemus" comes to Jesus to ask questions, of a sort to prompt another question: "Art thou a master of Israel, and knowest not these things?" (John 3:10). But in his apparently simple questioning ("How can a man be born when he is old? can he enter the second time into his mother's womb, and be born?") Nicodemus is wiser than his fellows who persist in their blindness. Vaughan's language stresses both the vividness and the limitations of Nicodemus's experience; he is not granted the fullness of light that would make complete understanding possible, but such light "As made him know his God by night."

> Most blest believer he!
> Who in that land of darkness and blinde eyes
> Thy long expected healing wings could see,
>   When thou didst rise,
> And what can never more be done,
> Did at mid-night speak with the Sun!

(lines 7–12)

"The Night" is a carefully orchestrated series of contrasts that prepares us for the reversal of values and the acceptance of the limits of human understanding that it finally articulates. Vaughan does not juxtapose logical opposites—sun / moon; light / dark—but rather noon and moon, light and night, and he uses the rhymes that force the pairs together at the same time that they point up the oddness of the link. The first two stanzas form a rhythmic and dramatic sequence leading to the climax of extreme contrasts in line 12: "Did at mid-night speak with the Sun!" This vivid description, which acknowledges the incarnation, the presence of divinity within the world and grace in the realm of nature, shows up the inadequacy of the simpler notions of order and opposition with which we began the poem.

As we see in line 8 of "The Night," it is not only darkness but blindness that prevents men seeing. The external condition of nature reflects the internal state of man—"that land of darkness and blinde eyes"; healing comes to those who have faith. Vaughan's position here as elsewhere recalls that of the Cambridge Platonist John Smith, who wrote: "We cannot see divine things but in a divine light; God only, who is the true light, and in whom there is no darkness at all, can so shine out of himself upon our glassy understandings, as to beget in them a picture of himself, his own will and pleasure and turn the soul as the phrase is 'like wax or clay to the seal' of his own light and love."[43] To call Vaughan a Platonist is perhaps to underestimate his eclecticism,[44] but there are affinities between certain of the Platonists' views and his, particularly his emphasis on vision over submission and his relatively slight stress on human depravity. In their assertion of the rational basis of religion the Cambridge Platonists argued, in words relevant to "The Night," that our failure to understand God is not the result of his obscurity but of "the disproportion of the faculty of our understanding."[45] Vaughan does not disavow Paul's words, "We walk by faith, not by sight" (2 Cor. 5:7), but as in his biblical text for lines 9–10 (Mal. 4:2), it is faith that creates sight: "But unto you that fear my name shall the Sun of righteousness arise with healing in his wings." Although God is the source of all light, light is not attributed solely to him, for as his light illumines their lives, men become "glo-worms" facing the moon. "Wise Nicodemus," whom the poet would emulate, is not passively overwhelmed by grace; rather, he is an active participant who responds to it.

Like Christ himself, who at once fulfills and overthrows the traditions of his people, Nicodemus has a dual status as he, a Pharisee and a ruler of the Jews, comes in secrecy by night to Jesus as his chosen rabbi. Appropriate to its subject, Vaughan's language in stanza 3 points in two apparently opposite directions: while it stresses the unlikely nature of Nicodemus's quest—"O who will tell me, where"—it also recalls the prophecy of the long-awaited Messiah who is now, miraculously and unexpectedly, at hand—"And there shall come forth a rod out of the stem of Jesse, and a Branch shall grow out of his roots" (Is. 11:1).

> O who will tell me, where
> He found thee at that dead and silent hour!
> What hallow'd solitary ground did bear
> So rare a flower,
> Within whose sacred leafs did lie
> The fulness of the Deity.
>
> No mercy-seat of gold,
> No dead and dusty *Cherub*, nor carv'd stone
> But his own living works did my Lord hold
> And lodge alone;
> Where *trees* and *herbs* did watch and peep
> And wonder, while the *Jews* did sleep.
>
> (lines 13–24)

In the tradition of Christian apologetics, Vaughan points to Jewish religious institutions that were intended as a means of communication between God and man but that have grown "dead and dusty." The mercy seat, the cherub, and the stone are all references to the Jewish tabernacle as described in Exodus 25–27, and the "Virgin-shrine" and "sacred vail" recall the Holy of Holies guarded by a veil in Exodus 26:31–33. Like the veil with which Moses covered his face after he had spoken with God on Mount Sinai, this veil of flesh protects men from gazing on something that would dazzle them. While it is a sign of man's inability to see clearly, it is also a means of revelation, for God is seen through the veil by those who could not otherwise see him at all: "Thou canst not see my face: for there shall no man see me, and live" (Ex. 33:20). But the immediate reference of "Virgin-shrine" is to Christ, who is himself the temple of God, in that he is God incarnate. The old means are superseded by "a new and living way, which he hath consecrated for us, through the veil, that is to say, his flesh" (Heb. 10:20). The previous dispensation depended on intermediaries, priests, animal sacrifices, and the formal ritual of the temple. As the fulfillment of these prophecies and precursors,

Christ is temple and high priest, prophet and king, mediator, sacrifice, and judge. The covenant is no longer to be written on stone tablets (Ex. 24:12) but in men's hearts and minds (Heb. 10:16), and the veil that covered the Holy of Holies has been rent (Luke 23:15).

Just as the original saving purpose of the temple has been perverted, so day and light, originally symbols of God, have been misused; day has become the time to serve Caesar rather than God. The recognition of these abuses prepares for the reversal in stanza 5, in which Vaughan turns all values upside down. He takes as his motto 1 Corinthians 3:19: "The wisdom of this world is foolishness with God" and shows that whatever seems best in ordinary contexts, in the logic of this world, is in fact antithetical to the goals of the spirit:

> Dear night! this worlds defeat;
> The stop to busie fools; cares check and curb;
> The day of Spirits; my souls calm retreat
>   Which none disturb!
> Christs progress, and his prayer time;
> The hours to which high Heaven doth chime.
>
>   (lines 25–30)

This stanza brings us wholly into the world of the night and into communion with heaven itself. "The hours to which high Heaven doth chime" may have been suggested by Herbert's "A kind of tune, which all things heare and fear" and "Churchbels beyond the starres heard" in "Prayer I"; Vaughan uses the image to suggest that the hours of prayer—matins, vespers, compline—are not merely human institutions but have something of literally universal validity; they are that to which "high Heaven," in its response to its Lord on earth, "doth chime."

In meditating on the physical darkness in which Nicodemus went to see Christ, itself a reflection of the spiritual darkness of the Jews, Vaughan comes to see that such physical darkness is a corrective to the spiritual darkness that now prevails even in the daylight. He moves from the historical night in which Nicodemus saw God to the mystical, permanent night in which men may still do so. In following Nicodemus through the night, in making the night, as Christ did, his prayer time, Vaughan enters the heavenly realm, not in ecstasy, but in sympathy and unity, in a more stable and enduring mode than that achieved in his earlier poems.

Gods silent, searching flight:
When my Lords head is fill'd with dew, and all
His locks are wet with the clear drops of night;
   His still, soft call;
His knocking time; The souls dumb watch,
When Spirits their fair kinred catch.

Were all my loud, evil days
Calm and unhaunted as is thy dark Tent,
Whose peace but by some *Angels* wing or voice
   Is seldom rent;
Then I in Heaven all the long year
Would keep, and never wander here.

                                              (lines 31–42)

Vaughan here goes beyond the otherworldly negatives of lines 25–28 to the positive spiritual realm—the world of the Song of Solomon, the garden in which, according to traditional exegesis, the soul meets God and Christ the Spouse meets his Bride the Church. The sensuous oriental atmosphere of the garden resembles that created in "Regeneration," in which "the aire was all in spice," or in "Unprofitablenes," in which Vaughan claimed, "I flourish, and once more / Breath all perfumes and spice." These lines from "The Night" also represent the poet's fullest participation in a world which, as we see in stanza 8, is not always accessible, yet is not, as one might have thought from stanzas 1 and 2, merely past history. While the first two stanzas describe an incident in the past, one that can never be recaptured, the question of stanza 3—"O who will tell me, where"—suggests that the experience may be available to the poet, for as we learn in stanza 4, it was in nature that Christ was found, and night and nature are still with us. Accordingly in stanzas 5 and 6 the poet participates fully in this realm, daring to speak twice in the first-person possessive: "my souls calm retreat" and "my Lords head." Thus even though the final stanza of the poem—"O for that night! where I in him / Might live invisible and dim"—seems to cry out for something not granted, the penultimate stanzas indicate that Vaughan seeks permanently what is here only intermittent.

Although he is exposed to the darkness of daylight partly by his own consent ("I . . . by this worlds ill-guiding light, / Erre more then I can do by night," lines 47–48), his closing prayer represents his reorientation to the true light found only in darkness. True to the paradoxes of the poem, this last stanza is Vaughan's most brilliant.

> There is in God (some say)
> A deep, but dazling darkness; As men here
> Say it is late and dusky, because they
> See not all clear;
> O for that night! where I in him
> Might live invisible and dim.

(lines 49–54)

Partly because of its brilliance and complexity, partly because of its resemblance to the writings of Pseudo-Dionysius and John of the Cross, "The Night" is sometimes made to sound like an exceedingly clever manipulation of paradox in which the poet is scarcely involved. But it seems to me that Vaughan wishes to demonstrate precisely the reverse: man is not master and explorer of paradox; he is at the mercy of his own limitations and of God's grace. Vaughan is not making a statement about the nature of God at all, for he, with Pseudo-Dionysius, believes that it is beyond human capacity to do so, but rather a statement about our perception of him, and in this he anticipates the attitudes and concerns of Traherne. "As men here / Say it is late and dusky, because they / See not all clear" does not denote a state that men have power to change. But God does "see all clear" and has it in his power to make one a "most blest believer" who can "at mid-night speak with the Sun."

Vaughan tells us at the beginning of "The Night" that the poem celebrates "what can never more be done," but the very paradoxes of his poem testify to a way of finding light in darkness, of seeing not with the eyes of this world but with those of faith. What began as paradox—that light might exist in darkness (stanzas 1–4)—now becomes the underlying assumption of the poem: night is the time of true light, the "day of Spirits" (stanzas 4–8). "The Night," among the last poems of *Silex Scintillans*, stands as a counterpart to "Regeneration," the first; both see divinity within the shadows of this life; both look forward to a more complete revelation. Yet "Regeneration" hopes for vision in this life, whereas "The Night" more actively recreates that vision in prayer.

In the paradoxes and reversals of "The Night" Vaughan not only transforms the reader's vision and understanding; he also demonstrates the transformation of his own understanding. He who had prayed for a moment of divine illumination now prays "for that night! where I in him / Might live invisible and dim." The poet who is left in darkness, despite all his prayers for light, learns to understand darkness in a new way. This understanding, the ability to see connections where before he had perceived only broken links, is the basis of Vaughan's later and most satisfying poems. In them not only light, but also darkness, is the shadow of God.

III

The Splendor of Eternity

TRAHERNE

THOMAS TRAHERNE, shoemaker's son of Hereford and Bachelor of Divinity of Oxford, was, like Donne, Herbert, and Vaughan, a poet for whom light was the shadow of God. More than any of the other metaphysical poets, more even than Vaughan, Traherne seems to have attained the illuminating vision of the divine. In consequence, some critics have preferred to call him, like his predecessor, a mystic, while others deny that he attained the highest unitive state.[1] But though the evidence of ecstatic experience is greater for Traherne than for Vaughan, the usefulness of such information for judging his poetry is distinctly limited. To conclude, as Alison Sherrington does, that Traherne's thoughts rather than his verses are poetic is not only to confuse the nature of poetry and biography but to ignore altogether the chief question—that of his work. A.L. Clements more wisely bypasses the issue of Traherne's private spiritual experience to consider the poetry itself in the light of the Christian mystical tradition.[2]

But any label, whether "metaphysical," "mystical," or some other, may give the deceptively comforting impression that we have placed and understood a poet, and it may tempt us to view the extraordinary as traditional and merely ordinary. The most extraordinary feature of Traherne's poetry, and that which most clearly links him with earlier metaphysical poets, is his dual vision of reality. This perception is vividly articulated in the passage that has done most for Traherne's reputation as a writer of luminous prose, *Centuries* 3.3, in which he writes: "Eternity was Manifest in the Light of the Day, and som thing infinit Behind evry thing appeared: which talked with my Expectation and moved my Desire. The Citie seemed to stand in Eden, or to be Built in Heaven." The confusion of location, the speaker's doubt whether he is on earth or in heaven, may recall Herbert's description of man's first innocence:

> For sure when Adam did not know
> To sinne, or sinne to smother;
> He might to heav'n from Paradise go,
> As from one room t'another.
>
>   ("The H. Communion," lines 33–36)

But despite the apparent similarity of motif, there is a basic and important difference between Herbert and Traherne: Herbert describes the ease with which Adam could move only in order to point out how much more circumscribed his own state is: "Give me my captive soul, or take / My bodie also thither"; whereas Traherne, in saying "The World resembled his Eternitie" ("Wonder," line 6), describes not life before the Fall but his own experience, in which as a child he recaptured the innocence of Adam. Unlike his predecessors, Traherne does not see eternity through time, distantly and symbolically, but in time; he does not so much deduce or intuit what is beyond from what is seen here, but sees through the present to the beyond: "Som thing infinit Behind evry thing appeared." To the child's unclouded sight, infinity itself is visible in this present life.

Traherne's description of the relationship between the finite and the infinite, like much else in his writing, seems to echo Plotinus, who spoke of the "Divine Mind—how beautiful, most beautiful! Lying lapped in pure light and clear radiance; the original of which this beautiful world is a shadow and an image."[3] In the seventeenth century the reading of the Book of Creatures, the examination of the world that was a shadow and an image, was more often methodical than ecstatic, and the Spanish Jesuit Juan Eusebius Nieremberg, some of whose works were translated by Henry Vaughan, converted Plotinus's image of the world as a poem to that of the world as a labyrinth.[4] Yet the striking thing about Traherne is that, although he would agree with Plotinus and perhaps even with Nieremberg in their statements on creation as the image of God, his poetry is not at all emblematic. For Donne, seeing man as a microcosm and finding a trinity of lives in a flea, for Herbert, disciplining the shape of his poems and his life to his Master's will, for Vaughan, finding the resurrection in a flower and fidelity in a stone or a cock, "the whole sensible universe," was, in Berkeley's words, "a system of signs."[5] For Traherne the universe was not for the most part a puzzle or a labyrinth, not the truth obscured, but rather a luminescent and satisfying vision. To be sure, Traherne distinguishes between the physical universe and the deity, but he does not dwell on the insufficiency of the one as a representative of the other: "When Amasis the King of Egypt sent to the Wise Men of Greece, to Know, Quid Pulcherrimum? upon due and Mature Consideration, they answered, The WORLD. The World certainly being so Beautiful that nothing visible is capable of more. Were we to see it only once, that first Appearance would amaze us. But being daily seen, we observ it not. ancient Philosophers hav thought GOD to be the *Soul of the World*" (C 2.21).

In this passage from *Centuries*, Traherne goes on to enumerate some of the qualities of God as revealed in creation, but both his descriptions of these qualities and the inferences to be drawn from them are extremely general. Rather than gleaning something particular from a specific object or experience, as Herbert does in his hard-won battles with himself or Vaughan in his meditations on nature, he is simply dazzled by the whole. Nor does Traherne's apparently effortless ecstasy much resemble the patient progress described by Saint Bonaventure in *The Mind's Journey to God*. [6] The strangely impersonal, yet enthusiastic conclusion to this meditation is perhaps closer to the thought of an eighteenth-century Deist than to that of the early seventeenth-century metaphysicals: "GOD . . . hath drowned our Understanding in a Multitude of Wonders: Transported us with Delights, and Enriched us with innumerable Diversities of Joys and Pleasures. The very Greatness of our felicity convinceth us, that there is a GOD" (C 2.21). One need scarcely say that for Donne, Herbert, and Vaughan whether there was a God was not the question, but rather whether one might as a sinner approach him, might hope for redemption and reconciliation, might be granted a vision of him.

In striking contrast to Vaughan and even to Herbert, there are in Traherne very few descriptions of natural objects perceived as images of spiritual truth. Traherne may begin with the created world (as for example in C 2.8), but he does not make an emblem of it; instead he quickly shifts to man's proper perception of this creation. The movement of *Centuries* 1:27–30 may be taken as typical:

You never Enjoy the World aright, till you see how a Sand Exhibiteth the Wisdom and Power of God: And Prize in evry Thing the Service which they do you, by Manifesting His Glory and Goodness to your Soul, far more then the Visible Beauty on their Surface, or the Material Services, they can do your Body. Wine by its Moysture quencheth my Thirst, whether I consider it or no: but to see it flowing from his Lov who gav it unto Man. Quencheth the Thirst even of the Holy Angels. To consider it, is to Drink it Spritualy. (C 1.27)

You never Enjoy the World aright, till the Sea it self floweth in your Veins, till you are Clothed with the Heavens, and Crowned with the Stars: and Perceiv your self to be the Sole Heir of the whole World. (C 1.29)

Till your Spirit filleth the whole World, and the Stars are your Jewels, till you are as Familiar with the Ways of God in all Ages as with your Walk and Table: till you are intimatly Acquainted with that Shady Nothing out of which the World was made: till you lov Men so as to Desire their Happiness, with a Thirst equal to the zeal of your own: till you Delight in GOD for being Good to all: you never Enjoy the World. (C 1.30)

There is of course a progressive pattern here, reflected in the repetition of "You never Enjoy the World aright" and in the movement to successively higher levels of understanding, but the progression is rhythmic and ec-static, not patient and logical. The poet moves from smaller things to greater, from the grain of sand to the stars; he also moves from physical enjoyment to understanding to ecstasy. Yet what he understands is less the world as the image of God or as a means to come to him than the world as man's glorious inheritance. His ecstasy is not a losing of himself in God but an expansion of self by means of this inheritance.

Man, central to Traherne's universe, is able to comprehend God's creation. For Herbert such a claim would have been the arrogant illusion of a persona; for Donne, the blasphemous boast of a lover; for Vaughan, despite all his longings, an impossibility. But in Traherne the claim is curiously matter-of-fact, as a reading of his poetic manifesto, "The Author to the Critical Peruser," emphasizes. At first Traherne's poetic aims and means seem like those of his predecessors: much in his stated prefer-ence for plain language recalls Herbert's "Jordan" poems or even Sidney's declarations of poetic sincerity:

> No curling Metaphors that gild the Sence,
> Nor Pictures here, nor painted Eloquence;
> No florid Streams of Superficial Gems,
> But real Crowns and Thrones and Diadems!
> .   .   .   .
> An easy Stile drawn from a native vein,
> A clearer Stream than that which Poets feign,
> Whose bottom may, how deep so'ere, be seen,
> Is that which I think fit to win Esteem.
> ("The Author to the Critical Peruser," lines 11–14, 17–20)

Traherne has no intention of repealing "the goodly exil'd traine / Of gods and goddesses" (cf. lines 25–36), and his avoidance of "Things that amaze, but will not make us wise" (line 24) may recall Vaughan's refusal to satisfy his reader's curiosity rather than attending to his spiritual needs.[7] But Traherne's repeated emphasis on the veracity and sincerity of his verse in such lines as "real Crowns and Thrones and Diadems" (line 14), "Not verbal Ones, / But reall Kings, exalted unto Thrones; / And more than Golden Thrones" (lines 33–35) goes beyond Sidney's artful insistence on artlessness in the injunction "look in thy heart and write." It even goes beyond the struggle for modest and truthful verse of Vaughan or Herbert, in the sense that Traherne scarcely seems to feel himself a poet at all; that is, he hardly distinguishes between the reality of God's truth and the reality of his own verse: " 'Tis this I do, / Letting Poëtick Strains and Shadows go" (lines 35–36).

Whereas Herbert in the "Jordan" poems disavows unnecessary ornament and complication, he is keenly aware of the greatness of his subject and never presumes to do it justice: "Nothing could seem too rich to clothe the sunne, / Much lesse those joyes which trample on his head" ("Jordan II," lines 11–12). Rather he casts himself in the role of the lowly, honest shepherd, the simple lover who copies out "a sweetnesse readie penn'd" (line 17). Traherne, by contrast, gives no sense of being unequal to his subject nor of difficulty in finding language suitable to it. In his hands the highest and most mysterious things become clear:

> The naked Truth in many faces shewn,
> Whose inward Beauties very few hav known,
> A Simple Light, transparent Words, a Strain
> That lowly creeps, yet maketh Mountains plain,
> Brings down the highest Mysteries to sense
> And keeps them there; that is Our Excellence:
> At that we aim; to th' end thy Soul might see
> With open Eys thy Great *Felicity*,
> Its Objects view, and trace the glorious Way
> Wherby thou may'st thy Highest Bliss enjoy.
> ("The Author to the Critical Peruser," lines 1–10)

These lines are full of paradoxes and impossibilities; every couplet turns on making apparent what is evident but strangely unperceived. Yet although Traherne takes as his subject divine mysteries and the soul's felicity, these are not to be merely glimpsed fleetingly or partially but seen "with open Eys," seen, in fact, with eyes of sense. Traherne's promise that his "strain" will make "Mountains plain" is a daring echo of the biblical prophecies of the coming of the Messiah when "every valley shall be exalted, and every mountain and hill shall be made low" (Is. 40:4), but it is something that few Christian poets had claimed for themselves.

Although Traherne freely employs paradoxes in "The Author to the Critical Peruser" and in the poems that follow, he neither acknowledges nor seems to sense the difficulty, according to ordinary conceptions, of what he proposes. On only one occasion did Vaughan dare to state "I saw Eternity the other night," and even so critics have hardly believed him;[8] the long arduous struggle of *The Temple* was needed before Herbert could at last submit his will to the vision of eternity; but Traherne conceives it as man's by nature: "Few will believ the Soul to be infinit; yet Infinit is the first Thing which is naturaly Known" (C 2.81). This attitude explains Traherne's emphasis on the childhood vision and his apparently uncritical use of the persona of the child. Nowhere does he encourage us, as Herbert does, to draw back from the persona and judge his judgment, for it is the persona who has the true vision; nor does Traherne share Vaughan's nostalgia for "those first white days" of his own life, for Traherne's point is that the early joy is easily attainable—if we will but see. Thus he proposes to treat "The naked Truth in many faces shewn, / Whose inward Beauties very few have known."

But the problem of seeing eternity in time which appears disquietingly easy for the poet remains difficult for the reader of Traherne's poems. Is Traherne merely simplistic and naïve? Are his ecstatic declarations the product of a unique and—for all its extravagant claims—curiously limited experience? Has he taken any thought for the reader? Are these poems for us as for him a form of spiritual exercise? Are they simple, flat, and one-dimensional, or are they in the full sense metaphysical? To answer these questions we must look not just at individual poems, but at the body of Traherne's work.

Traherne was not only the latest of the metaphysical poets to live and write but also the latest to appear in print: his poems were not known until the publication of the Dobell Folio in 1903 and the Burney Manuscript by Sir Idris Bell in 1910.[9] The reputation of Traherne's poetry has always suffered by comparison with his prose, but now that the *Centuries* (and other prose works yet in manuscript) are receiving critical attention rather than mere adulation, it appears that the difference in their quality, as in their thought and method, is not so great as was once supposed.[10] Traherne's prose may show better in excerpted form than his verse, but it will not do to take the vivid concretion of *Centuries* 3.3, the most famous passage in all his work, as typical of his prose and set it against the ecstatic climax of "My Spirit," which depends on its context for its effect, as representative of his verse. The bulk of Traherne's prose is by no means so glowing and vivid as the passage beginning "The Corn was Orient and Immortal Wheat," nor the body of his poems entirely lacking in sensuous detail. But more important, both prose and verse are cyclic and climactic. They aim, in the words of "The Demonstration," to overwhelm the reader with "Extremities of Blessedness" and thus "Compell us to confess / A GOD indeed." It is perhaps true that in his poems Traherne tends to rejoice in his blessedness and in his prose more fully to recreate it for the reader, and it is perhaps significant that the meditations were originally intended for a specific reader, presumably Susanna Hopton, whereas the poems, with the exception of some of those written in couplets, are chiefly lyric and ecstatic, aiming more at expression than persuasion.

Nevertheless the reader of the poems, though he may resist or resent Traherne's apparently boundless optimism, though he may find that Traherne underestimates the miseries of human existence, will, if he persists, be subjected to an experience more moving and convincing than has usually been granted and to a body of poetry far more coherent than is generally recognized. The *Centuries*, as Martz shows in *The Paradise Within*, comprise a grand cycle;[11] they are also a series of cycles—sometimes local, concentrated within a single meditation, sometimes within several meditations. The same is true of the poems, as I hope in the course of this study to demonstrate; they too force the reader to follow the leaps and circles of Traherne's mind, and hence their effect is not gauged by any single unit but by the combined impact of the whole. One may well gasp with astonishment at the extravagant claims Traherne makes for his own experience, and by implication, for all men; but before one can absorb such claims one is assaulted in rapid sequence with several more, even more appalling—or exhilarating.[12] Where Donne forces the reader step by step into logical impossibilities, Traherne overwhelms him with simple assertions of what one would certainly take for paradox, did the poet not appear to consider it so plainly evident. Traherne's apparent refusal to recognize our objections may or may not be naïve; it might as well be deliberate, for it is certainly consistent with his conviction that finally evil does not matter, that the world is good if we will but see it aright. Like one who has found the pearl of great price, Traherne cannot stay for lesser matters; it is his task to demonstrate "Incredibles alone."

Until very recently, the adverse judgment of Traherne's poetry, in contrast to his prose, has been greatly influenced by confusion about what Traherne actually wrote,[13] in particular by a failure to distinguish between the two manuscripts, the one very much more reliable than the other, in which his poems exist. The first, the Dobell Folio (Bodleian MS. Eng. Poet. c. 42) is an autograph text of thirty-seven of Traherne's poems with numerous corrections in the hand of his brother Philip Traherne; the second, the Burney Manuscript (British Museum MS. Burney 392) is entirely in Philip's handwriting, apparently compiled by him from a manuscript that has since been lost. It contains some of the poems (twenty-two poems and two stanzas of another) found in Dobell but includes thirty-eight poems for which we have no other source.[14] A comparison of the poems that appear in both manuscripts shows that Philip in copying his brother's poems made a great many changes, occasionally improving the meter, but most often taming the sense, trying to make Thomas's ecstatic verse acceptable to conventional taste and orthodox opinion. The result, often very flat indeed, casts serious doubt on the text of those poems preserved only in the Burney Manuscript.

Most recent critics have preferred to base their judgment of Traherne's work on the Dobell Folio, and several scholars have argued that it constitutes a unified and structured work.[15] John Malcolm Wallace finds in the Dobell poems an example of the form of Jesuit meditation outlined by Louis Martz, dividing them into composition of place, pre-meditation, and a three-part analysis based on memory, understanding, and will. Clements sees a threefold structure representing the spiritual progress of man through innocence, the Fall, and redemption.[16]

Although a strong case may be made for the Dobell Folio as a coherent whole, one may question whether these are wholly adequate descriptions of its structure. Wallace himself plants the seeds of doubt: "So skillfully has Traherne insured the continuity of these sections that it would not always be easy to fix the demarcation between them had not the titles of the poems indicated the exact lines of division."[17] The reader who, like myself, finds no such clear indications in the titles will be the more dubious about this scheme. As for the threefold progression Clements outlines, it of course reflects the traditional Christian pattern of spiritual development, but it does not follow that this is Traherne's own pattern—or indeed that the poems are arranged in any sort of narrative, chronological sequence.

The Dobell poems do, I would argue, reflect Traherne's own spiritual development, not in the form of a simple linear progression, but in a virtuoso treatment of time and perspective. They do not merely represent innocence followed by its loss and restoration, but an ever-widening perception of the meaning of that original state and a recapitulation of the child's vision from the broader, maturer perspective of the adult poet. Although many have found in Traherne's insistence on his own radiant vision and in his use of the first person a forgetfulness of anyone and anything else, the Dobell Folio is in fact a carefully didactic and persuasive whole by which Traherne tries to bring the reader to see as he sees. His technique involves a manipulation of persona and tense, not as in Herbert to create distance between reader and persona, but rather to create identity.

The first poem in the Dobell Folio, "The Salutation," is a bold instance of this method, a kind of frontal assault, surprising in being addressed not to the reader, not even to God, but to the speaker himself, and that in a kind of sublime unawareness of every other reality. This poem differs from the familiar seventeenth-century dialogues between the body and soul in that the elements in this interior dialogue are not yet clearly defined, for the poem represents the child's awakening to himself, to the individual parts of his body, at the point of his coming into the world.

> These little Limmes,
> These Eys and Hands which here I find,
> These rosie Cheeks wherwith my Life begins,
> Where have ye been,? Behind
> What Curtain were ye from me hid so long!
> Where was? in what Abyss, my Speaking Tongue?
>
> (lines 1–6)

Traherne does not, like Vaughan in "The Retreate," envision a state of blissful previous existence but rather a state of nothingness from which he now awakens.[18] The supposed naïveté with which Traherne is often reproached has a positive function here: it forces upon the reader as directly as possible the experience of the childhood vision. If such is Traherne's aim, the adjectives "little" and "rosie" may seem disturbing and inconsistent; but though these words assume bases of comparison unavailable to the infant in his first moments of existence, they are a linguistic compromise by which the poet communicates those moments to the adult reader.

"The Salutation" reveals a gradually developing awareness of the self and of its place in the universe, and in this sense it is an embryonic version of the poems to follow. At first the poet—the child—is aware only of his physical being; gradually he begins to place himself in time (stanza 2), then to appreciate his body in relation to the whole world (stanzas 3–4), and then in relation to the God who created world, body, and soul (stanzas 5–6). The last stanza is a kind of retrospective in the present perfect tense in which the speaker judges the whole sequence as "strange all . . . yet brought to pass."

"Wonder," the next poem, continues this movement from past to present, from simple being to a greater awareness of that being. It begins in the past tense, as a narrative, thereby acknowledging the existence of someone or something outside the speaker, and proceeds to place some distance between the speaker and his earliest experiences.

> How like an Angel came I down!
> How Bright are all Things here!
> When first among his Works I did appear
> O how their GLORY me did Crown?
> The World resembled his *Eternitie*,
> In which my Soul did Walk;
> And evry Thing that I did see,
> Did with me talk.
>
> (lines 1–8)

The movement from the past tense of line 1 to the present tense in line 2 effectively emphasizes the enduring truth of the child's vision, for what once was, still is. Traherne makes this connection by virtue of syntactic juxtaposition rather than explicit use of a conjunction: "How like an Angel came I down!" leads to "How Bright are all Things here!" The relationship is in fact one of cause and effect: what we are determines what we see. It is part of Traherne's strategy to suggest the truth of relationship in the early poems—to make us experience it as the child does—and only later to state it explicitly, in the poems that represent adult comprehension and recreation of the initial state of wonder.

Although Traherne has not been noted for the precision of his language,[19] the ambiguities in the first stanza of "Wonder" embody Traherne's own metaphysical vision, expressing at once the uncertainty of our present lives and the ultimate certainty, the transcendent basis, of them. The vision of this stanza, like so much in Traherne, is embryonic—at once partial and complete. The word "first" of line 3 represents the child's perspective and designates a chronological stage in his own experience: "When first among his Works I did appear"; but by the end of line 4, "O how their GLORY me did Crown," we realize that man is "first among his Works" in another sense—that he is the chief among God's creatures. The child's word and his perception are truer than he or we originally realized, and his speech, recapturing the experience of Adam, unites two moments of time in a moment of eternity. Similarly, in lines 5–6 ("The World resembled his *Eternitie*, / In which my Soul did Walk;"), the relative "which," syntactically exact but in effect puzzling, allows the reader either to make a leap of faith or to draw back, to question whether the poet's soul walked in this world or in eternity, and to begin to see that, truly perceived, the two readings may be one. Besides the beauty of this first vision Traherne emphasizes also its vitality: it flows from a living force, from the spirit of God within him; thus in the lines, "The Skies in their Magnificence, / The Lively, Lovely Air" (lines 9–10), the order of the adjectives is crucial, for it is because of life, that divine source, that the air—like all creation—is beautiful.

These first poems represent a developing awareness not only of self but of the world and the evil in it. At first, amid the splendor of the child's early vision, in the poems "Wonder," "Eden," and "Innocence," the other side of reality is represented by negation, in an account of what the poet did *not* see.

> Harsh ragged Objects were conceald,
> Oppressions Tears and Cries,
> Sins, Griefs, Complaints, Dissentions, Weeping Eys,
> Were hid: and only Things reveald,
> Which Heav'nly Spirits, and the Angels prize.
>
> ("Wonder," lines 25–29)

These negatives, present in "Wonder" only in stanzas 4 and 7, take up an ever larger part of successive poems until they dominate entirely; yet the images of evil, repeated and strengthened in "Eden," are also held firmly in control by Traherne's technique.

> I knew not that there was a Serpents Sting,
>   Whose Poyson shed
>   On Men, did overspread
> The World: nor did I Dream of such a Thing
>   As Sin; in which Mankind lay Dead.
> They all were Brisk and Living Weights to me,
> Yea Pure, and full of Immortalitie.

("Eden," lines 8–14)

Traherne's statement "nor did I Dream of such a Thing" may be taken in the simple sense—"I could not even imagine such a thing"—as a testimony to his innocence and as a distinction between himself and the rest of mankind. What might well be the reader's natural response—that it does not matter whether the child was aware of sin and evil or not; that they do exist and must be reckoned with; that any other view is naïve or obscurantist—is counteracted by the progression in lines 11–12 from dream, with its suggestion of sleep, to death. This sequence implies that sin is a dream, something less real, less true than the goodness and innocence in which the child exists. As Traherne maintains elsewhere, sin is primarily an illusion, a failure to see God's truth; but it is a fatal illusion, for in it "Mankind lay Dead." Here, he suggests, it is not the child but the world that dreams, and its dream of sin brings death, even as the temporary image of sleep prefigures the finality of death. But Traherne too joins the fallen human race as, at the end of "Innocence," the third poem in this sequence, he acknowledges his final separation from the early blissful state at the same time that he indicates the possibility of a return to it: "I must becom a Child again."

Traherne's emphasis on the innocence of childhood has led to a great deal of discussion of his attitude toward the doctrine of original sin, and many modern critics have been at pains to lift this seventeenth-century cleric and theological controversialist above suspicion of heresy; but to assert with A.L. Clements and W.H. Marshall that Traherne's basic position agrees with the Thirty-Nine Articles seems to me very misleading.[20] According to the words of the Ninth Article, "Original Sin . . . is the fault or corruption of the nature of every man, that naturally is engendered of the Offspring of Adam, whereby man is very far gone from Original Righteousness, and is of his own nature inclined to evil, so that the Flesh lusteth always contrary to the Spirit, and therefore in every Person born into the World it deserveth God's wrath and Damnation." Traherne, in the *Centuries*, strikes a very different emphasis:

I clearly find how Docible our Nature is in natural Things, were it rightly entreated. And that our Misery proceedeth ten thousand times more from the outward Bondage of Opinion and Custom, then from any inward corruption or Depravation of Nature: And that it is not our Parents Loyns, so much as our Parents lives, that Enthrals and Blinds us. . . . But I speak it in the presence of GOD and of our Lord Jesus Christ, in my Pure Primitive Virgin Light, while my Apprehensions were natural, and unmixed, I can not remember, but that I was ten thousand times more prone to Good and Excellent Things, then evil. But I was quickly tainted and fell by others. (C 3.8)

Traherne is more carefully orthodox in *Christian Ethicks,* which he intended to publish and which attempts a systematic theological statement, than he is in his poems or his meditations; yet even that treatise leaves some doubt of his full acceptance of the doctrine of original sin. In a listing of "natural doctrines," Traherne, while acknowledging man's corruption, also admits the possibility of human merit:

That there is a felicity and a Supream Felicity appointed for man: that he is a free Agent, and may lose it, if he pleases: that misery is the Consequent of the Loss of Felicity: that GOD delighteth in all those that Love and practice Vertue: that he hateth all those that drown their Excellencies in any Vice: that Sorrow and Repentance are necessary for all those that have offended GOD: that there is Hope to escape the Punishment of Sin, if we endeavour to live as piously as we ought. (*CE*, pp. 118–19)

The hope of achieving salvation by endeavoring "to live as piously as we ought" is in marked contrast to the doctrine of natural depravity of the Ninth Article and totally opposed to the thrust of *The Temple,* which is to point up the ultimate inconsequence of such efforts. The modern editors of *Christian Ethicks* are unquestionably right in finding in Traherne "much more emphasis than was then usual upon innocence."[21]

But however interesting Traherne's theology may be to his critics, his poems concern not dogma but the truth of experience; they reflect his point of view rather than articulate the argument for it. Yet his description of his own experience is also a statement about the truth itself: what sounds like the child's limitation—that he knows only the good—is also a statement about reality—that the world is divine:

A Native Health and Innocence
Within my Bones did grow,
And while my GOD did all his Glories shew,

I felt a Vigour in my Sence
That was all SPIRIT. I within did flow
With Seas of Life, like Wine;
I nothing in the World did know,
But 'twas Divine.

("Wonder," lines 17-24)

Once again Traherne's syntactic ambiguity points to the leap of faith that one must make in order to see the truth. What has seemed to many a form of obscurantism or naïveté is to Traherne the truest form of seeing,[22] for the child does not see "the Works of Men" but "the Glorious Wonder of the DEITIE" ("Eden," lines 48-49).

The child's peculiar vision is the direct result of his own angelic nature, as Traherne makes clear in these lines from "Wonder":

Cursd and Devisd Proprieties,
With Envy, Avarice
And Fraud, those Feinds that Spoyl even Paradice,
Fled from the Splendor of mine Eys.

(lines 49-52)

Thus his vision is not passive but active, for his innate goodness banishes the sight of evil, a point that Traherne's brother Philip, in revising line 52 to read "Were not the Object of mine Eys," missed entirely.

But despite the dominance of the child's vision, which exerts an influence on what he sees, the things of this world are not for Traherne objects of one's eyes in Philip's and our conventional sense of the term; they do not merely receive his sight but rather exude a positive light.

Proprieties themselvs were mine,
And Hedges Ornaments;
Walls, Boxes, Coffers, and their rich Contents
Did not Divide my Joys, but shine.

(lines 57-60)

Whereas for Philip all these things merely "to make me Rich combine," Thomas's language implies reciprocity between the shining world and the splendor of the child's eyes. Neither the world nor the luminous vision can exist without the other, as we will be told more plainly in later poems, but already Traherne's apparently contradictory and extravagant statements are preparing us for that fuller articulation, for the adult vision of the truth contained in embryo in the luminescent vision of the child.

Traherne's poetry, to the embarrassment of some of his critics, is marked by repetition: successive poems again and again recount the few central events of his life. His method is not simply to record occurrences but to recreate progressively his experiences for the reader, even as his own childhood visions were recreated by his adult mind. Not only the event but his own reaction to it occupies him, until the sequence of his poetry becomes a kind of kaleidoscope of his life, seen from a variety of perspectives. In the course of the Dobell Folio, Traherne represents the development of the child's initial awareness of himself and his universe in a way that anticipates the final contemplation of God reached in his last poems. He rises from a keen sense of the physical world as an embodiment of the divine to an ever higher level of abstraction, but one that never loses touch with its roots. He also develops the principle of "circulation" or reciprocity, by which the persona comes to understand God and man not singly but in intimate relation with each other, and that in ways that might have offended Donne, Herbert, or Vaughan.

Traherne's poems are a series of backward glances—first to original innocence and then, from a greater distance but with a renewed vision, through the time of obscurity once again back to original innocence. Traherne begins, as we saw in "The Salutation" and "Wonder," with the most immediate and positive impressions; gradually these recede, first in the shift from present to past tense, then in the increasing dominance of negative elements, and finally in the adoption of an adult perspective on childhood. In all of this the key word is perspective: it is not so much the speaker's situation that has changed as his understanding of it. There is astonishingly little mention of sin, certainly no intense or personal sense of it, and if there is here a reenactment of the Fall of Adam and Eve, it is not in a repetition of transgression, of the act of sinning, but in a coming to the knowledge of good and evil.

Yet there is in the Dobell Folio no section that in fact represents the fallen perspective. There are of course references to it, but they are oddly brief and disproportionately few by seventeenth-century standards. "The Instruction," which begins, "Spue out thy filth, thy flesh abjure," seems so out of place and character that Margoliouth believes it may be a last-minute insertion.[23] "The Improvment" speaks of the joys "which now our Care and Sin destroys" (line 76), but the poem itself is a celebration of God's wisdom rather than a lament for man's loss. "The Approach" records a time in which God

> often visiteth our Minds,
> But cold Acceptance in us ever finds:
> We send him often grievd away;
> Els would he shew us all his Kingdoms Joy.
>
> (lines 9–12)

Yet although Traherne says "My Heart did Hard remain / Long time" (lines 20–21), this period of obstinacy, it seems, is already past, and the poem rejoices in the return to intimacy:

> But now with New and Open Eys,
> I see beneath as if above the Skies;
> And as I Backward look again,
> See all his Thoughts and mine most Clear and Plain.
>
> (lines 25–28)

Just as the Dobell Folio shows us little of the Fall, so it has nothing to correspond to the bitter disappointment, the failure of vision, and the agony that Donne, Vaughan, and Herbert all experienced. There is nothing even to match the temporary distress of "Solitude" (in the Burney MS), when Traherne felt no sense of the divine, or its prose counterpart in *Centuries* 3.23. Rather, in the Dobell sequence, as soon as the earliest external vision begins to fade, the process of regeneration begins. This process is marked by the withdrawal inward which is both the characteristic of the child, cut off from the outside world of language and enthralled with his inner vision, and the sign of the adult who recreates what he sees. In both cases the self is focal and primary—for the child instinctively so,[24] for the adult as the result of an ever-increasing understanding of his importance in the scheme of things. The note of withdrawal is first sounded in "Innocence":

> A Serious Meditation did employ
> My Soul within, which taken up with Joy
> Did seem no Outward thing to note, but flie
> All Objects that do feed the Eye.
>
> (lines 13–16)

It is repeated in "Silence," in which the adult voluntarily recaptures the original state of "Dumnesse" described in the preceding poem:

> A quiet Silent Person may possess
> All that is Great or High in Blessedness.
> The Inward Work is the Supreme: for all
> The other were occasiond by the Fall.
>
> ("Silence," lines 1–4)

The child at first perceives nothing beyond himself:

> Then was my Soul my only All to me,
> A Living Endless Ey,
> Far wider then the Skie
> Whose Power, whose Act, whose Essence was to see.
>
> ("The Preparative," lines 11–14)

But the poet soon comes to understand his own role in creating what he sees:

> Tis not the Object, but the Light
> That maketh Heaven; Tis a Purer Sight.
> Felicitie
> Appears to none but them that purely see.
>
> ("The Preparative," lines 57–60)

On the one hand, Traherne emphasizes the power that is within man to make the good appear, describing a creative act parallel to God's own: "I saw moreover that it did not so much concern us what Objects were before us, as with what Eys we beheld them; with what Affections we esteemed them, and what Apprehensions we had about them. All men see the same Objects, but do not equaly understand them" (C 3.68). On the other hand, he stresses the essential goodness of creation, indicating that if we do not perceive it, we pervert the truth: "I began to believ that . . . evry Creature is indeed as it seemed in my infancy: not as it is commonly apprehended. Evry Thing being Sublimely Rich and Great and Glorious" (C 3.62). Such paradoxes are found again and again in Traherne: goodness is in the eye of the beholder; goodness is in the world if we will but see. This is not finally a contradiction but one more aspect of the reciprocal relationship between divine goodness and human appreciation figured in Traherne's verse. The height of God's creation is not in its mere existence but in its order—the design by which it was ordained to serve man; and conversely, creation cannot fully serve that function unless man so understands it.

Traherne believed that man exercises his truest humanity not in action but in contemplation, and not in anything that savors of the Fall but rather in all that recalls the glory of the first creation. The child in his first state of self-absorption imitates the state of Adam, of whom Traherne says:

> The first and only Work he had to do,
> Was in himself to feel his Bliss, to view
> His Sacred Treasures, to admire, rejoyce
> Sing Praises with a Sweet and Heavnly voice,
> See, Prize, Give Thanks within, and Love
> Which is the High and only Work, above
> Them all.
>
> ("Silence," lines 21–27)

In our earliest activity, in which we may imitate our first father, there is not only something noble, but something resembling the divine (lines 33–38). Indeed, in contrast to Herbert, who believed that although his life might reflect God's goodness (e.g. "The Odour"), it could never resemble it, Traherne derives his conception of the deity directly from his experience of himself, and his beliefs about the nature of God from his understanding of the nature of man. His often-exclamatory poems record a discovery that advances step by step to statements ever bolder, and, some might say, more blasphemous. Traherne has often been associated with the Cambridge Platonists,[25] but in his ecstatic sense of the glory of man, made in the image of God, he in fact exceeds their more moderate views on man's essential rationality. Even the twentieth-century reader, whether or not he can accept Traherne's theism, may well be dumbfounded by his claims for man. In "Silence" he ecstatically apostrophizes his infant state: "O happy Ignorance of other Things, / Which made me present with the King of Kings, / And like Him too!" (lines 43–45).

The ingenuousness of that last clause, with its note of revelation, eradicates the caution of centuries of theological distinction. By contrast, Nathanael Culverwell, Traherne's contemporary and a Cambridge Platonist, though he speaks of certain kinds of likeness, explicitly denies others, and stops short of Traherne's enthusiasm: " 'Tis the greatest honour that a creature is capable of, to be the picture of its creator. . . . Though an eye be enabled to behold the Sun, yet this does not make it at all one with the Sun, but it keeps its own nature still as much as it did before."[26] Warning against human presumption, Culverwell carefully distinguishes image from essence: "They must have very low and dishonourable thoughts of God that make any creature partner or sharer with him in his essence, and they must have high and swelling thoughts of the creature" (p. 104).

For Traherne, who makes no such distinctions, self-discovery and the correlative discovery of God's infinity and goodness hinge on two points—the movement of man's mind and man's position as the crown of creation. He begins with his sense that the objects he perceives are in fact within his own being ("My Spirit," stanza 3) and from this infers that since man's mind can take in all things, it can extend everywhere. Since thoughts are more real than things (see "Dreams," lines 52–56),[27] the freedom of man's mind marks his essential freedom—wherever man's mind can roam, in effect, there man is. That such language recalls biblical statements of divine omnipresence is not accidental but essential to Traherne's thought (cf. Ps. 139:1–13).

> The Sun ten thousand Legions off, was nigh:
> The utmost Star,
> Tho seen from far,
> Was present in the Apple of my Eye.
>
> ("My Spirit," lines 59–62)

Because his mind can range throughout time and space, Traherne finds in himself (and by implication in all men) an infinite capacity; and infinity, of course, is the mark not of man but of God: "My Soul a Spirit infinit! / An Image of the Deitie!" ("My Spirit," lines 71–72). In "My Spirit," Traherne's description of his own spirit comes astonishingly close to Aquinas's definition of God as Pure Act: "Its Essence is Transformed into a true / And perfect Act" (lines 25–26). The poet finds "Act" and "Power Infinit" to be not only within himself but also of himself (lines 105–8). Equally startling, later in the poem, the ancient definition of God—a circle whose center is everywhere and whose circumference is nowhere—has become the formula for man.[28]

> A Strange Extended Orb of Joy,
> Proceeding from within,

Which did on evry side convey
It self, and being nigh of Kin
    To God did evry Way
Dilate it self even in an Instant, and
Like an Indivisible Centre Stand
At once Surrounding all Eternitie.

("My Spirit," lines 86–93)

The contrast between Traherne's delight in infinity and Herbert's sense of a limited universe has been noted by Marjorie Nicolson and Rosalie Colie. The cause, according to Robert Ellrodt, who points out that Nicholas Cusanus felt such an attraction for infinity before Copernicus and Giordano Bruno before Galileo, is in Traherne's temperament as much as in the new philosophy.[29] However, Ellrodt notes, Cusanus distinguished between the "relative infinity" of the created universe and the "absolute infinity" of God. Though Traherne makes a similar distinction in *Centuries* 2.21, he does not dwell on the point but rather takes the infinity of the universe as evidence of the infinity of God and proceeds from the one to the other with little apparent sense of the barrier he has crossed. Finding no difficulty in conceiving eternity, he thus finds infinity within himself.

While Traherne, if pressed, might have agreed with the precise theological position of Culverwell, which distinguishes sharply between God and man, it is clear that the whole force of his poetry works to eliminate such distinctions rather than to make them. Traherne's new sense of the easy kinship between man and God would seem to eliminate the sense of distance, the tension on which metaphysical poetry depends. The wit of metaphysical poetry may be compared to an electrical charge leaping a distance, establishing a connection between two unlike but mutually attracting poles: if the distance is too great, the contact cannot occur; if it is too small, the charges will be more easily and less spectacularly dissipated. The poetry of Donne, Herbert, and Vaughan is strongly marked by such a sense of distance, so much so that the poet often doubts that the contact can be made: the result in Donne is often a spectacular conjunction, in Vaughan sometimes a genuine failure, in Traherne perhaps too easy a union. Traherne lacks Donne's sense of sin, Herbert's feeling of inadequacy, and Vaughan's frustration with the imperfect representation of spirit in matter. Even the idea of man as microcosm, so dear to earlier metaphysical poets, has little appeal for Traherne, and the Book of Creatures, that imperfect but telling representation of divinity, is transformed in his eyes from evidence about God into the very glory of God.

We have seen how in Vaughan and Herbert the nature of religious longing and the structure of belief—the desire to see and the desire to submit—shape their poems. In Traherne, one might be tempted to think (and one would certainly be supported in this by the weight of critical opinion), that the loss of a sense of distance, of metaphysical tension, produces flat and shapeless verse. But while very different in structure from the poems of Vaughan and Herbert, Traherne's poems too are shaped to his experience, an experience that is uniquely one of discovery and ecstasy, and though we miss in Traherne the sense of man as a microcosm of the created universe, we find a new sense of relationship—a sense of the spirit of man as a microcosm of the divine spirit.

Traherne's subject—infinity (or eternity, as he interchanges the two)—seems an impossible one for a poetic that thrives on limits and paradoxes, as metaphysical poetry has been claimed to do. How can one celebrate limitlessness? What can stand in relation to it? What is to prevent the poem imitating its subject and becoming in Traherne's phrase "a Narrow Endless Length" (C 2.21)? Traherne's answer is that man is by nature related to limitlessness; man, discovering himself and hence his Maker, becomes the unifying center of his poems. Thus it is that so many of his poems begin at the same point—at the awakening to consciousness or at the more abstract assertion of the proper function of man—and move out from it in ever-widening circles of comprehension. His exclamatory style, so often criticized, is the voice of the discovering spirit, and the short ecstatic bursts embody successive stages of perception.[30] As Traherne discovers the magnitude of his own being he cries:

> O Wondrous Self! O Sphere of Light,
> O Sphere of Joy most fair;
> O Act, O Power infinit;
> O Subtile, and unbounded Air!
> O Living Orb of Sight!
> Thou which within me art, yet Me! Thou Ey,
> And Temple of his Whole Infinitie!
> O what a World art Thou! a World within!
> All Things appear,
> All Objects are
> Alive in thee! Supersubstancial, Rare,

Abov them selvs, and nigh of Kin
To those pure Things we find
In his Great Mind
Who made the World! tho now Ecclypsd by Sin.
There they are Usefull and Divine,
Exalted there they ought to Shine.

("My Spirit," lines 103–19)

The persona who can contain the endless reaches of space within his own soul discovers also that the whole creation exists to serve him. In discovering this blessing and in praising God for it, he becomes involved in a reciprocal relationship between God and man that manifests the most basic principle of the universe. God, "infinitly Prone to Lov," has created man, a being "infinitly Lovly" (C 1.67). The cycle of love, loving, and beloved that operates between God and man bears a striking resemblance to Traherne's account of the three Persons of the Trinity in *Centuries* 2.39–48, and the concept of circulation there articulated is one that pervades Traherne's work.

God is "that Life and that Being which is at once the fountain, and the End of all Things" (C 2.46), but speaking in terms of the earthly analogue, Traherne finds that it is man who is "the end / Of all his Labors!" ("The Vision," lines 52–53) and the creatures that flow from God as fountainhead. God is the End of creation in Aristotle's and Augustine's sense, that Being or *Telos* toward whom all things tend, while man is the end of the creation in the sense that it was ordained for his pleasure; yet the use of this term in close conjunction to apply to both God and man is curious. In lines 41–46 of "The Vision," "the End" clearly refers to God and represents the highest of all things, but by lines 52–53—"my self the End / Of all his Labors!"—the term again refers to man. Such usage seems deliberate rather than careless, for if one follows closely the movement of *Centuries* 2.50, in which Traherne first describes God, then the soul without God, and at last the loving soul, one sees that in loving man is united with God in a degree that approaches identity. Of all creation it is in man that God may most clearly be seen, and it is in comprehending the shape of creation and finding himself at the center that man beholds God.[31]

To see a Glorious Fountain and an End
To see all Creatures tend

To thy Advancement, and so sweetly close
    In thy Repose: To see them shine
In Use in Worth in Service, and even Foes
    Among the rest made thine.
To see all these unite at once in Thee
    Is to behold Felicitie.

                    ("The Vision," lines 33–40)

The climax of Traherne's idea of reciprocity between man and God is reached in *Centuries* 2.90, in which Traherne undertakes to show "that the Idea of Heaven and Earth in the Soul of Man, is more Precious with GOD then the Things them selvs, and more Excellent in nature." The world would have been created in vain, says Traherne, if it were not enjoyed by man. Moreover, in thinking of God's world man in fact improves upon the physical creation, and because thoughts are higher than things, man, himself a creator, returns to God a better gift than was given him: "The World within you is an offering returned. Which is infinitly more Acceptable to GOD Almighty, since it came from him, that it might return unto Him. Wherin the Mysterie is Great. For GOD hath made you able to Creat Worlds in your own mind, which are more Precious unto Him then those which He Created: And to Give and offer up the World unto Him, which is very Delightfull in flowing from Him, but much more in Returning to Him" (*C* 2.90). This section of *Centuries* goes beyond the poet's vision and discovery as seen in the early poems to emphasize the voluntary nature of his offering to God. The process of praise and recreation of the world within the mind here described is the business and the goal of the remaining poems in the Dobell Folio, as the poet moves to an ever fuller understanding of the truth so brilliantly glimpsed in the early poems, and as he moves from things to thoughts, toward a higher—in the sense of more conscious and more abstract—spiritual experience.

Although it is tempting in arguing the cyclical nature of the Dobell poems to try to divide the work into parts, to define an orderly progression in its thematic development, such an attempt in fact contradicts the very nature of this spiraling work, which turns in on itself and returns to its central focus even as it moves onward. Each stage both anticipates what is to come and recapitulates what has gone before; individual poems are paradoxes of completeness and incompleteness, moments of eternity in time. Traherne's verses, in imitation of his religious experience, trace a long journey to their point of origin, but though they involve repetition, they are not redundant, for such a movement conforms to Traherne's vision of a universe in which all proceeds from and returns to God. The ideas of infinite extension and perpetual return to which Traherne frequently refers also determine the structure of his poems, which represent an ongoing revelation, as they return to their focus in the discovering soul and its reciprocal relation with its creator. Traherne's reference in "The Approach" to "deep Abysses of Delights" and to "present Hidden Precious Benefits" is an apt description of his vision and his method: by tracing his own developing vision he forces on our attention the obvious truth—God's love and glory—that we would otherwise ignore.

"Fullnesse," one of Traherne's most finely constructed poems, finds eternity in a grain of sand, the whole of bliss in whatever part of it may now be experienced, at the same time that it combines images of circularity and reflection with images of upward movement. In this respect it epitomizes not only the poet's experience but the movement of the poems of the Dobell Folio, which are always repeating and reinterpreting past experiences and so moving forward to a more complete understanding, which in itself is a reflection of the ultimate vision of eternity. The form of the poem splendidly imitates this movement:

> That Light, that Sight, that Thought,
>   Which in my Soul at first He wrought,
> Is sure the only Act to which I may
>   Assent to Day:
>   The Mirror of an Endless Life,
>   The Shadow of a Virgin Wife,
> A Spiritual World Standing within,
>   An Univers enclosd in Skin.
> My Power exerted, or my Perfect Being,
> If not Enjoying, yet an Act of Seeing.
>   My Bliss
>   Consists in this,
>   My Duty too
>   In this I view.
>   It is a Fountain or a Spring,
>   Refreshing me in evry thing.
> From whence those living Streams I do derive,
> By which my Thirsty Soul is kept alive.

The Centre and the Sphere
Of my Delights are here.
It is my Davids Tower,
Where all my Armor lies,
The Fountain of my Power,
My Bliss, my Sacrifice:
A little Spark,
That shining in the Dark,
Makes, and encourages my Soul to rise.
The Root of Hope, the Golden Chain,
Whose End is, as the Poets feign,
Fastned to the very Throne
Of Jove.
It is a Stone,
On which I sit,
An Endless Benefit,
That being made my Regal Throne,
Doth prove
An oracle of his Eternal Love.

This evocative catalogue of epithets recalls the poetic technique (*aenigma*) of Herbert's "Prayer," but Herbert's images stretch to bind together the opposition of heaven and earth, while Traherne's images easily epitomize and reflect. "Fullnesse" turns on central images that represent the focal points of the poet's life and that in turn merge as one: "That Light, that Sight, that Thought, / Which in my Soul at first He wrought" becomes the point from which all of his experiences—past, present, and future—radiate. At the center of the poem Traherne finds in "That Light," which has since become a fountain, "The Centre and the Sphere / Of my Delights"; and in the concluding lines this same "little Spark" "Doth prove / An oracle of his Eternal Love." Like Marvell's image of the drop of dew, the images that form the nodal points of Traherne's poem express eternity while longing for it, while the visual effect of contrasting long and short lines emphasizes the idea of self-containment and extension, like the "endless Sphere" image Traherne so often uses.

Traherne's verse is harmonious enough to be appropriate to heaven, yet varied enough to be acceptable to earthly ears. The lines are remarkably musical, ringing changes on vowel and consonant sounds, repeating metric and phrase patterns, and using alliteration and repetition of words for emphasis, as well as a succession of close rhymes with some internal rhyme. Yet Traherne avoids monotony by variation in line length, by breaks in the metrical pattern, and by alteration of the normal aabbcc rhyme scheme. His rhymes emphasize connections that extend beyond the immediate links in the chain: the eternal deity, first dimly apprehended as Jove (line 31), is finally seen in full as love (line 37), in a rhyme that concludes the poem; the rhyme on "Sacrifice" and "rise," lines 24 and 27, underscores the unexpected relation between these two apparently opposite actions.

The more closely one examines it, the more intricate the structure of "Fullnesse" appears, until it seems almost a virtuoso display of the qualities of control and craftsmanship that Traherne is supposed to lack. Metaphysical in the most complete sense, it acknowledges the distance between heaven and earth, yet finds the one in the other, not simply but paradoxically: "A Spiritual World Standing within, / An Univers enclosd in Skin." Traherne perfectly balances his present partial experience of felicity against the final achievement of it, matching contemplating against enjoying; in so doing he is linked to that Being who is Pure Act, whom he knows by oracle rather than in the fullness of his Being: "My Power exerted, or my Perfect Being, / If not Enjoying, yet an Act of Seeing." Traherne's use of the terms "Enjoying" and "Seeing" here is philosophically exact, denoting the difference between our as yet distant perception of divinity—though for Traherne far less distant than for most—and the enjoyment of Him in eternity. Such language might seem flat and unevocative, but, though abstract and technical, it is in fact unusually concise, yielding up its meaning on examination. Traherne uses even such philosophical terminology as part of his ecstatic movement upward, and here too, as part of a cycle, it has power, acquiring more force with each successive poem.

The images of the circle, of reflection, and of arising so central to the Dobell Folio govern the following poems as well. "Nature" again retells the story of childhood, but in a way that, in a sharp divergence from the tradition of Hooker, Donne, and Herbert, effortlessly links the realms of body and spirit, nature and grace. As in "Fullnesse," there is a "Secret self" within that on "Angels Wings" "guided me to all Infinitie" (lines 18–30). Repeatedly Traherne emphasizes the ease and naturalness of this movement, first theoretically, in the alternately rhymed pentameter stanzas of "Ease," then more persuasively in the beautiful images of "Speed."

> The Liquid Pearl in Springs,
> The usefull and the Precious Things
> Are in a Moment Known.
> Their very Glory does reveal their Worth,
> (And that doth set their Glory forth;)
> As soon as I was Born, they all were Shewn.
>
> ("Speed," lines 1–6)

In this universe governed by the principle of circulation, appearance and reality are mirror images of each other (lines 4–5). Thus meaning is not something to be puzzled out or elaborately articulated as in Vaughan or Donne or Herbert; it is rather instantly perceived in the glory of precious objects. For once, Traherne makes full use of the sensuous and evocative power of poetry, using run-on lines, liquids, and sibilants to convey the impact of an experience:

> True Living Wealth did flow,
> In Chrystall Streams below
> My feet, and trilling down
> In Pure, Transparent, Soft, Sweet, Melting Pleasures,
> Like Precious and Diffusive Treasures,
> At once my Body fed, and Soul did Crown.
>
> (lines 7–12)

That the emphasis is on the poet's impressions rather than on the object itself is clearly evident in the series of adjectives of line 10, which take us from the relatively objective stance of sight to the greater physical participation of touch and taste, and finally to the total involvement of "Melting Pleasures." The metrical balance of line 10 makes us pause before the spondaic foot and final trochaic descent of "Soft, Sweet, Melting Pleasures," and the liquid sounds and feminine ending of that line underscore the poet's total receptivity to his experience. Traherne's final line (with the simultaneity of "At once my Body fed, and Soul did Crown") makes explicit what the reader must surely feel: here there is no conflict between the pleasures of the body and the joys of the soul.

However much we might like Traherne to remain on this plane, reveling in enjoyment of the senses, it does not fit his design to do so. Rather he moves from the contemplation of a single beautiful object to the contemplation of categories, which as truly beautiful in themselves, need no glorifying adjectives.[32] The opening lines of stanza 3 show a physical elevation (we have moved from contemplating a spring in stanza

2 to thinking of a throne in stanza 3) that parallels an elevation of the understanding:

> I was as High and Great,
> As Kings are in their Seat.
> All other Things were mine.
> The World my House, the Creatures were my Goods,
> Fields, Mountains, Valleys, Woods,
> Floods, Cities, Churches, Men, for me did shine.
>
> (lines 13–18)

The level of discourse rises in stanza 4 to a still higher level of abstraction; this is the constant motion of Traherne's poetry, in accordance with the notion that thoughts rather than things represent the highest truth. As before, Traherne moves from the object to his perception of it, as appropriate to his title—"Speed"—which celebrates a manner and a motion rather than an object:

> Great, Lofty, Endless, Stable,
> Various and Innumerable,
> Bright usefull fair Divine,
> Immovable and Sweet the Treasures were,
> The Sacred Objects did appear
> Most rich and Beautifull, as well as mine.
>
> (lines 19–24)

Although the last two stanzas of "Speed" continue this upward movement of language and sense, reaching at last to heaven itself, they also contain a countermovement, as they acknowledge the effects of sin, and as Traherne compares the vanished perfect vision with his present obscurity:

> New all! New Burnisht Joys;
> Tho now by other Toys
> Ecclypst.
>
> (lines 25–27)

The last stanza of "Speed" touches briefly on a theme common to many of Vaughan's poems, the decline from an earlier state of communion with God, though the emphasis on loss and darkness is here very much muted, for one never feels in Traherne's mature work Vaughan's sense of despair and alienation.[33]

The cyclic pattern of rising and falling that characterizes intercourse between heaven and earth is also the pattern of Traherne's verse, as he alternates between ecstasy and meditation, between assurance and questioning, between contemplation of God's beneficent action and man's response. This upward movement of glorification is not a single one but a rhythmic pulsation of contrasting attitudes, emotions, and poetic techniques. Thus, whereas "Speed" depicts man's ascension, "The Designe" opens with the counterstroke of God's condescension: "When first Eternity Stoopd down to Nought, / And in the Earth its Likeness sought" (lines 1–2). By the end of the poem Eternity's gifts have raised man up again so that in "The Person," which follows, he can once more, as at the beginning of "Speed," contemplate his own physical being with joy. As before Traherne begins with the concrete and moves to the more abstract, but this time the process extends over several poems. The delight in the body of "The Person" gives way to a sense of the body's limitations in "The Estate"; but that questioning leads not only to reaffirmation of the physical being but to a vision of the entire physical universe that surrounds the body as God's gift to man. This hymn of praise yields in "The Enquirie" to a further question, one that, as before, tests the limitations of the blessing just celebrated.

"The Circulation," which presents a good many specific examples, both social and physical, of the cyclical nature of the universe, forms a central link in Traherne's thought. Its opening stanza suggests that the poet is beginning to apprehend on a quite different level from the immediate physical and intuitive sensation of "The Salutation," "Wonder," and "Eden," and also that he is no longer speaking only in the first person, of his own experience, but of the experience of the human race.

> As fair Ideas from the Skie,
>   Or Images of Things,
> Unto a Spotless Mirror flie,
>   On unperceived Wings;
> And lodging there affect the Sence,
> As if at first they came from thence;
> While being there, they richly Beautifie
> The Place they fill, and yet communicat
> Themselvs, reflecting to the Seers Ey,
>   Just such is our Estate.
> No Prais can we return again,
> No Glory in our selvs possess,

But what derived from without we gain,
From all the Mysteries of Blessedness.

("The Circulation," lines 1–14)

Traherne's beautiful floating lines with their open rhymes suggest a movement from things to thoughts and an advance over earlier and simpler forms of perception, but they also retain a sense of that first vision, and of its partiality, that make us realize that even the present state is incomplete: the "or" of line 2, the "as if" of line 6, the images of the mirror, the reflection, and the "unperceived Wings" all contribute to this uncertain, yet magical quality. We now know enough to know that we do not know; we face the "Mysteries of Blessedness."

"The Circulation" represents a further advance over earlier poems in that the poet who has so exulted in the glory of man now understands that his glory is derivative. This realization of human limitation and of divine limitlessness is a milestone of Traherne's verse: for the first time it sets a boundary between the poet's sense of himself and of God. But in the dynamic process of Traherne's poetry such conclusions give way to new inquiries. He moves dialectically from a true but limited vision to a realization of its limitations, to a greater awareness that incorporates the truth of the first vision. Although God is by theological necessity sufficient unto himself, there is nevertheless a relationship between God and man that gratifies the Creator as well as the creature: man is, Traherne finds, "a Glorious Spring/Of Joys and Riches to my King" ("Amendment," lines 29–30). The poems that follow "Amendment" develop the idea of the two parallel and interrelated cycles—the one within the Deity and the other between God and man—as they work at last to reconcile two apparently incompatible concepts: that God is infinite and self-sufficient, and that he is dependent on man.

The first of these poems, "The Demonstration," despite its prosaic title, is one of Traherne's most daringly paradoxical poems. Like "The Circulation" it deals with the modes and the validity of perception; it is concerned not only with what we know but with how:

> The Highest Things are Easiest to be shewn,
> And only capable of being *Known.*
> A Miste involvs the Ey,
> While in the Middle it doth lie;
> And till the Ends of Things are seen,
> The Way's uncertain that doth stand between.

As in the Air we see the Clouds
Like Winding Sheets, or Shrouds;
Which tho they nearer are obscure
The Sun, which Higher far, is far more Pure.
("The Demonstration," lines 1–10)

Traherne's image of the sun as the only thing we may truly see recalls
Plato's allegory of the cave and seems an encouragement to raise our
sights to the highest truth. But Traherne differs from Plato in his apparent
sense that we may view that sun without being dazzled, or rather, if we are
overwhelmed, it is in a thoroughly positive way. Traherne's language, as
violent but not so explicit as that of Donne's "Batter my heart," or of
Crashaw's description of the divine ravishment of Saint Teresa, cele-
brates the deity who overwhelms man through the excess of his glory.

Its Beams by violence
Invade, and ravish distant Sence.
Only Extremes and Hights are Known;
No Certainty, where no Perfection's shewn.
Extremities of Blessedness
Compell us to confess
A GOD indeed. Whose Excellence,
In all his Works, must needs exceed all Sence.

And for this Caus Incredibles alone
May be by Demonstration to us shewn.
(lines 13–22)

Yet though God's excellence exceeds all sense, the senses are not antithet-
ical to the workings of the spirit, for it seems to be through the senses that
we learn of his glory.

Traherne differs still more strongly from Plato in his emphasis on the
small things of this earth as giving us a view of divine splendor, not in the
sense of a dark vision but rather a true epitome:

Those Things that are most Bright
Sun-like appear in their own Light.
And Nothing's truly seen that's Mean.
(lines 23–25)

Traherne's argument is difficult, shifting from one point of a paradox to
the next: at first he seems to say, "No mean thing may be truly seen" (as in
stanza 1) and then, upon examination, he seems to suggest, "If we see

anything in creation as mean, we have not seen it truly." The reader may at first have had the impression that he is being urged to fix his mind on glorious objects, but it then appears that Traherne intends a radical shift in the notion of brightness. The smallest and most trivial things as well as the greatest may be among the most glorious, though the source of this glory is not specified. Whereas the preceding lines suggested an innate splendor, the next imply a beauty that comes from without:

> Be it a Sand, an Acorn, or a Bean,
> It must be clothd with Endless Glory,
> Before its perfect Story
> (Be the Spirit ne're so Clear)
> Can in its Causes and its Ends appear.
>
> (lines 26–30)

Throughout the Dobell Folio, Traherne establishes both sides of this paradox: beauty is in the object and in the eye of the beholder. This is the truth initially experienced by the child, but it is now grasped much more fully by the adult who realizes that the value of God's creation is both inherent in it and enhanced by man's appreciation of it.

> His Gifts as they to us com down
> Are infinit, and crown
> The Soul with Strange Fruitions; yet
> Returning from us they more value get.
>
> ("The Demonstration," lines 37–40)

The final triumphant lines of "The Demonstration," their short phrases and repeated words suggesting an ever-closer interlocking between God and man, achieve the boldest demonstration of all—the reconciliation of the God who is sufficient in himself to the God who depends for his felicity on man. Traherne's description of men in line 71 dramatically adapts and reverses the biblical account of the God in whom "we live, and move, and have our being" (Acts 17:28) to make the Creator almost blasphemously dependent on his creation.

> In them he sees, and feels, and Smels, and Lives,
> In them Affected is to whom he gives:
> In them ten thousand Ways,
> He all his Works again enjoys,
> All things from Him to Him proceed

By them; Are His in them: As if indeed
His Godhead did it self exceed.
    To them He all Conveys;
    Nay even Himself: He is the End
To whom in them Himself, and All things tend.

(lines 71–80)

The process of discovery works dialectically: the principle of "The Circulation," earlier found inapplicable to the Divine Being because incompletely understood, is now reasserted as truth, and the circle of discovery, which began in the child's discovery of his own being and through it his discovery of the nature of God, concludes with God's seeking of himself through his creatures.

Traherne's last poems, like his earlier ones, proceed by repetition, moving through familiar patterns in a spiral that leads to an ever more rarefied atmosphere. They also alternate in mood and temper, shifting between the meditative or theoretical and the ecstatic as the poet's thoughts climb ever higher. Margoliouth (2:393) notes the alternation of the four "Thoughts" poems with "two outer pairs with abstract titles ('Love,' 'Blisse' and 'Desire,' 'Goodnesse') and a middle poem without a title but, in effect, an ecstatic 'Thoughts' poem." The "Thoughts" poems celebrate the superiority, indeed the all-sufficiency of thoughts; they represent an elevation already achieved, a freedom from all limitations. The four poems with which they alternate, by contrast, are full of passionate desire and represent a strenuous upward movement of the spirit. This pattern of upward movement reverses that of the earliest poems, in which negative reality comes ever more to dominate. Then the child saw eternity in time in that he looked at this earth and believed it to be eternal (C 3.2; "Wonder," stanza 1; "Eden," stanza 2); now the poet sees eternity in time in that he rises by thought to contemplation of the eternal. The cycle moves from the nature of God ("The Anticipation") to man's response to it ("The Recovery"), from increasing comprehension of the nature of thought as a bond between man and God (chiefly in the "Thoughts" poems) to longing for the highest (as in "Love" and "Desire"). Of the nine last poems, "Blisse" celebrates the pure uncorrupted joy of Adam; "Goodnesse" represents the recapturing of that bliss.

Both "Love" and "Desire" are, in comparison with the whole of Traherne's work, unusually highly structured poems. Each follows upon a poem more meditative and philosophical than itself and each begins with a burst of emotion. The extended ecstatic apostrophe with which

"Love" opens (likely to annoy anyone who disapproves of Traherne's rapturous, exclamatory style) may have its origin in the pietistic notion of the Divine Being who functions on earth only through the works of men. Medieval and Renaissance piety stressed the pathetic elements in this theme, showing a Christ who suffers with his people, but in Traherne's hands it is expanded into a metaphysical principle whose implications are resoundingly positive. In men God not only performs all earthly functions, but in them he seeks an otherwise unfulfillable part of himself.

The terms applied to love in this first stanza suggest a kind of paradoxical epitome of the universe—both "Abridgement of Delights" and "Kingdom Wide"; both "God" and "Bride of God"; "King" and "Queen of Sight." In stanza 2 the mode of the poem shifts quickly from such abstractions to a more personal, meditative exploration of the furthest reaches of the poet's imagination and confesses the ultimate satisfaction of his desires in "Such a King, / The fountain Head of evry Thing!" But the reality the poet perceives so far exceeds even such expectations that in stanza 3 he can hardly believe his good fortune; he cites two parallels from classical myth that at once exemplify and fall short of his experience.

> . . . Jove beyond the Fiction doth appear
> Once more in Golden Rain to come.
> To Danae's Pleasing Fruitfull Womb.
>
> His Ganimede! His Life! His Joy!
> Or he comes down to me, or takes me up
>   That I might be his Boy,
> And fill, and taste, and give, and Drink the Cup.
>
> (lines 28–34)

Though Traherne's unwonted excursion into sensuous myth has caused some embarrassment among his critics,[34] the pair of legends—of Danae and Ganymede—together convey (as line 32 indicates) not only God's goodness but his movement down to man and man's movement up to God—in other words, the mutual relationship, the pattern of circulation that is a chief theme of Traherne's verse.

The concluding lines of "Love" are an extraordinary balance between high claims and limitation, between extension and tight structure. The simple listing of epithets in metrically restrained lines contrasts with the swirling images of lines 31–34; yet one comes to realize that despite

Traherne's careful control, the claims these final lines make for man exceed anything in the preceding ecstasies of the poem:

> But these (tho great) are all
> Too short and small,
> Too Weak and feeble Pictures to Express
> The true Mysterious Depths of Blessedness.
> I am his Image, and his Friend.
> His Son, Bride, Glory, Temple, End.
>
> (lines 35–40)

The last two lines encapsulate the Christian and classical language of the poem, boldly combining what before had seemed contradictory, implying that no term does justice to the mysterious relationship between God and man. The lines move by balance and contrast: the abstract "Image" is tempered by the homely and biblical "Friend"; "Son" and "Bride," which are contradictory if one takes either the myth of Ganymede or of Danae as final, are here united in the context of the Bible, in which the classical "Jove beyond the Fiction doth appear" and which uses both concepts to express man's intimacy with God. Man's claim to be made in God's image, which has both classical and biblical foundations, is balanced against the far bolder claim to be the "End" of the Deity with which Traherne concludes the poem.

"Desire" is the last of the four passionate poems that alternate with the "Thoughts" poems, and as with "Love," the emotion it expresses is part of the upward drive of the whole cycle. It recapitulates the poet's experience from a new, elevated perspective and goes even further than preceding poems to make man in God's image. The single pulsating sentence of stanza 1, so appropriate to its subject, looks back on the poet's earliest days, no longer simply as a time of peace and glory, but as the first stage in his spiritual development.

> For giving me Desire,
> An Eager Thirst, a burning Ardent fire,
> A virgin Infant Flame,
> A Love with which into the World I came,
> An Inward Hidden Heavenly Love,
> Which in my Soul did Work and move,
> And ever ever me Enflame,
> With restlesse longing Heavenly Avarice,

That never could be satisfied,
That did incessantly a Paradice
Unknown suggest, and som thing undescried
Discern, and bear me to it; be
Thy Name for ever praisd by me.

(lines 1–13)

This picture of the poet's childhood as filled to an unpleasant degree with passion and longing is very different from that of the earliest poems, in which he seemed far more satisfied than restless. But if the two images seem inconsistent, Traherne's method is not, for by repeatedly looking back on the same experiences from new perspectives, he finds that they reveal new truths, indeed that they become quite different experiences. The child's vision is perfect in that it is an epitome of eternal bliss, but it is not intended as a state of rest, and as the mature poet moves closer to the final state, that fact—and hence the partial quality of his early joy—is more clearly apparent.

"Desire" is the poem by Traherne most likely to remind the reader of Vaughan; the resemblance is strongest in the second stanza, which describes a far less happy aspect of that emotion than the first. "Parched my Witherd Bones / And Eys did seem: My Soul was full of Groans" (lines 14–15). But in striking contrast to Vaughan, Traherne, who is ever sure of reaching the goal, in the very moment of longing declares himself in bliss: "O Happiness! A Famine burns, / And all my Life to Anguish turns!" (lines 25–26). These lines are either nonsense or a reflection of the ecstatic pursuit of unearthly bliss—the time of spiritual dryness that Saint John of the Cross called "the Dark Night of the Soul." In Traherne's relentless search, which telescopes the past, the old delights of the earth embraced in the early poems and in the *Centuries* are no longer a source of pleasure:

Alass, all these are poor and Empty Things,
    Trees Waters Days and Shining Beams
Fruits, Flowers, Bowers, Shady Groves and Springs,
No Joy will yeeld, no more then Silent Streams.
    These are but Dead Material Toys,
    And cannot make my Heavenly Joys.

(lines 34–39)

We are witnessing a repetition, at a higher level, of the theme of "The Instruction"—the rejection of the material for the spiritual. Appropriately, Traherne's present response recalls that of "The Vision," which, following the negative "The Instruction," reinterpreted this world in the light of heaven. "Flight is but the Preparative," said Traherne then ("The Vision," line 1); now we are much closer to the goal, close enough to realize that it is not to be reached at the end of time (i.e., through an external event), but rather through the means of thought:

> Thoughts are the privileged Posts that Soar
> Unto his Throne, and there appear before
> Our selvs approach. These may at any time
> Abov the Clouds, abov the Stars may clime.
>
> ("Thoughts IV," lines 5–8)

Louis Martz in his discussion of Traherne in *The Paradise Within* argues that the movement of the *Centuries* parallels the three stages of Saint Bonaventure's *Journey of the Mind to God*: seeking God in the external world, in the self, and in contemplation of the essential attributes of the Trinity.[35] The claim could equally well be made of the Dobell Folio, whose inner movement parallels that of the *Centuries* and whose inner dynamic is both more effective and more complex than has been recognized. And Martz's description of Traherne's method, though he makes no such claim for it, applies as much to his verse as to his prose: "Traherne's book develops in a way very close to that found in Augustine's *Confessions* and in his *De Trinitate*: through the concatenation of repeated words and phrases, repeated always in a slightly different context, with a gradual increment of meaning, as the mind explores the central issues represented by these repeated words and phrases" (p. 43).

The final resemblance between the two works is to be seen in their conclusions. Because the Fifth Century contains only ten meditations, followed by the number 11, Gladys Wade thought it had been cut short by Traherne's death, though Margoliouth and Martz have since disagreed.[36] A supporting argument for the completeness of the *Centuries* is that the Dobell Folio—a work often considered mysterious but never deemed unfinished—concludes on a strikingly similar note. The last meditation of *Centuries*, culminating a series on the infinity and eternity of God, celebrates man's joy in divine omnipresence:

Our Bridegroom and our King being evry where, our Lover and Defender watchfully governing all Worlds, no Danger or Enemie can arise to hurt us, but is immediatly prevented and supprest, in all the Spaces beyond the utmost Borders of those unknown Habitations which he possesseth. Delights of inestimable valu are there preparing. For evry thing is present by its own Existence. The Essence of God therfore being all Light and Knowledg, Lov and Goodness, Care and Providence, felicity and Glory, a Pure and simple Act; it is present in its Operations, and by those Acts which it eternally exerteth, is wholly Busied in all Parts and places of his Dominion, perfecting and compleating our Bliss and Happiness. (C 5.10)

Like *Centuries* 5.10, "Goodnesse" contemplates the omnipresent glory of God in which our bliss mingles with his own. It is a very different poem from the preceding "Thoughts IV," which, true to the generally abstract character of the "Thoughts" poems, ends with a heavenly vision divorced from all earthly considerations:

> O give me Grace to see thy face, and be
> A constant Mirror of Eternitie.
> Let my pure Soul, transformed to a Thought,
> Attend upon thy Throne, and as it ought
> Spend all its Time in feeding on thy Lov,
> And never from thy Sacred presence mov.
> So shall my Conversation ever be
> In Heaven, and I O Lord my GOD with Thee!
>
> ("Thoughts IV," lines 95–102)[37]

These lines would seem to represent the culmination of the Dobell Folio, with its Platonic emphasis on spirit over matter, and its almost Berkeleyan insistence that things unperceived do not exist; they also conform more closely to the Augustinian pattern outlined by Martz. But this is not Traherne's final vision, for "Goodnesse," though it begins abstractly, turns from the contemplation of God to the contemplation of humanity. Not simple spirituality but beneficence is God's chief quality: "He is an Act that doth Communicate" ("The Anticipation," line 99); and man must join in this communication.

> The Bliss of other Men is my Delight:
> (When once my Principles are right:)
> And evry Soul which mine doth see
> A Treasurie.
>
> ("Goodnesse," lines 1–4)

"Goodnesse" embodies in fullest form the universal principle of reciprocity articulated in "The Circulation" and binds heaven and earth in perfect harmony. It ends in a vision of eternity that grows directly out of a vision of time, an image of the spiritual that proceeds from the sensuous. The things of this world, all of which Traherne saw as ministering unto him, become the joys of heaven, as they participate in the communion of saints in which he joins. The two final stanzas transform Christ's earthly metaphor, "I am the vine, ye are the branches" (John 15:5), to a heavenly one, but one nevertheless warmed by the poet's rich sensations.

> The Soft and Swelling Grapes that on their Vines
>   Receiv the Lively Warmth that Shines
>   Upon them, ripen there for me:
>   Or Drink they be
> Or Meat. The Stars salute my pleased Sence
> With a Derivd and borrowed Influence
>   But better Vines do Grow
>   Far Better Wines do flow
>   Above, and while
>   The Sun doth Smile
> Upon the Lillies there, and all things warme
> Their pleasant Odors do my Spirit charm.
>
> Their rich Affections do like precious Seas
>   Of Nectar and Ambrosia pleas.
>   Their Eys are Stars, or more Divine:
>   And Brighter Shine
> Their Lips are soft and Swelling Grapes, their Tongues
> A Quire of Blessed and Harmonious Songs.
>   Their Bosoms fraught with Love
>   Are Heavens all Heavens above
> And being Images of GOD, they are
> The Highest Joys his Goodness did prepare.
>
>   (lines 49–70)

This is no cold pastoral, no ethereal abstraction, but of all Traherne's poems perhaps the one most filled with the joys of earth, so that at the last, it is most truly by understanding this world that man understands the divine. The last lines link heaven and earth by raising man to fellowship with God and his saints, but the movement—for all that it has been the goal of the preceding poems—is an easy one, anticipated previously in the thoughts of the adult and the visions of the child, and lacking even the "letting go," the release of tension, of Herbert's "So I did sit and eat." "Goodnesse," like so many of the poems that precede it, describes a great circle—a figure that in Traherne's hands is both complete and infinitely extended—in imitation of the unceasing movement between heaven and earth that he celebrates. Each poem represents a particular point on the spectrum, but it is also often a retrospective that includes other moments. Each poem must end, and the cycle itself is concluded, but in a way that continues to reach out to infinity. The pattern traced by these poems recalls that of the *Centuries*, but, I would argue, rather than extending toward the stasis of mystical repose, they strive to participate in the eternal dynamic of divine goodness.

IV

The Endless Sphere
TRAHERNE

THE Dobell Folio, which, as we have seen, has a significant structure, one that reflects the movement of the poet's mind rather than external or logical categories, has been judged by most recent critics of Traherne to be the superior version of his poems and closest to his original intentions; but we cannot ignore the other major manuscript of his poems, British Museum Burney MS. 392. This manuscript, entitled "Poems of Felicity," is a volume of sixty-one poems prepared for the press by Philip Traherne but never published. It contains twenty-two poems already present in the Dobell Folio, one ("News") found also in *Centuries*, and thirty-eight poems for which we have no other source. A comparison of the poems that exist in both versions shows enough alarming and insensitive revisions by Philip to restrain us from making negative judgments of Traherne's verse on the basis of these poems; yet the number of very fine and markedly individual poems found only in the Burney Manuscript makes it impossible simply to reject that text as unsatisfactory. [1]

Although Philip Traherne included twenty-two Dobell poems in the projected "Poems of Felicity," he omitted fourteen others, presumably intending to include them in a second volume. [2] Whether the Burney Manuscript conforms to Thomas's or to Philip's design is uncertain. Some critics have approved it: Margoliouth considers "Philip's arrangement of the poems . . . on the whole a good one" (1:xv) and Jean-Jacques Denonain believes that the order of the Burney Manuscript may reflect Thomas's own wishes. But although, as Stanley Stewart notes, Philip in his interpolation for the most part preserved the original Dobell sequence, [3] the resulting cycle is not very satisfactory, and it is based on quite different assumptions from those of the Dobell Folio. Only the titles could have persuaded Philip that "The Apprehension," which refers to the preceding dazzling vision of "My Spirit," should follow "Right Apprehension," a tirade against the values of this world and the barrenness of gold. In placing "An Infant-Ey" and "The Return" between "Innocence" and "The Preparative" Philip apparently sought to join poems of like themes but in so doing disrupted his brother's rhythmic pattern of shifting perspectives and moods.

The judgment of Margoliouth and Denonain notwithstanding, the Burney Manuscript as it stands seems less clearly and meaningfully structured and more repetitive than either the Dobell Folio or the *Centuries* would lead one to expect of Traherne. Yet that group of thirty-nine poems found in Burney but not in Dobell taken by themselves do have a kind of coherence.[4] They differ in emphasis from the Dobell cycle: they are somewhat less ecstatic and place a greater stress on sin and man's fallen state.[5] Where in the Dobell sequence only the discordant "The Instruction" is fully devoted to the fallen perspective, such Burney poems as "Solitude" and "Poverty" record the poet's full sense of loss and abandonment. Even the two poems that open the sequence, "An Infant-Ey" and "The Return," do not, like "The Salutation" or "Wonder," record the present experience of bliss but rather an event placed firmly in a past that, as one reads, seems to recede ever further. "An Infant-Ey" describes generally and objectively the child's vision and its decline; by the time the poem shifts to the first person in stanza 3 it is to lament a past that the poet can only ache to recapture. Curiously, although "The Return" opens positively (and paradoxically), "To Infancy, O Lord, again I com, / That I my Manhood may improv," each successive stanza brings less, rather than more, hope of attaining that newborn state of security; and "Solitude" moves from a narrative past tense to a present (and by implication a future) still filled with longing. On the whole, then, the effect of the Burney cycle is far less positive and optimistic than that of the Dobell Folio.

The Burney poems tend also to be more one-dimensional than the Dobell poems, lacking the kind of complicated double perspective, the simultaneous sense of two kinds of experience that emerges in "The Salutation" or "Wonder." Like the Dobell Folio, the Burney poems move from things to thoughts, but the closing poems do not show the breathless alternation of meditation and ecstasy that allows the Dobell sequence to soar so high. There is evidence that such a pattern may have existed in Thomas's original order but that it was eliminated by Philip's leveling mind.[6] Such poems as "Insatiableness" and "Hosanna" are of course expansive, but "The Review," which concludes the sequence, looks back to the childhood vision, dwelling on the ways man can go astray rather than incorporating that first glow into a mature and heavenly repose as does "Goodnesse." The central apocalyptic vision is not that of the reciprocal "Circulation" between God and the poet, but of that essentially social structure, the New Jerusalem, the conception of which arises from the child's wonderings about "Christendom."

In comparison with the Dobell Folio, the Burney poems are also somewhat more conventional[7]—whether as the result of Philip's revisions or of his selection we do not know—and they place a greater emphasis on religious institutions. Though the poet rejects mere external rites in "Solitude," he finds in "Churches" joy in the physical structure that praises God and in "Bells" an exemplum of man's duty. The poet is in Burney clearly involved in mankind: he finds solace not in a unique and radiant vision, but in the Bible, given to all. The search for happiness in "Dissatisfaction," which is a movement from material goods to social life, then to education, and finally to philosophy and maturity, could be that of Everyman; and in "Bells" the speaker sounds like any pious churchman. The progression from "The Bible" to "Christendom" is logical but prosaic, revealing nothing unique in the poet's experience, whereas in Dobell the poet focuses first on the discoveries of an "I" who is the center of creation and only then extends this claim to all mankind.

The Burney poems should not, I believe, be interspersed with the Dobell sequence as they are in Philip Traherne's arrangement in the Burney Manuscript but read as a parallel to them, just as we read several successive versions of Traherne's central experiences in *Centuries*. The Burney poems are perhaps most closely allied to the Third Century, which is more personal and less philosophical and theoretical than the Second and Fourth Centuries. One of the finest of the Burney poems, "News," appears in the Third Century; there are clear parallels in *Centuries* 3.23 and 3.16 to "Solitude" and "Poverty"; and an expanded version of the desire for a heavenly book met by the Bible is found in *Centuries* 3.27–35 (one case in which Traherne's verse is more economical than his prose). As the Burney poems move to praise God in thoughts and to exult at man's limitless mind, so the Third Century praises God after the example of, and sometimes in the words of, King David.

Considering the impossibility of recovering a reliable text, we cannot hold Traherne fully responsible for the infelicities of the Burney poems. Some of them have a kind of mechanical unity (e.g., "Insatiableness"); others are arbitrary in structure (e.g., "The Apostacy," "The City"). Yet although the cycle as a whole is less marked by Traherne's distinctive spirit than the Dobell Folio, there are a number of fine poems within it, including several that invite comparison with the poems of Donne, Herbert, and Vaughan and thus help us mark Traherne's distance from the earlier metaphysicals and his movement toward eighteenth- and nineteenth-century modes of thought.

One of the most important and distinguishing features of Traherne's work is his religious and philosophical optimism, seen as he records the decline of his first bright vision and the return to communion with the divine. Like Vaughan, Traherne understands his own situation in the context of the religious history of the human race as recorded in the Old Testament, but where Vaughan looks back on an irrecoverable time of communion between God and man, Traherne identifies himself with the innocent perceptions of Adam:

> The Sun as bright for me doth shine;
> The Spheres abov
> Do shew his Lov,
> While they to kiss the Earth incline,
> The Stars as great a Service do;
> The Moon as much I view
> As *Adam* did, and all God's Works divine
> Are Glorious still, and Mine.
>
> ("The World," lines 5–12)

The great loss which the speaker experiences is not, despite the brief statement "Sin spoil'd them" (line 13), seen as the consequence of disobedience but of a misjudgment of value. The child's first judgment is expressed in vivid, concrete terms, and in a stanza form whose consecutively longer lines and even rhythm suggest the process of weighing:

> One Star
> Is better far
> Than many Precious Stones:
> One Sun, which is abov in Glory seen,
> Is worth ten thousand Golden Thrones:

A juicy Herb, or Spire of Grass,
In useful Virtu, native Green,
An Em'rald doth surpass;
Hath in't more Valu, tho less seen.

("The Apostacy," lines 1–9)

The stanza structure also represents the slow process by which the child
learns to misunderstand creation:

But I,
I knew not why,
Did learn among them too
At length; and when I once with blemisht Eys
Began their Pence and Toys to view,
Drown'd in their Customs, I became
A Stranger to the Shining Skies,
Lost as a dying Flame;
And Hobby-horses brought to prize.

(lines 55–63)

Traherne's language vividly conveys the physical qualities of its object—
the "juicy Herb" and "Shining Skies"—as it suggests the true values that
the child perceives. The "Spire of Grass" recalls not only the slender
shape of a blade of grass but the place of worship of which it is an emblem;
the pairing of "useful" and "Virtu" reinforces the original meaning of
virtue, which involves strength as well as goodness, to suggest the innate
power—the *virtu*—of natural objects; and the remarkably evocative "Lost
as a dying Flame" conveys the child's sense of deprivation and loneliness
through an image of light and of vision. The progression from the shining
skies to the dying flame, the latter akin to but separated from the former,
and finally to the earthly, material, and trivial hobbyhorse is subtle and
poignant. Traherne moves from a world in which the value of objects is
inherent, ordained by their divine creator and perceived by the child, to a
world in which connections are false or arbitrary and experience is di-
vorced from reality.

The brilliance and validity of the vision in "The Apostacy" are bal-
anced by the desolation of "Solitude," which follows. As before,
Traherne differentiates the persona's perception from the reality of his
situation; his physical loneliness is the outward sign of an inner state, in
particular his misapprehension of the truth.

My roving Mind
Search'd evry Corner of the spacious Earth,
From Sky to Sky, if it could find,
(But found not) any Mirth:
Not all the Coasts,
Nor all the great and glorious Hosts,
In Hev'n or Earth, did any Mirth afford;
I pin'd for hunger at a plenteous Board.

("Solitude," lines 17–24)

It is out of this distorted feeling of isolation and deprivation that the speaker's renewed sense of his place in the scheme of things arises, as he finds in "The Bible" the answer to "Dissatisfaction," as he realizes that "Jerusalem / Is *mine*, as 'tis my Maker's, choicest Gem," that he is part of "Christendom." "Churches" and "Bells," which in "Solitude" only accentuate his unhappy state, when rightly understood, become patterns for his thoughts and actions.

As in the Dobell Folio the poet moves from an appreciation of his own body (cf. "The Person" and "The Odour") to an ever-widening sense of his place in the universe ("Admiration" and "The Image"); indeed, he infers the nature of the universe from the nature of man as manifested in himself. The process of discovery begins with the eighteenth poem in the sequence, "The Odour," which tempts comparison with Herbert's poem of the same name. Herbert refers the reader to 2 Corinthians 2:15: "For we are unto God a sweet savour of Christ, in them that are saved, and in them that perish"; and his poem turns on the reflection of sweetness or "savour" from Christ to man.[8] Although both Herbert's poem and the passage from Corinthians may have prompted Traherne's poem, the differences are striking and characteristic of the two poets. Both Traherne and Herbert refer to a spiritual savor, and both use emphatically sensuous images to do so, but whereas Herbert's delight is in the "orientall fragrancie" of his Master's name and the qualities it represents, Traherne's delight is in his own body as a miracle of process. Herbert's poem is directed toward God, Traherne's poem, though full of praise of God's power, is directed toward himself. While drawing on Old Testament images of love and fertility, Traherne dwells on the theory of the body and its relation to the soul rather than on its physical qualities.

These Hands are Jewels to the Ey,
Like Wine, or Oil, or Hony, to the Taste:

These Feet which here I wear beneath the Sky
Are us'd, yet never waste.
My Members all do yield a sweet Perfume;
They minister Delight, yet not consume.

("The Odour," lines 1–6)

The images are sensuous, but the delight is spiritual; what most fascinates Traherne is the body's intermediate position between the transitory and the permanent.

Can melting Sugar sweeten Wine?
Can Light communicated keep its Name?
Can Jewels solid be, tho they do shine?
From Fire rise a flame?
Ye solid are, and yet do Light dispence;
Abide the same, tho yield an Influence.

Your Uses flow while ye abide:
The Services which I from you receiv
Like sweet Infusions throu me daily glide
Ev'n while they Sense deceiv,
B'ing unobserved: for *only Spirits see*
What Treasures Services and Uses be.

(lines 13–24)

The mystery that Traherne ponders, the relation between flow and permanence, process and stability, is akin to the mystery of God as he comes to understand it in "The Anticipation" (Dobell): God is "the Fountain Means and End"; "He is an Act that doth Communicate." In the Burney sequence too Traherne's first questionings and discoveries are the stepping-stones to the next level of understanding because the universe he discovers is a series of repeated patterns. Moreover, as in Dobell, his perception is as vital as the patterns he perceives. The ability to understand and value himself is crucial to the ability to comprehend the rest of God's beneficence. He addresses the "Services and Uses" of his body:

If first I learn not what's *Your* Price
Which are alive, and are to me so near;
How shall I all the Joys of Paradise,
Which are so Great and Dear,
Esteem? Gifts ev'n at distance are our Joys,
But lack of Sense the Benefit destroys.

("The Odour," lines 37–42)

Traherne finds in himself the kind of object lesson that Vaughan and Herbert had found in external nature, but the manner in which he urges study of this emblematic being provides an astonishing reversal of Herbert's image of man as the mirror of God.

> Liv to thy Self; thy Limbs esteem:
> From Hev'n they came; with Mony can't be bought,
> They are such Works as God himself beseem,
>   May *precious* well be thought.
> *Contemplat* then the Valu of this Treasure,
> By *that* alone thou feelest all the Pleasure.
>
> Like Amber fair thy Fingers grow;
> With fragrant Hony-sucks thy Head is crown'd;
> Like Stars, thine Eys; thy Cheeks like Roses shew:
>   All are Delights profound.
> Talk with thy self; thy self enjoy and see:
> At once the Mirror and the Object be.
>
>   (lines 43–54)

For Herbert whatever delight is to be found in man is only a reflection of the supreme sweetness of Christ; for Traherne, man is himself precious and delightful: his limbs are "such Works as God himself beseem." In understanding the glory of man, Traherne comes to understand the goodness of God; the one is an undimmed reflection of the other. Both poets see positive human qualities as divine gifts, but for Traherne man is in fact good; for Herbert he is good only by imputation. Herbert's poem is centered on God and shows sweetness moving from God to man back to God; Traherne's is centered in man and represents the poet's learning to delight in himself, to see the "End" of these "sacred Uses." Furthermore, for Traherne, all is meaningless without man, without his comprehension of the universe; all "is to no End, / If I *the Use* of each don't apprehend" ("The Odour," lines 65–66). Just as Herbert's tightly structured poem reflects the strict economy of his universe, so Traherne's less tidy verses seem to grow directly out of the uneven processes of discovery of the insatiable self and of the endless universe.

Like the Dobell cycle, the Burney poems reflect the poet's ever-increasing comprehension. The sense of man's great value to man developed in "The Odour" is extended in "Admiration" to an awareness of man's value to heavenly creatures: "What is Man that he / Is thus admired like a Deity!" (lines 43–44). The poet's exploration of the universe, physical and moral, continues through his mental processes—first the "sweet Mistakes" of "unexperienc'd Infancy" in "Shadows in the Water" and "On Leaping over the Moon"; later in the adult perceptions of "Walking," "The Dialogue," "Dreams," and "The Inference." These poems move ever further into the abstract, from things to thoughts, and again man is the center that holds the sequence together.

Traherne's ability to make dramatic connections between heaven and earth is sometimes undercut, as we have noticed in *Centuries* and the Dobell poems, by his tendency to see little distinction between them. An example of this lessening of metaphysical tension among the Burney poems is "The Evidence," which, in its use of metaphors of business and contracts, recalls Herbert's sonnet "Redemption." The comparison is perhaps unfair, for "Redemption" is one of Herbert's finest poems, whereas "The Evidence" is not one of Traherne's best; yet the differences between them are characteristic of the two poets. "Redemption" is remarkably tight and economical, even for Herbert; it builds swiftly and inexorably to the finality of the last line. Except for the title and the words "in heaven at his manour" (line 5), Herbert's terminology and expectations are wholly mundane—to "make a suit unto him, to afford / A new small-rented lease, and cancell th' old" (lines 3–4). The phrase "rich Lord" of line 1 is nicely ambiguous, and part of the irony of the poem results from the persona's confusion about the nature of his Lord's wealth and of his own debt: "I . . . knowing his great birth, / Sought him accordingly in great resorts" (lines 9–10). Only with the stunning last line does the universe of the poem come sharply into true perspective:

> At length I heard a ragged noise and mirth
> Of theeves and murderers: there I him espied,
> Who straight, *Your suit is granted*, said, & died.

In "The Evidence," by contrast, doubt about the level of discourse can last at most two lines, for the poet himself elaborates his metaphor for us rather than using it to surprise.

> His *Word* confirms the Sale:
> Those Sheets enfold my Bliss:
> Eternity its self's the Pale
> Wherin my tru Estate enclosed is:
> Each ancient Miracle's a Seal:
> Apostles, Prophets, Martyrs, Patriarchs are

The Witnesses; and what their Words reveal,
Their written Records do declare.
All may well wonder such a 'State to see
In such a solemn sort settled on me.

(lines 1–10)

The first line might allude to a verbal agreement, but we soon recognize the pun on the written word, the Bible. "Bliss" may at first seem to refer to the highest earthly happiness, but by line 3 there can be no doubt of the nature of the poet's inheritance. Yet Herbert's specific, economical, earthly discourse shocks us into seeing the heavenly meaning of his words, while Traherne's continued emphasis on the spiritual leads, oddly enough, to a less transcendent (and less effective) conclusion. There is a kind of ambiguity in Traherne's lines, but one that releases tension rather than builds it, as in the course of the second stanza, God's works, which at first seemed further evidence of a spiritual estate, now become the estate itself:

Did not his *Word* proclaim
My Title to th' Estate,
His *Works* themselvs affirm the same
By what they do; my Wish they antedate.
Before I was conceiv'd, they were
Allotted for my great Inheritance;
As soon as I among them did appear
They did surround me, to advance
My Interest and Lov. Each Creature says,
God made us Thine, that we might shew His Prais.

(lines 11–20)

Herbert, in compelling reader and persona to confront the Incarnation, forcefully represents the link between heaven and earth while Traherne, thinking persistently in abstractions, bypasses this central mystery almost completely. Even when, in the First Century, Traherne fixes his gaze upon the Crucifixion, he dwells not on the sufferings of Christ but on the benefits to man.

There may we see the most Distant Things in Eternity united: all Mysteries at once couched together and Explained. The only reason why this Glorious Object is so Publickly Admired by Churches and Kingdoms, and *so little thought of by Particular men* [emphasis mine], is becaus it is truly the most Glorious. It is the Root of Comforts, and the Fountain of Joys. It is the only Supreme and Sovereign

Spectacle in all Worlds. It is a Well of Life beneath in which we may see the face of Heaven abov: and the only Mirror, wherin all things appear in their Proper Colors. that is sprinkled in the Blood of our Lord and Savior. (C 1.59)

Even this scene, curiously abstract by comparison with the careful cultivation of the senses in so much sixteenth- and seventeenth-century meditation,[9] allows thoughts to prevail over things. It represents Christ, in the midst of his sufferings, more aware through thoughts of the beauty of the world than of his physical pain. "Was He not the Son of GOD and Heir of the Whole World? To this poor Bleeding Naked Man did all the Corn and Wine and Oyl, and Gold and Silver in the World minister in an Invisible Maner, even as he was exposed Lying and Dying upon the Cross" (C 1.60). The key to this strangely unemotional, one is tempted to say, oddly insensitive, view of the Crucifixion, is partly in Traherne's belief that abstraction is a higher level of truth, that perception is more important than physical reality.

Given this belief, it is not surprising that Traherne seems to find his true voice in the concluding poems of the Burney sequence, which celebrate man's limitless mind. This emphasis is also expressed early in the Burney sequence, as in the third poem, "News," and more sharply in the twenty-third and twenty-fourth poems, "Shadows in the Water" and "On Leaping over the Moon," in poems that stress the reality of dreams, illusions, and mistakings.

"News" is remarkable in combining a sense of rare excitement over the heavenly tidings, the "News from a forrein Country," with a firm control of persona and perspective. It portrays the child's eagerness to embrace the truth while it suggests the mystery of that which it embraces. Fine as the "News" of the Burney Manuscript is, we are fortunately able to recapture Thomas's original version, unrevised by Philip, in *Centuries* 3.26. The prose introduction it receives there highlights the poem's use of the foreign country as a metaphor for heaven, though it is a metaphor in which the poet does not distinguish clearly between tenor and vehicle, as indeed he does not seem ultimately to separate heavenly from earthly experience.

When I heard any News I received it with Greediness and Delight, becaus my Expectation was awakend with som Hope that My Happiness and the Thing I wanted was concealed in it. Glad Tidings you know from a far Country brings us our Salvation: And I was not deceived. In Jury was Jesus Killed, and from Jerusalem the Gospel came. Which when I once knew I was very Confident that evry Kingdom contained like Wonders and Causes of Joy, tho that was the fountain of them. As it was the First fruits so was it the Pledg of what I shall receiv in other Countries. (C 3.25)

One would expect of a devout seventeenth-century poet that salvation would be the climax of his hopes and of his prose meditation, but for Traherne the news from "Jury" is only an initial stage, the "Pledg" of "like Wonders and Causes of Joy" elsewhere in the world, as if the sacrifice of Christ might elsewhere be equaled. It is consonant with his view of the innocence of childhood and its receptivity to the heavenly vision that Traherne, as distinguished from many of his contemporaries, does not think of salvation as focused in a single redemptive act, but rather as consisting in the total blessings of life.

"News" itself does not specify the nature of the good tidings (and its prose context in *Centuries* reinforces this ambiguity); it simply indicates the soul's receptivity to them: the unknown good is not only as yet unknown but also to some extent unknowable. But in the Burney Manuscript, where "News" is set between "The Return" and "Felicity," in which the poet is "Prompted to seek my Bliss abov the Skies," the balance is tipped in favor of an explicitly spiritual meaning.

> News from a forrein Country came,
> As if my Treasure and my Wealth lay there:
> So much it did my Heart Enflame!
> Twas wont to call my Soul into mine Ear.
>   Which thither went to Meet
>   The Approaching Sweet:
>   And on the Threshhold stood,
> To entertain the Unknown Good.
>   It Hoverd there,
>   As if twould leav mine Ear.
> And was so Eager to Embrace
> The Joyfull Tidings as they came,
> Twould almost leav its Dwelling Place,
>   To Entertain the Same.
>
> As if the Tidings were the Things,
> My very Joys themselvs, my forrein Treasure,
>   Or els did bear them on their Wings;
> With so much Joy they came, with so much Pleasure.

My Soul stood at the Gate
To recreat
It self with Bliss: And to
Be pleasd with Speed. A fuller View
It fain would take
Yet Journeys back would make
Unto my Heart: as if twould fain
Go out to meet, yet stay within
To fit a place, to Entertain,
And bring the Tidings in.

(C 3.26, lines 1–28)

Traherne skillfully conveys energy and eagerness, bewilderment and hesitation; he uses parallel phrasing and anaphora to create balanced syntactical and metrical units, while dividing the lines by caesuras or interrupting the sense with the line ending. These devices reinforce Traherne's image of the soul torn between introverted and extroverted pleasure, between a desire to go out of itself to meet the unknown joy and to wait passively within.

The first two stanzas of the poem record the child's experience, without qualification or comment; only the past tense and the "as if" construction (lines 2 and 15) allow the possibility of another interpretation; but in stanzas 3 and 4 Traherne draws back from the child's involvement in his experience to wonder at and pronounce upon it, to point up its limitations, but also its remarkable completeness. The balance and energy that characterize the first two stanzas dominate also the third and fourth, which are less animated but no less forceful. Stanza 3 embodies two paradoxical emphases—the child's "Sacred Instinct" and his ignorance; stanza 4 represents the limitation of the child's vision and its final fulfillment. Stanza 3 is marked by questioning and longing, stanza 4, by statement and consummation. Both balance a preliminary statement or question against the forward thrust of a long sentence, which stretches over ten short lines, expressing in stanza 3 yearning, in stanza 4, the progressive fulfillment of desire.

What Sacred Instinct did inspire
My Soul in Childhood with a Hope so Strong?
What Secret Force movd my Desire,
To Expect my Joys beyond the Seas, so Yong?

Felicity I knew
Was out of View:
And being here alone,
I saw that Happiness was gone,
From Me! for this,
I Thirsted Absent Bliss,
And thought that sure beyond the Seas,
Or els in som thing near at hand
I knew not yet, (since nought did pleas
I knew.) my Bliss did stand.

(stanza 3, lines 29–42)

Traherne seems to distinguish in stanza 3 between felicity and happiness—felicity being the heavenly goal of which Augustine speaks—"Thou hast made us for thyself and we are restless until we find rest in Thee"[10]—and happiness being whatever joy may be found on earth. But for the child of "News" the two are also inextricably linked, for he finds no earthly happiness possible without true felicity (lines 33–37). Thus the child's hopes and frustrations confirm the connection of *Centuries* 3.25: "I was very Confident that evry Kingdom contained like Wonders and Causes of Joy, tho that was the fountain of them."

This link between happiness and felicity, between dream and truth, between tidings of heaven and tidings of earth, becomes the central point around which the poem turns as it reverses direction in the final stanza, as it triumphantly finds glory in an acorn and splendor in a grain of sand. One can now see the "as if" constructions in a new light: what at first seemed a form of prosaic understatement ("As if my Treasure and my Wealth lay there") now accommodates the greater truth that the persona is already in the midst of these gifts.

But little did the Infant Dream
That all the Treasures of the World were by:
And that Himself was so the Cream
And Crown of all, which round about did lie.
Yet thus it was. The Gem,
The Diadem,
The Ring Enclosing all
That Stood upon this Earthy Ball;
The Heavenly Ey,
Much Wider then the Skie,
Wher in they all included were

The Glorious Soul that was the King
Made to possess them, did appear
A Small and little thing!

(stanza 4, lines 43–56)

In this tightly constructed poem Traherne both recreates the child's ex-
perience and sets it in mature perspective; he allows us to participate
rhythmically and kinetically in the sense of division between two worlds
and the resolution of that conflict in the microcosmic condensation of the
last line. In subsequent poems he explores more fully the nature of the
"Small and little thing," the child's mind and his perceptions, with which
"News" concludes.

The relation between illusion and reality and the communication of
spiritual meaning through natural means first treated in "News" is more
sharply focused in "Shadows in the Water." Coming to "Shadows in the
Water" from Donne's "A Lecture upon the Shadow" or Milton's image of
Eve as Narcissus in *Paradise Lost* (4.449–76) or even Vaughan's "Regen-
eration," one will be struck by the unusual way Traherne understands
and employs his image. He neither audaciously forces his own meanings
on it like Donne, nor reinterprets classical myth to find a greater truth like
Milton, nor commonsensically rejects the reflected image as illusory;
instead he probes it for its hidden meaning, not just rhetorically, but
actually. Traherne's method of finding meaning, unexpectedly, within
the image itself—rather than reading meaning into it—is closer to
Vaughan than to his other predecessors; yet even in "Regeneration" and "I
walkt the other day" what the poet rediscovers are traditional biblical and
natural emblems, albeit mysterious ones, whereas "Shadows in the
Water" appears to derive its somewhat surprising meaning from a particu-
lar experience. To be sure, Traherne's poem has its roots in another
tradition, in the Platonic notion that the child's perception, though in
earthly terms mistaken, is nevertheless an image of a higher truth avail-
able to the mature and philosophic mind; yet Traherne's extended, sym-
pathetic, and quite moving representation of the child's perception sets
him apart from his predecessors. Traherne's sense of the numinous,
though vaguer and less specifically doctrinal than that of Donne or Her-
bert, is no less convincing. He does not, like them, play with uncertain-
ties and long for certainties; he claims, with Vaughan, to see not the truth
but only something that leads toward it; and yet he wins the reader's assent
by a persuasive presentation of partial knowledge.

> Of all the Play-mates which I knew
> That here I do the Image view
> In other Selvs; what can it mean?
> But that below the purling Stream
>   Som unknown Joys there be
>   Laid up in Store for me;
> To which I shall, when that thin Skin
> Is broken, be admitted in.

(lines 73–80)

Traherne, who sometimes creates distance between himself and his readers by failing to maintain any distance between himself and his speaker, appears in this poem both as a child and as an adult; he is thus able to stand back from or enter into the experience he describes in a way that gives the poem a peculiar force. In this case, he invites our confidence in his judgment by opening with the adult's perspective, which then yields gradually to the child's true understanding. "Shadows in the Water" begins with a general statement of its basically Platonic notion but quickly particularizes this notion as Traherne moves to his own experience.

> In unexperienc'd Infancy
> Many a sweet Mistake doth ly:
> Mistake tho false, intending tru;
> A *Seeming* somwhat more than V*iew*;
>   That doth instruct the Mind
>   In Things that ly behind,
> And many Secrets to us show
> Which afterwards we com to know.

(lines 1–8)

The distinction between "*Seeming*" and "*View*" (line 4) distinguishes the child who pursues a "sweet Mistake" from the adult who discerns the truth; the distinction between "show" and "know" (lines 7–8) separates the child's intuitive vision from the adult's comprehension. Yet it is the early seeming, the "sweet Mistake," that points to the final truth.

The poet's first description of his experience clearly marks it as fancy and illusion. His account of the child's perception is carefully qualified by such verbs as "think" (line 10), "abus'd" (line 12), and "fancy'd" (line 13).

> Thus did I by the Water's brink
> Another World beneath me think;
> And while the lofty spacious Skies
> Reversed there abus'd mine Eys,
>   I fancy'd other Feet
>   Came mine to touch and meet;
> As by som Puddle I did play
> Another World within it lay.

(lines 9–16)

But by the third stanza we have been drawn into an assertion of the world in the water as reality—though a reality governed by other physical laws than the ones we know.

> Beneath the Water Peeple drown'd.
> Yet with another Hev'n crown'd,
> In spacious Regions seem'd to go
> Freely moving to and fro:
>   In bright and open Space
>   I saw their very face;
> Eys, Hands, and Feet they had like mine;
> Another Sun did with them shine.

(lines 17–24)

Not by indulging in metaphysical assertions but simply by reproducing in detail the child's wondering observations Traherne comes far closer to recreating his experience for the reader than he does in many of the Dobell poems. Each individual stanza focuses on a single physical fact which, given our knowledge of the laws of optics, points of itself to something beyond. We as adults are once again drawn back into the childhood fantasy of being able to walk through a mirror into the world on the other side, "Where Peeple's feet against Ours go" (line 48).

> 'Twas strange that Peeple there should walk,
> And yet I could not hear them talk:
> That throu a little watry Chink,
> Which one dry Ox or Horse might drink,
>   We other Worlds should see,
>   Yet not admitted be;
> And other Confines there behold
> Of Light and Darkness, Heat and Cold.

(lines 25–32)

The child's notion of the tiny chink, through which one can see the vastness of other worlds, is vivid, concrete, even electrifying, in its precise linking of great and small, petty and significant. Traherne here finds an image of infinity more teasingly effective than the endless rooms (rather like a grand hotel) of "Nature," as he imagines that in the reflections he sees there are reflections of yet other worlds beyond. His questions tempt us to imagine an endless succession of such reflections.

> Look how far off those lower Skies
> Extend themselvs! scarce with mine Eys
> I can them reach. O ye my Friends,
> What *Secret* borders on those Ends?
> Are lofty Hevens hurl'd
> 'Bout your inferior World?
> Are ye the Representatives
> Of other Peopl's distant Lives?
>
> (lines 65–72)

The vision the poet makes us share imposes two further shifts of belief or judgment. First, we must accept that the reflected world, "Tho it did not to View exceed / A Phantasm, 'tis a World indeed" (lines 43–44), an actual place where "Earth by Art divine" (line 46)—no paradox in Traherne's terms—allows us to see wonders. Second, we must bypass what every adult knows—that the reflection is only a shadow of ourselves—to discover the truth of our link with all mankind, even with "yet unknown Friends" in worlds still undiscovered.

> O ye that stand upon the Brink,
> Whom I so near me, throu the Chink,
> With Wonder see: What Faces there,
> Whose Feet, whose Bodies, do ye wear?
> I my Companions see
> In You, another Me.
> They seemed Others, but are We;
> Our second Selvs those Shadows be.
>
> (lines 57–64)

The old truth is rediscovered by the child with a new wealth of meaning, a meaning that is not a commonplace of physics, as it was for the adult, but one that points to the spiritual communion of saints. In learning to "understand" earthly phenomena, the adult has overlooked the divine significance recovered by the child, upon the rightness of whose perspective Traherne here insists. He does not tempt us with a mistake like Herbert, or show a struggle between two views; but while firmly controlling his persona from without, he introduces the reader to that persona's experience.

Traherne similarly cultivates the child's perspective, vividly, yet with fine control in "To the same purpos" and "On Leaping over the Moon," insisting that the apparent illusions of these experiences in fact reveal the truth; they are mistakes "tho false, intending tru." He plays with spatial perspectives as delightedly as Donne with points of theology or chemistry, as he tells how his brother in jumping a stream "dar'd to swim . . . throu the Air" over "A little pearly River":

> He would not use nor trust *Icarian* Wings
> Lest they should prov deceitful things;
> For had he faln, it had been wondrous high,
> Not from, but from abov, the Sky:
>
> He might hav dropt throu that thin Element
> Into a fathomless Descent;
> Unto the nether Sky
> That did beneath him ly,
> And there might tell
> What Wonders dwell
> On Earth abov. Yet bold he briskly runs
> And soon the Danger overcoms;
> Who, as he leapt, with Joy related soon
> How *happy he* o'r-leapt the Moon.
>
> ("On Leaping over the Moon," lines 27–40)

As in "Shadows in the Water" our altered perceptions of the physical lead to altered metaphysical conceptions: innocence, because it is for Traherne a psychological rather than a theological state, can be recaptured in adulthood as we begin to see in a new light. Yet in contrast to other metaphysical poets, Traherne's new vision is not emblematic, distinct from physical sight, but rather almost inseparable from it.

The Burney poems, with their emphasis on illusions, dreams, and mistakings, come closer than much in Traherne to the sort of specific detail we might expect of autobiography; yet insofar as these illusions turn out to be glimpses of the truth, they give vigor to another emphasis of the Burney Manuscript—the institutions of Christianity. The child's true instincts, those by which he rejects the false distinctions between the divine and human spheres, lead him in "Christendom," not to the mundane abstraction by which an adult understands that word, but to a vision of the heavenly city, the New Jerusalem, toward which the earthly reality tends. The child's imagination is based on what he knows on earth—in this poem he comes trailing no clouds of glory—yet the language in which he describes his fantasy points beyond earthbound experience, even as "Glorious" and "Souls" are capable of both celestial and mundane interpretations.

> I thought it was
> A Glorious Place,
> Where Souls might dwell in all Delight and Bliss;
> So thought, yet fear'd lest I the Truth might miss.
>
> ("Christendom," lines 17–20)

The very understatedness of Traherne's lines makes the reader look beyond them as he imagines

> A Town beyond the Seas,
> Whose Prospect much did pleas,
> And to my Soul so sweetly raise Delight
> As if a long expected Joy,
> Shut up in that transforming Sight,
> Would into me its Self convey;
> And Blessedness
> I there possess,
> As if that City stood on reall Ground,
> And all the Profit mine which there was found.
>
> (lines 31–40)

Traherne's penultimate line—"As if that City stood on reall Ground"—is in the subjunctive, implying to our conventionally oriented minds that the city he sees is merely an illusion. But this vision, in contrast to the dream of sin of "Eden," is true as well as prophetic. Here the word "reall" functions as a kind of pun, pointing up the difference between two levels of truth and reality, forcing us to the idea that the heavenly city does stand on ground more real than the material substance to which we normally apply the phrase.

As this example suggests, the precise level of reference in "Christendom" is often confusing, for although Traherne offers nothing so simple

as an image of the heavenly city, he cannot resist suggesting that that is
what we are seeing:

> A sprightly pleasant Time,
> (E'vn Summer in its prime),
> Did gild the Trees, the Houses, Children, Skies,
> And made the City all divine;
> It ravished my wondring Eys
> To see the Sun so brightly shine:
> The Heat and Light
> Seem'd in my sight
> With such a dazling Lustre shed on them,
> As made me think 'twas th' New Jerusalem.
>
> (lines 61–70)

On the other hand, the vision is distinctly natural, much more so than
the city of golden streets and precious stones described in Revelation
21.[11] The whole of Traherne's vision seems infused with the living force
of divinity, represented by the vital forces of this world, and reminiscent
of the beauties of Hereford. Indeed it might well be Hereford, its red clay
and winding streets transformed by the force of divinity. The point is
precisely that "Christendom" is neither a heavenly nor an earthly city,
but heaven among us, the communion of saints in this world and the
next. As Traherne's mingling of the mundane and the celestial em-
phasizes, the world in which we live, when truly seen, is "Holy Ground
of great Esteem":

> Before I was aware
> Truth did to me appear,
> And represented to my Virgin-Eys
> Th' unthought of Joys and Treasures
> Wherin my Bliss and Glory lies;
> My God's Delight, (which givs me Measure)
> His Turtle Dov,
> Is Peace and Lov
> In Towns: for holy Children, Maids, and Men
> Make up the King of Glory's Diadem.
>
> (lines 111–20)

The close relationship between the divine and the natural that arises in
"Christendom" is developed even more fully in "On Christmas-Day," an
exuberant festival poem whose opening stanzas bear a surprising resem-

blance to Herrick's "Corinna's Going a Maying." The holiday festivities, joined by all levels of society, from the plowman, with his "gayer Weeds" and "neatest Shoos," to the magistrate, also recall Herrick's "The Hock-Cart." The two poets may simply, as country parsons, share the background of festival, though "On Christmas-Day" seems too much like the answer of true religion and festival to sham piety to be merely coincidental. Whereas Herrick's lover makes a religion of the thoroughly secular celebration of May in order to entice his mistress, Traherne, with equal fervor, addresses his own soul, urging it to join, not in mock but in true religion. Both Traherne's soul and Herrick's lady are out of touch with the spirit of holiday, a fact the more curious in the case of the ecstatic Traherne; yet both poems convey the energy and delight of the occasion through the persona's exhortations.

> Shall Houses clad in Summer-Liveries
> His Praises sing;
> And laud thy king,
> And wilt not thou arise?
> Forsake thy Bed, and grow (my Soul) more wise,
> Attire thy self in cheerful Liveries.
>
> ("On Christmas-Day," lines 25–30)

In Herrick

> each field turns a street; each street a Parke
> Made green, and trimm'd with trees: see how
> Devotion gives each House a Bough,
> Or Branch: Each Porch, each doore, ere this,
> An Arke a Tabernacle is
> Made up of white-thorn neatly enterwove. [12]

Traherne's spring, no less in evidence, is an image in the world of nature of the fields of grace.

> See how they run from place to place,
> And seek for Ornaments of Grace;
> Their Houses deckt with sprightly Green,
> In Winter makes a Summer seen;
> They Bays and Holly bring
> As if 'twere Spring!
>
> (lines 7–12)

Although Traherne, here matched against one of the masters of zestful, evocative detail, sometimes settles for too bland a word—for example the "pleasant Branches" and "cheerful Liveries" of lines 30–31—he conveys the festival air with almost Elizabethan vividness, especially in his description "Old Winter's Frost and hoary hair, / With Garland's crowned, Bays doth wear" (lines 43–44). [13] Traherne stresses the power of the green boughs of Christmas to make the town look as if it were spring, using pastoral language that, while recalling Herrick's, points to a deeper meaning—the power of divine grace to infuse life into man:

> Let pleasant Branches still be seen
> Adorning thee, both quick and green;
> And, which with Glory better suits,
> Be laden all the Year with Fruits;
> Inserted into Him,
> For ever spring.
>
> (lines 31–36)

The adornments sought (line 8) are not merely beautiful; they are the tokens of redemption, the "Ornaments of Grace." The "sprightly Green" of line 9 betokens life and spirit, as does the "quick" of line 32. The language of the vineyard, lines 31–36, recalls Christ's words: "I am the vine, ye are the branches: He that abideth in me, and I in him, the same bringeth forth much fruit: for without me ye can do nothing" (John 15:5). The entire poem is orchestrated around the central idea of divine vitality articulated by the key rhymes: "Thus He, who is thy King, / Makes Winter, Spring" (lines 23–24). Their repetition sets the whole poem and the whole countryside chiming, until in the final stanza "The whole Assembly sings; / The Minster rings" (lines 119–20).

As in Herbert's "Prayer" and Vaughan's "The Night," heaven and earth are here chiming in harmony. "On Christmas-Day" is a far looser, more exploratory, yet less daring poem than Herbert's; it is more social in subject than Vaughan's, yet more solitary in its effect, for the speaker seems the one outsider in this scene of festivity. Nevertheless Traherne's poem, though it lacks the inner tension of Herbert and the dazzling language of Vaughan, has a peculiar vitality, a vision of reality in which inanimate objects spring into being, in which ordinary reality is filled with new life. Winter does not simply become spring, in the usual fashion of the seasons, but winter *springs* (or so line 24 strongly suggests); life comes out of death through the power of him "who is thy King." Particular expressions of this attitude, for example, "The Minster rings," may be explained as simple synecdoche, a conventional rhetorical device, but the effects are too persistent to ignore. Even dead metaphors seem to spring into life, perhaps not even wholly under the poet's control, but certainly in harmony with his understanding of the universe, until, as Traherne insists, not only the bells, but the minster itself rings.

At the same time that they show the poet concerned with the earthly celebration of heavenly rites and with the institutions of the church, the Burney poems, like the poems of the Dobell Folio, show him moving to ever higher levels of abstraction and ecstasy. Even though they do not provide the kind of remarkably integrated vision that concludes the Dobell sequence, these last poems, characterized by a celebration of man's limitless mind and of the integration of heaven and earth, are among the best and most vigorous of the Burney sequence.

At first glance, there seems a peculiar discordance between the theme of "Insatiableness" and its tight rhyme and stanza structure. While the poet speaks of his endless desires, he does so through a series of rhetorical questions, caught within short lines and close rhymes, that seems instead to proclaim his limitations:

> No Walls confine! Can nothing hold my Mind?
> Can I no Rest nor Satisfaction find?
>   Must I behold Eternity
>   And see
>   What Things abov the Hev'ns be?
>   Will nothing serv the Turn?
>   Nor Earth, nor Seas, nor Skies?
>   Till I what lies
>   In Time's beginning find;
>   Must I till then for ever burn?

(lines 1–10)

But in fact the subject is not infinity but insatiableness, and the experience of confinement that the poem provides reveals the limitations of lesser satisfactions, of the things that surround man and would restrict him.

> Not all the Crowns; not all the heaps of Gold
> On Earth; not all the Tales that can be told,
>   Will Satisfaction yield to me.

(lines 11–13)

Only in the uttermost expanse of time and space does Traherne at last break free from this world and find the mystery he seeks. Yet even there a strangely confident expectation persists, for though the speaker seems to demand something ultimate beyond himself, he anticipates no difficulty in coping with it.

> Till I what was before all Time descry,
> The World's Beginning seems but Vanity.
> My Soul doth there long Thoughts extend
>   No End
> Doth find, or Being comprehend:
>   Yet somwhat sees that is
>   The obscure shady face
>   Of endless Space,
>   All Room within; where I
> Expect to meet Eternal Bliss.
>
> (lines 21–30)

I have noted the ease (coupled with amazement) with which Traherne feels ready to encounter God and the infinity of space: "Ease" is both the title of one of his poems and one of his recurrent themes. But his notion of infinity is also peculiarly conditioned by his seventeenth-century scientific and cultural context. His poems do not celebrate one great limitless vastness that is beyond human conception, but a kind of conditional infinity, an endless succession of steps.[14] The ability to conceive the individual steps, if not the whole, makes "infinity" accessible and less frightening. One may watch the process by which Traherne arrives at this concept of infinity in "Nature," a poem from the Dobell sequence. He begins his argument, not with his usual sublime assurance, but with a troublesome question about the universe:

> For all I saw beyond the Azure Round,
> Was Endless Darkness with no Beauty crownd.
> Why Beauty should not there, as well as here,
> Why Goodness should not likewise there appear,
> Why Treasures and Delights should bounded be,
> Since there is such a Wide Infinitie;
> Were the sad Doubts and Troubles of my Soul.
>
> (lines 43–49)

Traherne's questioning is prompted by his personal dissatisfaction with what he finds in creation—for his is the standard that must be met—and by his notion that infinity in itself is not worthy of God: beauty and goodness are also necessary. As Traherne wrote in *Centuries:* "An infinit Wall is a poor thing to Expresse his Infinity. a Narrow Endless Length is nothing: might be, and if it were, were unprofitable" (*C* 2.21). His doubts are resolved when he comes to understand infinity as something like Herbert's "box where sweets compacted lie," much extended; it is a "Cabinet / Of Joys," a realm for the fancy, not vast emptiness but a wealth of images.

> But yet there were new Rooms, and Spaces more,
> Beyond all these, Wide Regions ore and ore,
> And into them my pent-up-Soul like fire
> Did break, Surmounting all I here admire.
> The Spaces fild were like a Cabinet
> Of Joys before most Distinctly set:
> The Empty, like to large and Vacant Room
> For Fancy to enlarge in, and presume
> A Space for more, removd, but yet adorning
> These neer at hand, that pleasd me evry Morning.
>
> (lines 71–80)

Thus despite Traherne's assertions of delight in eternity, the obscure blank has been tamed and humanized, transformed into something matching the poet's own capacity and its empty spaces filled with creatures of his own imagination.

"Insatiableness II" does not so much portray the outer limits of the soul's explorations as its restless, incessant motion. Logically, the structure of this poem should be open-ended, like Herbert's "The Collar" without its repentant, yielding conclusion, but paradoxically, the ending of "Insatiableness II" is just as definite as that of "Insatiableness I" and its stanza structure equally confining. Yet this form may be appropriate, for the poem's point of reference is not "The obscure shady face / Of endless Space" (I, lines 27–28) but "This busy, vast, enquiring soul": Traherne's confidence about the universe proceeds from his confidence about himself. Nevertheless, the opening lines of "Insatiableness II" more successfully convey busyness than vastness, and the reader may be a little irritated by what seems the poet's pompous self-satisfaction. If so, he will be electrified by the poem's striking conclusion, in which Traherne dares not merely to postulate but to affirm a universe designed to please man, and to confine the infinite deity within four brisk syllables.

'Tis mean Ambition to desire
     A single World:
   To many I aspire,
 Tho one upon another hurl'd:
Nor will they all, if they be all confin'd,
     Delight my Mind.

This busy, vast, enquiring Soul
     Brooks no Controul:
   'Tis hugely curious too.
 Each one of all those Worlds must be
Enricht with infinit Variety
     And Worth; or 'twill not do.

'Tis nor Delight nor perfect Pleasure
     To have a Purse
   That hath a Bottom of its Treasure,
Since I must thence endless Expense disburse.
Sure there's a GOD (for els there's no Delight)
     One Infinit.

(lines 7–24)

One may well grumble that if the universe should fail to meet Traherne's specifications he will not be the first to be disappointed. But disappointment does not come, for as the alternating currents of this poetic cycle make clear, no matter how insatiable the desires of the soul, they are matched by the infinity and grandeur of God's universe: accordingly "Insatiableness" leads to "Consummation."

"Consummation" is of itself a more interesting poem than "Insatiableness." Traherne seems more aware of the problems of his subject and conveys its paradoxes in carefully balanced phrases:

   The Thoughts of Men appear
 Freely to mov within a Sphere
   Of endless Reach; and run,
 Tho in the Soul, beyond the Sun.
The Ground on which they acted be
Is unobserv'd Infinity.

("Consummation," lines 1–6)

Traherne's lines move between the opposing poles of freedom and limitation, expanse and restriction, in the sequences "Freely" / "Sphere" / "endless Reach" and "Ground" / "Infinity." He develops the paradox that infinity can be accommodated by man: "Tho in the Soul, beyond the Sun"; infinity is so natural to man as to be "unobserv'd," existing not only in time and space but in the secret recesses of man's mind.

Traherne shifts easily from infinity of space to infinity of time, not because he sees an inherent connection between them but because he focuses on the thoughts that so easily embrace them both:

> They, in their native Sphere,
> At boundless Distances appear:
> Eternity can measure;
> Its no Beginning see with Pleasure.
> Thus in the Mind an endless Space
> Doth nat'rally display its face.
>
> (lines 13–18)

The inconceivable, it seems, is easily conceived: man can "Its no Beginning see with Pleasure." The universe holds no terrors for Traherne, though reading this poem one can hardly believe he has fully grasped its grandeur. But as in "Nature" man comes to terms with the frightening emptiness by filling it with his thoughts, so in this case Traherne populates it with the fantasy of the constellations:

> Wherin becaus we no
> Object distinctly find or know;
> We sundry Things invent,
> That may our Fancy giv content;
> See Points of Space beyond the Sky,
> And in those Points see Creatures ly.
>
> (lines 18–24)

Not only is man godlike in his power to conceive infinity; his creation through thought strongly resembles God's own creative activity. The consummation that Traherne envisions at the end of time is in a sense modeled on Paul's words: "For now we see through a glass, darkly; but then face to face" (1 Cor. 13:12). Yet Traherne's lines do not convey the image of a dazzling revelation to those hitherto in darkness, but rather a confirmation of what was already known, an actual seeing of what has already been vividly imagined:

> At last shall in a glorious Day
> Be made its Objects to display

And then shall Ages be
Within its wide Eternity;
All Kingdoms stand,
Howe'r remote, yet nigh at hand;
The Skies, and what beyond them ly,
Exposed unto evry Ey.

Nor shall we then invent
Nor alter Things; but with content
All in their Places see,
As doth the Glorious Deity;
Within the Scope of whose Great Mind,
We all in their tru Nature find.

(lines 41–54)

Appropriately, Traherne's "Hosanna," which follows, gives thanks for a consummation that has already been achieved, long before the apocalypse and without exceptional divine intervention.

No more shall Walls, no more shall Walls confine
That glorious Soul which in my Flesh doth shine:
No more shall Walls of Clay or Mud
Nor Ceilings made of Wood,
Nor Crystal Windows, bound my Sight,
But rather shall admit Delight.
The Skies that seem to bound
My Joys and Treasures,
Or more endearing Pleasures
Themselvs becom a Ground:
While from the Center to the utmost Sphere
My Goods are multiplied evry where.

(lines 1–12)

Traherne's exuberant lines with their eager rhythms and repeated phrases do not, like the shorter lines of "Insatiableness," make us feel the soul chafing at limits but rather bursting beyond them—even as line 1 moves beyond the phrase "No more shall Walls," even as it does not end with "confine" but, lacking an end stop, moves on to "That glorious Soul which in my Flesh doth shine" in line 2. The same principle obtains in the nonlimiting "bound" of line 7, which only seems to enclose but leads instead to "Joys and Treasures." The lines of stanza 1 move easily from the earthy opacity of clay or mud, to the greater dignity of wood, to the transparent beauty of glass; from walls to ceilings to windows, raising our thoughts from images of restraint to those of freedom, until what might have been a barrier becomes a means to "admit Delight."

The ability to experience delight is the focus and the fulcrum of "Hosanna," the first three stanzas of which alternate between a desire to burst all bonds and a desire to take all things unto oneself. The first stanza is expansive, the second, receptive; such alternating movement recalls that of the last Dobell poems between declarations of joy and meditation. By stanza 3 the apparent bounds to the poet's felicity are seen to be mere illusions—"Cloud," "Shades," and "Husks"; thus to escape from limitations is not to move physically but to elude the false creations of the mind. The poem no longer expresses vigorous outward and inward motions: the opposition between them is reconciled in a single movement of the understanding. It is now a matter of indifference whether one is "*Within* the Skies, or els *abov*" because "Both Worlds [are] one Heven made by Lov" (lines 29–30).

Having ascended to a heavenly realm in stanza 3, Traherne proceeds in stanza 4 to discover heaven within earthly experience. His method, as in "The Person," is to "Glorify by taking all away," for the adornments he rejects are seen to be a form of bondage.

> No more shall Trunks & Dishes be my Store,
> Nor Ropes of Pearl, nor Chains of Golden Ore;
>   As if such Beings yet were not,
>   They all shall be forgot.
>   No such in Eden did appear,
>   No such in Heven: Heven here
>   Would be, were those remov'd.
>
> ("Hosanna," lines 37–43)

The theme of this stanza—the loss of innocence through the acquisition of false values—recalls "The Apostacy." By a mingling of tenses Traherne eradicates the present state of evil by bringing together past innocence and future cleansing (lines 39–40; 41–42); and even more curiously, in lines 44–45, he suggests for a moment, by using the present tense ("The Sons of Men / Liv in Jerusalem") rather than the more usual subjunctive, the persistence of that innocence. Our fallen state is brought back to us in line 46—"Had they not Baubles lov'd"—but we have had a vision of Eden that the poem as a whole reaffirms.

Traherne's conception of the universe is of a dynamic whole existing for man, in an order designed for his delight, and fulfilling its purpose ultimately only in man's enjoyment of it. Man exercises a creative faculty in his appreciation of his central position: in saying "While I, that I the Center am, admire" (line 24), he performs an act of communion, an act of giving life:

> Like sprightly Streams
> My Thoughts on Things remain;
> Or els like vital Beams
> They reach to, shine on, quicken Things, and make
> Them truly Usefull; while I *All* partake.

(lines 56–60)

In both the Burney and the Dobell poems Traherne's vision centers on the individual's self-discovery, expressed in the first person, in a way that appears almost narcissistic and solipsistic, but in *Centuries* Traherne explores more fully and at far greater length how all men exist for the glory and enjoyment of each man and how the multiplication of souls leads to the multiplication of love. In "Hosanna" Traherne, though he does not fully articulate this principle of the increase of love, glances at it and emphasizes the joy it brings:[15]

> For Me the World created was by Lov;
> For Me the Skies, the Seas, the Sun, do mov;
> The Earth for Me doth stable stand;
> For Me each fruitful Land
> For Me the very Angels God made *His*
> And *my* Companions in Bliss.

(lines 61–66)

The final poem of the Burney sequence, "The Review," closes the cycle on a meditative note. Though at first glance this alternation of mood from the expansive temper of "Hosanna" suggests the analogous movement of the Dobell Folio, "The Review" is in a minor key, far removed from the joyful integrated harmonies of the final Dobell poem, "Goodnesse." Traherne opens with a familiar question:

> Did I grow, or did I stay?
> Did I prosper or decay?
> When I so
> From *Things* to *Thoughts* did go?

("The Review," lines 1–4)

From all that has gone before, one would expect the answer to be resoundingly positive, but Traherne so qualifies his thought throughout the poem that he succeeds only in blurring the point:

> Wise ones are a sacred Treasure;
> Tru ones yield Substantial Pleasure:
>   Compar'd to them,
>   I *Things* as *Shades* esteem.
> False ones are a foolish Flourish,
> (Such as Mortals chiefly nourish)
> When I them to *Things* compare,
> Compar'd to *Things*, they Trifles are.

(lines 16–23)

The distinction between thoughts and things, complicated by a subdivision into true and false, wise and foolish, leads to the conclusion that foolish thoughts are inferior to true things. Though commonsensical, this notion is uncharacteristic of Traherne, who elsewhere affirms the supremacy of thoughts over things. While it is perhaps too much to blame these clumsy and repetitive lines wholly on Philip Traherne, we may guess that their jingling meter and prosaic sentiments would have pleased him.

The second part of "The Review," a return to childhood, is much more positive, but it still lacks altogether the complexity of the Dobell Folio. The poet simply reverts to a former state; he has not learned to view life in a way that synthesizes the adult's and the child's experience. The contrast may be seen in several lines that flatly echo "The Approach," a poem found early in the Dobell sequence. There the persona finds himself ". . . enveloped in more then Gold; / In deep Abysses of Delights, / In present Hidden Precious Benefits" ("The Approach," lines 34–36). By contrast, in "The Review" his imagination ". . . makes my Life a Circle of Delights; / A hidden Sphere of obvious Benefits" (lines 9–10). The benefits made obvious, the subtlety has vanished from the lines; the paradox becomes crude and unpersuasive, lacking altogether the sense of time and illumination that gave the other lines their force. Traherne goes on to find in these "obvious Benefits" a rough source of satisfaction; they are "An Earnest that the Actions of the Just / Shall still revive, and flourish in the Dust" (lines 11–12). Such lines draw a moral from the situation in the manner of many a meditative poem; they do not, like the best of Traherne, find meaning luminescent within it.

The Burney sequence, somewhat more personal as well as somewhat more conventional than the Dobell cycle, nevertheless parallels it in many respects—in its reflection of the religious development of the poet from childhood to adulthood, in its alternation of moods, in its rising to higher levels of consciousness and abstraction. Philip Traherne's selection and ordering of poems as well as his revision of his brother's text may in some measure account for the differences between the two sequences, and for the flatness of the conclusion of the Burney sequence; yet enough of the original remains to testify to the cyclic, dialectic character of Traherne's vision and to contribute to our understanding of him as a metaphysical poet, one who even more clearly than his predecessors saw the light of eternity before it faded into the light of common day.

The striking contrasts in form and technique between Traherne and earlier metaphysical poets derive not only from his theological views but also from his religious experience; the differences may consist not so much in his ultimate position as in the way he achieves it. In some sense for Herbert and Vaughan as well as for Traherne, "Eternity was Manifest in the Light of the Day, and som thing infinit Behind evry thing appeared" (C 3.3); but in Herbert, despite a strong sense of the universe as emblematic, this vision is fully achieved only in the last poems, after arduous struggle. Vaughan's belief in (and longing for) the light of eternity and his experience of it are, to his sorrow, often quite distinct; the consequences of this fact are a complexity and to some extent an uncertainty in poetic structure and handling of images. Traherne's poetry is shaped not by the tension of a dialogue or an external difficulty, but by the discovery of a truth within him that corresponds to the truth without; hence his is the verse of harmony and delight rather than of longing and submission. Yet different as Traherne is from Donne, Herbert, and Vaughan, he is intimately related to them, for although he begins by denying the distinctions that his predecessors struggled to overcome, and although he seems to have little sense of the extravagance of his own claims, his poetry in fact benefits from its metaphysical contexts, because he makes easy what earlier poets found difficult, and thus their sense of tension and of relationships gives force to Traherne's own unusual ease of perception.

In the closing years of the seventeenth century ease of perception came not, as for Traherne, in a sense of the eternal now, or in doubts about whether "The Citie seemed to stand in Eden, or to be Built in Heaven" (C 3.3), but in a loss of the dual vision of metaphysical poetry, in a resolution of paradox, in a strong preference for earthly reality. Dryden's religious poems are public declarations, not private meditations; Cowley's lyrics retain the surface of metaphysical poetry without the substance; Pope articulates truth to which all men of sense can assent. But Traherne, like his great predecessors, offers us a fleeting glimpse of a vision now altogether lost:

> The Sons of Men
> Liv in Jerusalem,
> Had they not Baubles lov'd.

Abbreviations

C	Traherne, *Centuries*
CE	Traherne, *Christian Ethicks*
ELR	*English Literary Renaissance*
HLQ	*Huntington Library Quarterly*
JEGP	*Journal of English and Germanic Philology*
JHI	*Journal of the History of Ideas*
JWCI	*Journal of the Warburg and Courtauld Institutes*
MLQ	*Modern Language Quarterly*
MP	*Modern Philology*
PBSA	*Papers of the Bibliographical Society of America*
PMLA	*Publications of the Modern Language Association of America*
PQ	*Philological Quarterly*
RES	*Review of English Studies*
RM	Browne, *Religio Medici*
SEL	*Studies in English Literature, 1500–1900*
SP	*Studies in Philology*
TLS	[London] *Times Literary Supplement*

Notes

Introduction

1. Kermode, *The Romantic Image* (London: Routledge and Kegan Paul, 1957), chap. 8.

2. On this subject see the discussion by James Smith, "On Metaphysical Poetry," in *Determinations*, ed. F. R. Leavis (London: Chatto and Windus, 1934), pp. 10–45.

3. Bennett, *Four Metaphysical Poets: Donne, Herbert, Vaughan, Crashaw*, 2d ed. (Cambridge: Cambridge Univ. Press, 1953), p. 6.

4. *Religio Medici* in *The Works of Sir Thomas Browne*, ed. Geoffrey Keynes (London: Faber and Faber, 1964), 1:45. This edition of Browne's works is cited throughout; *Religio Medici* is hereafter abbreviated *RM*.

5. For a full discussion of this current of ideas see Ruth Wallerstein, *Studies in Seventeenth-Century Poetic* (Madison: Univ. of Wisconsin Press, 1950), pp. 181–277.

6. Bonaventure, *The Mind's Road to God*, trans. George Boas (Indianapolis, Ind.: Bobbs-Merrill, 1953), p. 20; *Mysterium Magnum*, in Jacob Böhme's *Sämtliche Werke*, ed. K. W. Schiebler (Leipzig: Verlag Johann Ambrosius Barth, 1843), 5:10; Nieremberg quoted by Mario Praz, *Studies in Seventeenth Century Imagery* (London: Warburg Institute, 1939), p. 19. Several of Nieremberg's works were translated by Henry Vaughan.

7. And of course by the emblematists as well, as Rosemary Freeman in *English Emblem Books* (London: Chatto and Windus, 1948), and Mario Praz have demonstrated.

8. Gracián, *Agudeza y Arte de Ingenio*, ed. Eduardo Ovejero y Maury (Huesca: Ivan Nogue, 1648), Discurso 2.

9. J. A. Mazzeo, "Metaphysical Poetry and the Poetic of Correspondence," *JHI* 14 (1953): 228. See also Mazzeo, "A Seventeenth-Century Theory of Metaphysical Poetry," *Romanic Review* 42 (1951): 245–55; "A Critique of Some Modern Theories of Metaphysical Poetry," *MP* 50 (1951): 88–96; "Analogy and Renaissance Culture," *JHI* 15 (1954): 299–304. I am deeply indebted in the writing of this introduction to Mazzeo's explication of seventeenth-century ideas of wit and to an article by S. L. Bethell, "The Nature of Metaphysical Wit," *Northern Miscellany of Literary Criticism* 1 (1953): 19–40.

10. Cf. S. L. Bethell, *The Cultural Revolution of the Seventeenth Century* (London: Dennis Dobson, 1951) and Patrick Grant, *The Transformation of Sin: Studies in Donne, Herbert, Vaughan, and Traherne* (Amherst: Univ. of Massachusetts Press, 1974).

11. Quoted by James Smith, "On Metaphysical Poetry," p. 16.

12. Martz, *The Poetry of Meditation*, rev. ed. (New Haven, Conn.: Yale Univ. Press, 1962).

13. White, *The Metaphysical Poets* (1936; rpt. New York: Collier-Macmillan, 1962), pp. 25–26.

14. "Affliction IV," in *The Works of George Herbert*, ed. F. E. Hutchinson (Oxford: Clarendon Press, 1941), lines 5–6. This edition of Herbert's works is cited throughout.

15. "My Spirit," in *Thomas Traherne: Centuries, Poems, and Thanksgivings*, ed. H. M. Margoliouth (Oxford: Clarendon Press, 1958), 2:54, line 71. This edition of Traherne's works is cited throughout, as Margoliouth.

I. *Between Two Worlds:* HERBERT

1. *The English Works of George Herbert*, ed. Palmer, 3 vols. (Boston: Houghton Mifflin, 1905), 1: 190–91. Palmer has an even bolder, if not more vulnerable, successor in Stanley Fish, who in *The Living Temple: George Herbert and Catechizing* (Berkeley: Univ. of California Press, 1978), argues for the catechetical structure of *The Temple*.

2. The Williams Manuscript (MS. Jones B62 in Dr. Williams's Library, Gordon Square, London) contains seventy-three poems that reappeared in the later Bodleian Manuscript (MS. Tanner 307) and the edition of 1633, though with a number of important changes. Hutchinson, *Works of Herbert*, pp. l–lvi, gives an account of the two manuscripts, outlining the insertion of later poems into the order of the Williams Manuscript and the rearrangement of the order. He also takes issue, pp. lxvii-lxix, with Palmer's ordering of Herbert's poems. Mary Ellen Rickey, *Utmost Art: Complexity in the Verse of George Herbert* (Lexington: Univ. of Kentucky Press, 1966), pp. 103–47, treats the differences between the Williams and Bodleian Manuscripts in her discussion of Herbert's poetic development. Amy Charles, "The Williams Manuscript and *The Temple*," *Renaissance Papers* (1971): 59–77, finds the reasons for Herbert's rearrangement "personal, intuitive and allusive," but has no doubt that the order is Herbert's own and intentional.

3. Palmer first noted that the Williams Manuscript contains no poems referring to Herbert as a member of the priesthood and guessed that it had been completed by 1628 or 1629, at any rate before Herbert arrived at Bemerton in 1630.

4. Izaak Walton, "The Life of Mr. George Herbert," in *The Lives of John Donne, Sir Henry Wotton, Richard Hooker, George Herbert & Robert Sanderson*, ed. G. Saintsbury (London: Oxford Univ. Press, 1927), p. 314.

5. Brewster S. Ford, "The Influence of the Prayer Book Calendar on the Shape of George Herbert's *The Temple*" (Ph.D. diss., Univ. of Virginia, 1964), develops this point most fully, although it is also made by Rosemond Tuve, *A Reading of George Herbert* (Chicago: Univ. of Chicago Press, 1952), chap. 1; Joseph Summers, *George Herbert: His Religion and Art* (Cambridge, Mass.: Harvard Univ. Press, 1952), pp. 86–87; and Sara W. Hanley, "Temples in *The Temple*: George Herbert's Study of the Church," *SEL* 8 (1968): 121–35.

6. Ford, in his often informative and useful discussion, makes many forced connections as he tries to account for virtually every poem in relation to the Prayer Book. Tuve and Summers, though noting the influence of the liturgical year, do not suggest it as anything like a complete basis of *The Temple*. Cf. also Helen Gardner, ed., *The Poems of George Herbert* (London: Oxford Univ. Press, 1961), p. xviii.

7. Ford notes, pp. 21–22, that the Prayer Book Calendar is in fact three calendars: its list of daily readings begins with January 1, its list of Moveable Feasts, with March 25, and its list of Sunday cycles and Communions, with Advent. I concur with his view that "in beginning *The Temple* with the sequence of events leading from the Passion through Easter, Herbert may simply have been choosing what seemed to him primary" (p. 22).

8. John David Walker, "The Architectonics of George Herbert's *The Temple*, *ELH* 29 (1962): 289–305; and Stanley Stewart, "Time and *The Temple*," *SEL* 6 (1966): 97–110.

9. See Walker; Valerie Carnes, "The Unity of George Herbert's *The Temple*: A Recon-

sideration," *ELH* 35 (1968): 505–26; Sara W. Hanley, "The Unity of George Herbert's *The Temple*" (Ph.D. diss., Univ. of Notre Dame, 1966).

10. Mary Ellen Rickey, pp. 5–9, finds in this order a reflection of the classical temple, but surely Herbert would be more likely to follow the Christian pattern. The suggestion of Ford (n. 37), that all liturgical services opened penitentially, and of Fish, that *The Temple* has a catechetical structure (a point that Ford also makes in connection with the tone of "The Church Porch"), seems more pertinent.

11. Summers, cited above; Fish, *Self-Consuming Artifacts* (Berkeley: Univ. of California Press, 1972), chap. 3. See also Rosalie Colie, "George Herbert and *Caritas*," *JWCI* 22 (1959): 303–31.

12. Freer, *Music for a King: George Herbert's Style and the Metrical Psalms* (Baltimore: Johns Hopkins Press, 1972), p. 1; Stein, *George Herbert's Lyrics* (Baltimore: Johns Hopkins Press, 1968), p. 210; Vendler, *The Poetry of George Herbert* (Cambridge, Mass.: Harvard Univ. Press, 1975), pp. 231–33.

13. Fish, *Self-Consuming Artifacts*, p. 216. Fish's study, from which I have learned a great deal, while apparently concentrating on the reader's response to a work, actually emphasizes to an equal degree the poet's struggle in creating the work and the work as a reflection of that struggle. But despite the subtlety and insight of Fish's readings, it finally seems overingenious to find suspect, as he does, a poet's accomplishment of his explicitly stated and ardently sought goal.

14. Vendler, pp. 237–41. Vendler seems to have no sense of how heretical Herbert would find this notion. Making God in his own image is something Herbert's personae frequently do, but Herbert himself, never.

15. Melissa C. Wanamaker has an interesting interpretation of Herbert's own use of the word "plain" in "Jordan I" in *Discordia Concors: The Wit of Metaphysical Poetry* (Port Washington, N.Y.: Kennikat Press, 1975), pp. 43–46.

16. Rickey, pp. 101–2, notes the simplicity of such titles in contrast to more puzzling ones; she does not note how deceptive even such simple ones can be.

17. Cf. Fish, *Self-Consuming Artifacts*, p. 207.

18. *The Works in Verse and Prose Complete of Henry Vaughan, Silurist*, ed. Alexander B. Grosart (The Fuller Worthies Library, 1871), 1:xciv; Enright, "George Herbert and the Devotional Poets," in *From Donne to Marvell*, vol. 3 of *A Guide to English Literature*, ed. Boris Ford (Baltimore: Penguin Books, 1956), pp. 146–47; Knieger, "The Purchase-Sale: Patterns of Business Imagery in the Poetry of George Herbert," *SEL* 6 (1966): 111.

19. These eleven poems are "The Altar," "The Sacrifice," "The Thanksgiving," "The Reprisall," "The Agonie," "The Sinner," "Good Friday," "Redemption," "Sepulchre," "Easter," and "Easter-wings." Stanley Fish's discussion of "letting go" in Herbert is particularly applicable to these early poems, if perhaps overstated with regard to the whole of *The Temple*.

20. "The Altar" has of late been the subject of much critical comment which I will not duplicate here. See especially Fish, *Self-Consuming Artifacts*, pp. 207–15, Rickey, pp. 9–16, Summers, pp. 140–43, and Vendler, pp. 61–63.

21. Herbert, *The Country Parson, Works*, p. 231.

22. Summers, chap. 7.

23. Among the meanings of *wave, waive,* and *waver* (OED) are to wander, to stray; to abandon (a task), to evade (doing something); to refuse (something offered); to relinquish (a right); to refuse to accept (some provision made in one's favor). Cf. Hutchinson, *Works of Herbert*, p. 517, who takes *waive* as the dominant sense.

24. OED and Hutchinson, *Works of Herbert*, p. 517.

25. Elizabeth Stambler, "The Unity of Herbert's *Temple*," *Cross Currents* 10 (1960):

251–66; Rosalie Colie, "*Logos* in *The Temple*: George Herbert and the Shape of Content," *JWCI* 26 (1963): 336; Fredson Bowers, "Herbert's Sequential Imagery: 'The Temper,'" *MP* 59 (1962): 202.

26. "Dialogue" of course is not one of the passion sequence, but one of the later poems that continue the patterns seen in embryo in the first two poems.

27. The elaboration of the meaning of synecdoche in Thrall, Hibbard, and Holman, *A Handbook to Literature* (New York: Odyssey, 1960), points up the persona's mistake: "In order [for the synecdoche] to be clear . . . the part selected to stand for the whole must be the part most directly associated with the subject under discussion. Thus . . . we speak of infantry on the march as *foot* rather than as *hands* just as we use *hands* rather than *foot* for men who are at work at manual labor."

28. When Helen Vendler speaks of Herbert's excessive self-abasement, and argues that Herbert's soul could never be called "brutish" (pp. 153, 231ff.), she ignores Herbert's adherence to the doctrine of natural depravity, according to which all men, not just unpleasant ones, stand condemned and in need of divine grace.

29. As in "Affliction I," lines 35–36: "Thus thinne and lean without a fence or friend, / I was blown through with ev'ry storm and winde."

30. Cited by Hutchinson, *Works of Herbert*, p. 490.

31. See especially Rom. 3:19–27 and 6:14–20.

32. On the ambiguities of language after the Fall see Christopher Ricks, *Milton's Grand Style* (Oxford: Oxford Univ. Press, 1963), pp. 109–17.

33. I remain unconvinced by the argument of Bill Smithson, "Herbert's 'Affliction' Poems," *SEL* 15 (1975): 125–40, that these poems must be rearranged in order to show Herbert's spiritual growth.

34. *Devotions upon Emergent Occasions*, ed. Anthony Raspa (Montreal: McGill-Queen's Univ. Press, 1975), Meditation XVII, p. 87.

35. Vendler, pp. 168–70, finds "Mortification" gruesome, an instance of the poetic mind tainted by a blighting and useless perception; I would call it electrifying. Death for the poet means not extinction but eternal life; yet it is only by full awareness of the presence of death in life that he attains life in death. Such paradoxes are common in the seventeenth century: for example, Jeremy Taylor's *Rule and Exercises of Holy Dying* is a treatise on how to live well, while his *Holy Living* instructs the reader in preparation for death.

36. The final vision is the vision of the last poems of *The Temple* though not limited to them; the misperception that one must act is especially dominant in early poems but by no means limited to them. "The Crosse" is an instance of a poem late in the sequence in which this misperception occurs.

37. Vendler, pp. 38–39, among others, comments on this aspect of the poem.

38. A combination of *aenigma* and *asyndeton*. On the form of "Prayer," see Virginia R. Mollenkott, "George Herbert's Epithet-Sonnet," *Genre* 5 (1972): 131–37; and E. B. Greenwood, "George Herbert's Sonnet 'Prayer': A Stylistic Study," *Essays in Criticism* 15 (1965): 27–45.

39. As maintained by Vendler, p. 39.

40. *Devotions upon Emergent Occasions*, ed. Raspa, Expostulation XIX, p. 102.

41. *A Defence of Poetry*, in *Miscellaneous Prose of Sir Philip Sidney*, ed. Katherine Duncan-Jones and Jan Van Dorsten (Oxford: Clarendon Press, 1973), p. 79.

42. From the Canticle for Easter-tide, based on 1 Cor. 5:7–8.

II. *The Shadow of Time*: VAUGHAN

1. See Hutchinson's account of the text of *The Temple* in *Works of Herbert*, pp. lii–lvi, and the discussion in Rickey, *Utmost Art*, pp. 103–33; on Vaughan see *The Works of Henry*

Vaughan, ed. L. C. Martin, 2d ed. (Oxford: Clarendon Press, 1957), pp. xx, xxiv. This edition is cited throughout.

2. At the same time he discourages a merely biographical interest: "In the *Perusal* of it, you will (peradventure) observe some *passages*, whose *history* or *reason* may seem something remote; but were they brought *nearer*, and plainly exposed to your view, (though that (perhaps) might quiet your *curiosity*) yet would it not conduce much to your greater *advantage*" (*Works of Vaughan*, p. 392).

3. "They are all gone into the world of light," lines 39–40; "Chearfulness," line 17.

4. This has been the subject of a great deal of critical attention. Among those who have seen Hermetic influences in Vaughan are Alexander C. Judson, "The Source of Henry Vaughan's Ideas Concerning God in Nature," *SP* 24 (1927): 592–606; L. C. Martin, "Henry Vaughan and 'Hermes Trismegistus,' " *RES* 18 (1942): 301–7; E. C. Pettet, *Of Paradise and Light: A Study of Vaughan's Silex Scintillans* (Cambridge: Cambridge Univ. Press, 1960); and Patrick Grant, *The Transformation of Sin*, pp. 154–68. On Platonism in Vaughan, see Merritt Y. Hughes, "The Theme of Pre-existence and Infancy in 'The Retreate,' " *PQ* 20 (1941): 484–500 and L. C. Martin, "Henry Vaughan and the Theme of Infancy," in *Seventeenth Century Studies Presented to Sir Herbert Grierson* (Oxford: Clarendon Press, 1938), pp. 243–55.

5. See Florence Sandler, "The Ascents of the Spirit: Henry Vaughan on the Atonement," *JEGP* 73 (1974): 209–26; Grant, *The Transformation of Sin, chap.* 5; D. P. Walker, *The Decline of Hell* (London: Routledge, Kegan Paul, 1964).

6. By early I mean simply early in the printed sequence of poems in *The Temple* and *Silex Scintillans*. I have already noted studies of the order of *The Temple*. In the case of Vaughan, there is no basis for dating particular poems, though it seems likely that the poems that first appeared in the second edition of *Silex Scintillans*, published 1655, were written later than those in the first edition, published 1650.

7. Among modern critics who use the term mystic to apply to Vaughan are Helen C. White, *The Metaphysical Poets*, p. 283; Itrat Husain, *The Mystical Element in the Metaphysical Poets of the Seventeenth Century* (Edinburgh: Oliver and Boyd, 1948), p. 193; R. A. Durr, *On the Mystical Poetry of Henry Vaughan* (Cambridge, Mass.: Harvard Univ. Press, 1962). This judgment has been most vigorously disputed by E. L. Marilla, "The Religious Conversion of Henry Vaughan," *RES* 21 (1945): 15–22; Marilla, "The Mysticism of Henry Vaughan: Some Observations," *RES* 18 (1967): 164–66; Frank Kermode, "The Private Imagery of Henry Vaughan," *RES* n.s. 1 (1950): 206–25; James D. Simmonds, *Masques of God: Form and Theme in the Poetry of Henry Vaughan* (Pittsburgh, Pa.: Univ. of Pittsburgh Press, 1972).

8. Cf. D. C. Allen, *Doubt's Boundless Sea* (Baltimore: Johns Hopkins Press, 1964), pp. 132–34.

9. L. C. Martin (*Works of Vaughan*, p. 737) also notes the similarity of Herbert's "Whitsunday," which follows Herbert's two sonnets on "The H. Scriptures."

10. In *Magia Adamica*, Thomas Vaughan writes: "Hermes affirmeth that in the beginning the earth was a quagmire or quivering kind of jelly, it being nothing else but water congealed by the incubation and heat of the Divine Spirit." Then "the Holy Spirit, moving upon the chaos—which action some divines compare to the incubation of a hen upon her eggs, did together with his heat communicate other manifold influences to the matter. . . . He did therefore hatch the matter and bring out the secret essences, as a chick is brought out of the shell." *The Works of Thomas Vaughan*, ed. A. E. Waite (New Hyde Park, N.Y.: University Books, 1968), pp. 129–30.

11. These seem the natural divisions and have been related by Martz (*The Paradise Within*, p. 17) to "the three 'books' cultivated by the medieval Augustinians: the Book of Scripture, the Book of Nature, the Book of the Soul."

12. Speculation about the relationship between Wordsworth and Vaughan began with Vaughan's nineteenth-century editors, among whom the legend of influence grew and exfoliated. In *A Household Book of English Poetry*, published in 1868, Archbishop Trench noted the similarity between "The Retreate" and the "Intimations Ode," and in 1870 an unnamed correspondent provided him with evidence (which he apparently did not question) that Wordsworth had owned a copy of *Silex Scintillans*. No proof was demanded until 1935, when Helen McMaster, after a careful examination, rejected the story as a myth. See McMaster, "Vaughan and Wordsworth," *RES* 11 (1935): 313–25.

13. See Ross Garner's discussion of "Unprofitablenes" in *The Unprofitable Servant in Henry Vaughan*, Univ. of Nebraska Studies, n.s. no. 29 (Lincoln: Univ. of Nebraska Press, 1963), p. 10: "In 'Regeneration,' for example, one thing is said and another is meant. But in 'Unprofitablenes,' one thing is said and both it and something else are meant; what is expressly stated in the fictitious person of a flower is experienced in the poem as true not only of the flower but also of the spiritual life of the poet. And the spiritual fact is discovered in the natural fact and is given expression by it."

14. See John Hollander's excellent discussion of the relation between music and cosmic order in *The Untuning of the Sky* (Princeton, N.J.: Princeton Univ. Press, 1961), chap. 2.

15. This is the opinion of F. E. Hutchinson, *Henry Vaughan: A Life and Interpretation* (Oxford: Clarendon Press, 1947), pp. 95–97, 104–8, and 195–96; and Martin, *Works of Vaughan*, p. 731, on the basis of the date of William Vaughan's death (July 14, 1648), of the mention of his brother's death by Thomas Vaughan in *The Man-Mouse Taken in a Trap* (London, 1650), and of the untitled poems themselves. See also Jeffrey Ford, "Vision in Vaughan" (M.A. thesis, Columbia Univ.,1964), for a discussion of the evidence of the untitled poems.

16. *Anima Magica Abscondita*, in *Works of Thomas Vaughan*, pp. 115–16. Thomas Vaughan also wrote: "To speak then of God without Nature is more than we can do, for we have not known Him so; and to speak of Nature without God is more than we may do, for we should rob God of His glory and attribute those effects to Nature which belong properly to God and to the Spirit of God, Which works in Nature" (*Euphrates*, in *Works*, p. 395).

17. Stanza 6. The lines do not make Vaughan a Wordsworthian; they are simply an emphatic statement of the doctrine of the Book of Creatures. Many of course did still believe, among them John Ray, author of *The Wisdom of God Manifested in the Works of the Creation* (London, 1691).

18. Gracián, *Agudeza y Arte de Ingenio*, Discurso II.

19. It is of course difficult in many cases to categorize poems, especially since many of Vaughan's best poems combine both strains, but one may, for example, call "Abels blood" a biblical poem and "The Bird" a nature poem. When these distinctions are made there are in fact somewhat more biblical poems than nature poems, even if the former are less well known and sometimes less successful.

20. Simmonds, *Masques of God*, chap. 5.

21. On Vaughan's Hermeticism see especially Hughes and Martin, note 4 above; on his belief in man's essential innocence, see E. C. Pettet, who speaks of Vaughan's "idealization . . . of the innocence, purity, and vision of childhood" (p. 20), and cites W. Lewis Bettany, ed., *Silex Scintillans* (London: Blackie, 1905): "In 'Childhood' [the poet] calmly repudiates the orthodox Christian doctrine of original sin, and, in a beautiful fallacy, transfers to the childhood of the individual man that innocence which elsewhere he has predicated of the childhood of the race."

22. Cf. Martz's account of the differences between the two parts in *Paradise Within*, p. 4.

23. See Hutchinson, *Henry Vaughan*, chap. 8.

24. Cf. the somewhat different division outlined by Ross Garner in *Henry Vaughan: Experience and the Tradition* (Chicago: Univ. of Chicago Press, 1959), p. 58. Scholars of

Vaughan will recognize in the discussion that follows the coincidence of my view of "Regeneration" at a number of points with those of Garner, Durr, and Pettet, to whose comprehensive readings I am indebted.

25. The similarity of the image in this stanza to Quarles's emblem of the scales (*Emblems* 2.4) has been noted by many critics, including Rosemary Freeman, *English Emblem Books*, p. 150; Kermode, p. 215; Durr, pp. 160–61; Pettet, pp. 106–7. Garner, *Experience*, pp. 54–55, sees an extended similarity to Wither.

26. See the discussion of Paul in connection with "Sinne," above, pp. 28–30.

27. Cf. "Religion," lines 1–20; "The Search," lines 21–32; "Corruption," lines 21–28.

28. Cf. the statement of Richard Hooker: "The best things we do have somewhat in them to be pardoned. How then can we do anything meritorious and worthy to be rewarded?" in *Of the Laws of Ecclesiastical Polity* (London: J. M. Dent & Sons, 1954), 1:24.

29. Cf. Stanley Stewart's extended discussion of the garden *topos* in *The Enclosed Garden* (Madison: Univ. of Wisconsin Press, 1966). Chap. 4 specifically treats "Regeneration."

30. Garner, *Experience*, p. 60, takes a different view: "Allegorically, the fountain refers to the baptismal font, symbolically, to the fountain of the water of life" (Rev. 21:6).

31. *Anima Magica Abscondita*, in *Works of Thomas Vaughan*, p. 100.

32. See Herbert G. Wright, "The Theme of Solitude and Retirement in Seventeenth-Century Literature," *Études Anglaises* 7 (1954): 22–35; Maren-Sofie Røstvig, *The Happy Man* (Oxford: Basil Blackwell, 1954); cf. Simmonds, who denies that Vaughan retired from the world (p. 13), but who nevertheless finds (p. 110) that the success of the Puritan revolution had something to do with his turning inward.

33. A similar view is expressed by Wanamaker, p. 13.

34. See the discussion of this point by Simmonds, pp. 186–88.

35. Especially Is. 2:2–3; 4:2–6; 60:19–20; Micah 4; and of course the book of Revelation.

36. The syntax of lines 27–28 does not indicate clearly whether the foul storms are that which is darkened or that which darkens; both, probably, just as books and scribes seem to be dark and to create darkness.

37. Simmonds, pp. 93–98, probably rightly, sees in these lines a reference to contemporary events, to the Puritan storm under which Vaughan suffered.

38. Robert Sencourt, *Outflying Philosophy* (London: Simpkin, Marshal, Hamilton, Kent, [1925]) pp. 191–93; Sencourt, *Carmelite and Poet* (New York: Macmillan, 1944), pp. 145–56; White, pp. 277–78; Itrat-Husain, pp. 230–32; Garner, *Experience*, pp. 137–44; Durr, pp. 119–21; Pettet, p. 152; S. Sandbank, "Henry Vaughan's Apology for Darkness," *SEL* 7 (1967): 141–52.

39. John of the Cross, *Complete Works*, trans. P. Silverio de Santa Teresa, C. D., and ed. E. A. Peers (London: Burnes Oates & Washbourne, [1934]), 1:98–99. Vaughan never mentions John of the Cross explicitly, and there is no record of an English edition during Vaughan's lifetime, but he would have been well able to read the Latin (published in Cologne in 1622 and reprinted there in 1639). Louis Martz, *Poetry of Meditation*; Helen C. White, *English Devotional Literature, 1600–1640* (Madison: Univ. of Wisconsin Press, 1931); and Joseph B. Collins, *Christian Mysticism in the Elizabethan Age* (Baltimore: Johns Hopkins Press, 1940) have documented the impact of continental works of meditation on native English religious writings.

40. Trans. C. E. Rolt (London: Society for Promoting Christian Knowledge, 1920), 1:191.

41. Martin, *Works*, p. 750, notes the echoes of Vaughan's *Mount of Olives* and his translation of Nieremberg. Cf. also Kermode, p. 223.

42. See Leland H. Chambers, "Henry Vaughan's Allusive Technique: Biblical Allu-

sions in 'The Night,' " *MLQ* 27 (1966): 371–87, for a full account of biblical allusions in the poem. The prose passage quoted is a tissue of biblical passages, especially Job 5:15, Prov. 4:18–19, and Mal. 4:2.

43. *The Excellency and Nobleness of True Religion*, in *The Cambridge Platonists*, ed. Gerald R. Cragg (New York: Oxford Univ. Press, 1968), p. 96.

44. Florence Sandler (see n. 5), who seems to consider Platonism respectable and Hermeticism not, is eager to reclaim Vaughan as a Platonist, even though there are considerable areas of agreement between the two philosophies and though both were pervasive in the Renaissance. Louis Martz, *Paradise Within*, speaks more broadly of a great Platonic tradition that embraces Augustine (who also quoted Hermes Trismegistus), Bonaventure, Vaughan, and Traherne.

45. John Norris, *An Account of Reason and Faith*, in Cragg, p. 156.

III. *The Splendor of Eternity:* Traherne

1. Those who use the term mystic include Helen White, *The Metaphysical Poets*, pp. 326–28; H. M. Margoliouth, ed., *Thomas Traherne: Centuries, Poems, and Thanksgivings*, 1:xl; Anne Ridler, *Thomas Traherne: Poems, Centuries, and Three Thanksgivings* (London: Oxford Univ. Press, 1966), p. xvii; Alison J. Sherrington, *Mystical Symbolism in the Poetry of Thomas Traherne* (St. Lucia, Queensland: Univ. of Queensland Press, 1970), pp. 80–81; and Gladys Wade, *Thomas Traherne* (Princeton, N.J.: Princeton Univ. Press, 1944), pp. 215–38. K. W. Salter, in *Thomas Traherne, Mystic and Poet* (London: Edward Arnold, 1964), p. 30, on the basis of the categories of Evelyn Underhill's *Mysticism*, denies him that designation.

2. Sherrington, pp. 112–14; Clements, *The Mystical Poetry of Thomas Traherne* (Cambridge, Mass.: Harvard Univ. Press, 1969).

3. *Enneads* 3.8, in Grace H. Turnbull, ed., *The Essence of Plotinus: Extracts from the Six Enneads and Porphyry's Life of Plotinus*, based on the trans. of Stephen MacKenna (New York: Oxford Univ. Press, 1934). Compare Plotinus's statement in *Enneads* 1.6.9: "No eye ever saw the sun without becoming sun-like, nor can a soul see beauty without becoming beautiful. You must first become all god-like and all beautiful if you intend to see God and beauty" (Plotinus, *Enneads 1.1–9*, with an English trans. by A. H. Armstrong [London: Heinemann, 1966], p. 261), with Traherne, *Christian Ethicks:* "Every Like in Nature draweth to its Like, the Beautiful, and the Wise, and the Good, and the Aged; but especially the GOD-*Like* . . . . GODLINESS, or GOD-LIKENESS is the cement of Amity between GOD and MAN" (p. 285). This and all further references to *Christian Ethicks* (cited as *CE*) are to the edition of Carol L. Marks and George Robert Guffey (Ithaca, N.Y.: Cornell Univ. Press, 1968). Traherne himself quoted the passage from *Enneads* 1.6.9 as translated by Thomas Jackson, *A Treatise of the Divine Essence and Attributes* (London, 1628), p. 439, in his Commonplace Book, under "Preparation of Objects," f. 77.1 (noted by Marks and Guffey, *CE*, p. 375).

4. The statement by Nieremberg is quoted in the Introduction, p. 2; Mario Praz, p. 19, cites it as an example of the kind of attitude that gave rise to emblems and devices in such profusion. He notes (p. 16): "The century which produced the great mystics produced also the emblematists: they seem opposites, and frequently these opposites are found united in the same person."

5. Cited by Praz in a footnote, p. 18.

6. I do not dispute Martz's contention in *The Paradise Within* that Traherne is part of the Augustinian tradition as carried on by Saint Bonaventure, but the two manifestations of that tradition seem to me radically different.

7. See n. 2, chap. 2, above.

8. See, for example, Kermode, Marilla, and Simmonds, n. 7, chap. 2, above.

9. For a description of the manuscripts in which Traherne's poems exist, see Margoliouth's Introduction, 1:ix–xxiii.

10. When so perceptive a critic as Louis Martz, while upholding the received opinion on the relative value of Traherne's verse and prose (*Paradise Within*, p. 80), declares a journey through the whole of the *Centuries* fatiguing (p. 44), a revaluation may be at hand. For a discussion of some of the unpublished works, see Carol Marks, "Thomas Traherne's Commonplace Book," *Papers of the Bibliographical Society of America* 58 (1964): 458–65; Carol Marks Sicherman, "Traherne's Ficino Notebook," *PBSA* 63 (1969): 73–81; and James M. Osborn, "A New Traherne Manuscript," *TLS*, 8 Oct. 1964, p. 928.

11. Martz, pp. 43–102. Martz speaks also (p. 53) of "the continuous interrelationship of the meditations."

12. In a most perceptive article on Traherne's use of language, R. W. Hepburn ("Thomas Traherne: The Nature and Dignity of Imagination," *Cambridge Journal* 6 [1953]: 725–34) shows how Traherne both makes extravagant statements and makes them acceptable.

13. As pointed out by Clements, pp. 3–5. See also Stanley Stewart, *The Expanded Voice: The Art of Thomas Traherne* (San Marino, Calif.: Huntington Library, 1970), pp. 210–11.

14. There are thirty-nine poems in all that do not appear in Dobell, but one, "News," is also found in *C* 3.26.

15. See Clements, p. 5. Margoliouth (1:xv) says: "Philip's arrangement of the poems is on the whole a good one; his editing and changing of the text is a disaster."

16. Wallace, "Thomas Traherne and the Structure of Meditation," *ELH* 25 (1958): 79–89; Clements, p. 61. See also Jean-Jacques Denonain, *Thèmes et Formes de la Poésie Métaphysique* (Paris: Press Universitaires de France, 1956), p. 254–81.

17. Wallace, p. 80.

18. In this I concur with Margoliouth (2:337); for a different view see Malcolm M. Day, "Traherne and the Doctrine of Pre-existence," *SP* (1968): 81–97.

19. Clements's assertions to the contrary are the exception that proves the rule.

20. Clements, pp. 85–88; Marshall, "Thomas Traherne and the Doctrine of Original Sin," *MLN* 73 (1958): 161–65. See also notes to *CE*, ed. Marks and Guffey, p. 318.

21. *CE*, p. 318. Cf. also Anne Davidson, "Innocence Regained: Seventeenth-Century Reinterpretations of the Fall of Man" (Ph.D. diss., Columbia Univ., 1956), chap. 6. More recently, Patrick Grant, *Transformation of Sin*, chap. 6, argues that Traherne is neither Augustinian nor Pelagian but Irenaean in outlook, though Grant too finds Traherne's views consistent with the Thirty-Nine Articles.

22. For example, see Marks on the "Church's Year Book," *PBSA* 60 (1966): 72.

23. Margoliouth, 2:342. Cf. also Clements, pp. 97–98.

24. Robert Ellrodt, *L'Inspiration Personelle et L'Esprit du Temps chez Les Poètes Métaphysiques Anglais* (Paris: Librairie José Corti, 1960), 1.2.301, notes the similarity with the findings of Piaget.

25. Traherne's interest in Platonism, ancient and modern, is evident from passages in his Commonplace Book (Bodleian MS. Eng. poet c 42) and Notebook (Brit. Mus. Burney MS. 126) copied from Henry More's *Divine Dialogues* and Ficino's summary of Plato. See Carol Marks, "Thomas Traherne and Cambridge Platonism," *PMLA* 81 (1966): 521–34; T. O. Beachcroft, "Traherne and the Cambridge Platonists," *Dublin Review* 186 (1930): 278–90; and the articles by Marks cited n. 10 above.

26. An *Elegant & Learned Discourse of the Light of Nature* (London, 1652), pp. 101, 213.

27. Traherne's questioning of the existence of external reality, as Bertram Dobell and others have noted, made him a "Berkeleian before Berkeley was born" (*Poetical Works of Thomas Traherne* [London: Dobell, 1903], p. lxxx). Traherne is concerned not with the

philosophical problem of the objective cause of phenomena, but rather with human response and with inner reality.

28. Traherne uses the definition even more explicitly in the "Thanksgivings for God's Attributes," 2:318, lines 223–25. Margoliouth, 2:415, cites the *Oxford Dictionary of Quotations* on this famous definition: "Origin unknown: said to have been traced to a lost treatise of Empedocles"; but the most likely immediate source for Traherne is Thomas Jackson (*Divine Essence*), from whom in his Commonplace Book, under "Omnipotence," he copies the passage in which Jackson quotes with approval the definition "of *Trismegist, Deus est sphaera, cujus Centrum est ubiq., cujus peripheria nusquam.*"

29. Nicolson, *The Breaking of the Circle*, rev. ed. (New York: Columbia Univ. Press, 1962), pp. 180–82, 192, 196–203; Colie, "Thomas Traherne and the Infinite," *HLQ* 21 (1957): 69–82; Colie, *Paradoxica Epidemica: The Renaissance Tradition of Paradox* (Princeton, N.J.: Princeton Univ. Press, 1960); Ellrodt, 1.2.335.

30. However unlikely the comparison may seem, this technique resembles that of the earliest essays of Francis Bacon, whose apparently undigested bits and phrases represent the mind in pursuit of truth, and contrasts with the smooth prose of Dryden, which reflects the sociability of truth found.

31. Cf. Traherne's citation of Pico della Mirandola's *Oration on the Dignity of Man* in C 4.76.

32. See Clements, pp. 38–41.

33. On the other hand, as I point out in "The Origins of Ecstasy: Traherne's 'Select Meditations,' " *ELR* 9 (1979): 419–31, some of Traherne's earlier work contains a number of—for him—unusually conventional passages, and several expressions of distress that link his style much more closely with Vaughan's than one might gather from his published works.

34. See Wade, p. 173, and Sherrington, p. 101.

35. Martz, p. 57.

36. Wade, p. 173. Margoliouth wrote: "I cannot but look on V. 10 as a triumphant and perfect conclusion" (1:297); to which Martz added: "the number 11 reaches out to infinity, toward the silence of mystical repose" (p. 102).

37. These lines express a longing like Vaughan's, but one wonders whether it is only accidental that the transforming of a soul to thought, coupled with the rhyme on "ought" recalls the perhaps exaggerated piety and the sharp division between body and spirit of Marvell's "Dialogue between the Resolved Soul and Created Pleasure": "My nobler rest is on a thought / Conscious of doing what I ought."

IV. *The Endless Sphere:* TRAHERNE

1. See chap. 3, pp. 110–11, above, for further details of the differences between the two texts.

2. As suggested by the title, "Poems of Felicity, Vol. I." Stewart, pp. 156 and 226, suggests that Philip Traherne was working from three manuscripts—one something like Dobell, one with poems unique to Burney, and one containing a third sequence—and collating them to two; though it seems quite as likely that Philip had only two manuscripts—Dobell itself and another that contained both the poems unique to Burney and a number of other poems, some of them known to us only by title.

3. Denonain, *Thèmes et Formes*, p. 256; Stewart, p. 156.

4. Stewart argues, p. 156, that those Burney poems not found in Dobell constitute "a sequence of poems in many ways parallel to that in the other volume" and probably essentially true to Thomas's order.

5. In this I concur with Denonain, p. 256, though not with his judgment that these

poems represent a shift in Traherne's thinking. The difference in tone may result from Philip's selection or his revision; in any case we cannot date either group of poems.

6. The Dobell Folio, though in Thomas Traherne's autograph, also contains notes in Philip Traherne's handwriting that point to the ordering and selection of poems for "Poems of Felicity." After "Innocence," Philip wrote "An Infant-Ey. p. 1"; after "The Improvment," he wrote "The Odor, p. 124"; and in fact, in Burney "Innocence" precedes "An Infant-Ey," and "The Improvment" precedes "The Odour." Elsewhere Philip seems to have had more difficulty making up his mind. After "My Spirit," he wrote and deleted "Anatomy"; after "The Rapture," he wrote "Childhood p. 120 and 9. News p. 133" and then deleted "Childhood"; after "The Estate," Philip wrote "The Return. p. 2" and deleted it, and then wrote "The Evidence." In each case the final version corresponds to the order of "Poems of Felicity."

7. See Allan H. Gilbert, "Thomas Traherne as Artist," *MLQ* 8 (1947): 339, who cites the concurring opinions of Wade, Bell, and Iredale.

8. See discussion of "The Odour," above, chap. 1, pp. 38–40. That Traherne knew Herbert we are certain; he thought enough of "To all Angels and Saints" to copy it in "The Church's Year Book."

9. As so well documented by Martz, *The Poetry of Meditation*.

10. Augustine, *Confessions*, transl. Vernon J. Bourke (New York: Fathers of the Church, 1953), p. 4.

11. Traherne's vision is also surprisingly social, a reminder that for all the ecstasy of his poems, he thrived on human relations. One gets a sense of his need for company from *C* 4.14 and the Preface to *A Serious and Pathetical Contemplation*, quoted by Margoliouth, 1:xxxii.

12. "Corinna's Going a Maying," lines 30–35, p. 68, in *The Poetical Works of Robert Herrick*, ed. L. C. Martin (Oxford: Clarendon Press, 1968).

13. Margoliouth (2:370) suggests that Traherne may be combining memories of childhood Christmases with a post-Restoration celebration.

14. Newton shared this concept of infinity, which Max Jammer, *Concepts of Space: The History of Theories of Space in Physics* (Cambridge, Mass.: Harvard Univ. Press, 1954), p. 66ff., traces back to the Aristotelian idea of space as a continuum composed of parts that can be subdivided *ad infinitum*. Jammer contrasts this position with that of Nicholas of Cusa and Thomas Campanella—that space is homogeneous and undifferentiated—which he sees as the precursor of modern conceptions of infinity.

15. Margoliouth (2:387) notes the variation in the rhyme scheme of lines 67–70 but does not comment; one may wonder whether these lines, which stress so strongly that "they lov *Me*," are altogether as Thomas Traherne wrote them. Nevertheless, it is clear that while the passages from *Centuries* just quoted stress the universal implications of love, Traherne here sees and celebrates its personal application.

Index